Praise for *The Future Ain't What It Used To Be*

"[T]o achieve a competitive advantage in today's information-rich business environment, it is not enough to understand current consumer needs. You have to stretch out and imagine future needs that hopefully no one else has spotted. Iconoculture® has spotted forty, which leaves me green with envy but hungry to understand their application to our clients' brands."

> —N. J. Kendall
> Head of planning, Bartle Bogle Hegarty

"[T]hese three trend mavens are so far out there that they make you really uncomfortable, but then they tie their ideas back to basic life and business implications. Getting in touch with these cultural trends is key to creating the future, versus [just] tracking trends and watching the past in the rearview mirror."

> —P. Gayle Fuguitt
> Director, marketing research and business information
> and analysis, Big "G," General Mills, Inc.

"For those of us building lives and businesses that we want to be around 50 years from now, *The Future Ain't What It Used To Be* is a must read that clears the mind for proactive management of our future."

> —Donna Lopiano
> Executive director, Women's Sports Foundation

"Knowledge is power, and this book provides an incredible amount of usable knowledge."

> —Tom Gegax
> Founder and head coach, Team Tires Plus stores

"This book is just what I have come to expect from working with the team at Iconoculture®: perceptive analyses of what's coming next, supported by a wealth of cultural detail, and interpreted usefully by their years of marketing savvy."

> —Myra Stark
> Senior vice president and director of knowledge management
> and consumer insights, Saatchi & Saatchi

"Iconoculture® isn't just about telling you what's trendy, the chimera of cool that recedes as you approach it. They go one step further with surefire money-spinner applications for all of the trends they've spotted. But the real reason to read this book is its infectious enthusiasm for good old-fashioned observation. They make it look so simple it's like they've given us the tools of the trade. Pick up the paper, run off to the mall, and have your very own multiple Iconogasm.™"

> —Nigel Carr
> General manager, Kirshenbaum Bond & Partners

the future ain't
what it used to be

the **40** cultural trends transforming
your job, your life, your world

the future ain't what it used to be

the **40** cultural trends transforming
your job, your life, your world

Iconoculture® Inc.
Mary Meehan, Larry Samuel, Vickie Abrahamson

Riverhead Books
a member of Penguin Putnam Inc.
New York
1998

Iconoculture®, Inc.

Mary Meehan, Larry Samuel, Vickie Abrahamson

Iconoculture® is a registered trademark of Iconoculture, Inc. , Iconogasm™, and Signs of the Times also are trademarks of Iconoculture®, Inc.

Riverhead Books
a member of Penguin Putnam Inc.
200 Madison Avenue
New York, NY 10016

Library of Congress Cataloging-in-Publication Data
The future ain't what it used to be: the 40 cultural trends transforming your job, your life, your world / by Iconoculture, Inc.: Mary Meehan, Larry Samuel, Vickie Abrahamson.
   p. cm.
   Includes index.
   ISBN 1-57322-080-9 (acid-free paper)
   1. Marketing—United States. 2. Popular culture—United States. I. Meehan, Mary (Mary A.), 1955–. II. Samuel, Larry. III. Abrahamson, Vickie. IV. Iconoculture, Inc.
HF5415.1.F88   1998   97-22755 CIP
306' .0973—dc21

Copy editing by Jana Branch
Design by Michael Doyle and Shannon Pettini
Illustrations by Shannon Pettini
Selected illustrations by Michael Doyle

Printed in the United States of America
10 9 8 7 6 5 4 3 2 1
This book is printed on acid-free paper. ∞

To Yogi Berra, Yankee great and sage extraordinaire,
for inspiring the title of this book and for bestowing on us juicy nuggets of
trend wisdom: "You can observe a lot just by watching" and
"Prediction is difficult, especially about the future."

contents

introduction

There's definitely *one* thing we all can agree on—the future ain't what it used to be. You can always depend on Yogi to tell it like it is. Depend on this book to do the same.

Your job, your life, your world are changing at warp speed, making it more important than ever for you to know what's around the next cultural curve. This book helps you navigate the uncharted terrain ahead so you'll be in the right place at the right time with the right mindset to proactively manage your future.

Who are these Iconoculture smartypants, anyway?

Funny you should ask. Iconoculture is a group of three marketing renegades dedicated to helping turn trends into business opportunities. Think of us as a cultural weathercaster, reading the prevailing trendwinds to forecast marketing dewpoints. Based, but not frozen, in Minneapolis, Minnesota, Iconoculture has developed an international reputation by working with individuals, small-sized and *Fortune* 500 corporations, advertising agencies, universities, and the media to leverage trends into strategies for personal and business growth.

So what? Anyone and everyone is talking trends these days.

True. Often, reporting a trend is a no-brainer. Doing something with it, however, like building a new business; retooling out-of-touch business equities; creating and launching new brands; bonding viscerally with customers, kids, boomers, twentysomethings, or the balding (male *and* female) neighbors next door is the tricky part. It's that tricky part that is the key to thriving rather than merely surviving today's and tomorrow's tumultuous changes. And it's that tricky part—how to wisely capitalize on the forty cultural trends transforming your job, your life, your world—that makes *The Future Ain't What It Used To Be* an invaluable, kick-butt resource.

Doing what comes culturally

In 1992, Iconoculture—Mary Meehan, Larry Samuel, and Vickie Abrahamson—emerged from our respective marketing trenches, pooled considerable resources (pocket change, good brains), and twelve-stepped a shared addiction to popular culture into a trend newsletter and consulting partnership. Today, as in the beginning, our mission is to go inside trends, digging deeper to decode the values driving current and emerging culture. We prospect the juiciest part of the cultural landscape and translate the social *zeitgeist* into marketing opportunities.

How we do our digging is what most working stiffs would kill for. Each of us goes his or her separate way, spending days lockjawed to the TV screen, movie screen, computer screen; reading everything in sight from the *Iowa City Advertiser* to the *Willamette Weekly* to out-there news like *Transgender Tapestry* (how else would we learn the thirteen most asked questions about crossdressing?) and the timber-titillating *Loggers World*. Vickie Abrahamson crisscrosses the USA on backroads from Wolf Point, Montana, to Millinocket, Maine, stopping to chitchat with folks in cafés, co-ops, bowling alleys, at concerts, or midstream Gallatin River with hipwaders and flyrod as tools of the trade. Larry Samuel, with a Ph.D. in American Studies emblazoned on his trend scout uniform, sleuths the margins to see what shock waves are beginning to register on the cultural Richter scale. After a hard day of net trolling, Larry covers the night beat to check out what the heppest cats and coolest chicks are wearing, drinking, smoking, and grooving to. Mary Meehan is Iconoculture's resident media maven, known to have devoured whole networks in a single gulp. The quintessentially quirky cable access channel; the Westminster Dog Show; all the news that's fit to print; and movies, movies, and more movies are her craves. Back together, we make sense out of the cultural chaos, make key connections, and discuss the implications for individuals and marketers. In your wildest dreams, you could never imagine the sheer tonnage of snacks we snarf up while comparing notes. Yikes!

Are you ready for  an iconogasm™?

The Future Ain't What It Used To Be is divided into ten chapters identified by Iconoculture as America's passion points—**mind, body, spirit, experience, identity, society, nature, relationships, fear,** and **technology.** These passion points, fertile with lifestyle and marketing potential, are explored and documented within the framework of forty cultural trends, or what we call **signs of the times**™ Each sign has its own distinct personality punctuated by a curious name—**biomorphing, gray matter, toto too, beehiving, zentrepreneurism, altered states**—brought to life by a fascinating spectrum of people, places, and things all rocking the world as we speak. These forty cultural trends are literal signs of the times, guideposts that point the way for you to proactively manage your future. Think of signs as territories to stake with your career, business, or brand. Pay special attention to the many **iconogasms.** Each and every 'gasm cuts to the core of the trend and gives you an actionable idea as the **cultural climaxes/marketing opportunities** you've been yearning for.

It's for certain that the future is not what it used to be, but this book will help you turn the future into what you *want* it to be.

the future ain't
what it used to be

the **40** cultural trends transforming
your job, your life, your world

chapter 1: mind

$e=mc^2$

In the nineteenth century we conquered the machine, and in the twentieth century we conquered space. Now we are ready to conquer the mind. The twenty-first century will be the era of the brain, as we begin to chart this largely unmapped terrain. The first two millennia were much about perfecting the art and science of making things. The third millenium will be about figuring out how we did it.

Decoding the process of thinking is the Next Big Thing, with exciting research already pouring out on the subject of subjects. Rather than reading intelligence by IQ, for example, a new generation of scholars is proposing theories of alternative intelligences and even EQ (Emotional Quotient). Expect interest in the mind's inner workings to become a full-fledged obsession in the years ahead, the key to unlimited experience, discovery, and fantasy.

sign #1:  gray matter

So what, exactly, is going on above our necks, culturally speaking? Well, quite a lot, fortunately. Do not despair over talk of the dumbing-down of America or the flattening of our cognitive bell curve. As we satisfy our perpetual urge to assimilate new information, our collective *gray matter* continues to grow. *Gray matter* has much to do with the Information Age, which is driving our need to acquire more and more intellectual capital. On an individual level, the thirst for knowledge is part of the process of self-actualization, an idea that inspires baby boomers in particular.

Equally important is the shift toward self-education, part and parcel of our reduced reliance on "experts." Traditional forms of education and learning are being challenged by those dissatisfied with institutions, government, and authority in general. *Gray matter* will continue to take new shape as we live up to the creed that the mind is a terrible thing to waste.

Education

Adults have recognized that education is a continuous, lifelong experience rather than something limited to the young. The service-based, global, technology-driven economy of the twenty-first century is driving adults to create new *gray matter*. According to *Daedulus*, 89 percent of all jobs being created today require some sort of post-secondary education. Re-engineered adults are returning *en masse* to college to get more degrees, and continuing education programs are responding, offering classes in everything from Spying 101 to How to Put Up Drywall. Today adult learning is more often combined with social activities, creating a new form of edutainment. Book clubs have emerged as *fin de siecle* quilting bees, merging reading, discussion, and coffee-klatching.

On a larger scale, seniors are hustling off to Elderhostels every chance they get, in the belief that group learning is more rewarding than that lonely trek. Ten thousand Elderhostel courses at 1,000 host institutions are offered every year, in fact, as over-fifty-fivers spend $325 to $440 a pop to expand their *gray matter*. Go-go geezers immerse themselves in subjects such as regional culinary heritage, lives of eccentric authors, and the art and science of gemology.

Participation in travel clubs is another way people with common interests can develop new *gray matter* and have fun at the same time. Check out the turtles in the Galapagos Islands, or learn how to cook real Italian cuisine in Tuscany. Your wish is a travel agent's command.

For kids, education ain't what it used to be. More kids than ever are forgoing public education, heading off to charter schools or to the kitchen table for home schooling. The trend toward smaller, more intimate schools is consistent with today's educational mission of building kids' relationships with other kids and with their own self-esteem. Decentralized schools have allowed for more diverse curricula and greater leeway in educational mission. The result will be a future generation of adults with very different ideas about what constitutes intelligence.

Encouraging girls' *gray matter* has become a priority as schools finally create girl-friendly classrooms, where Sally is encouraged to develop her full potential. Parents' involvement in schools is taking a turn down a different hallway, as in the case of Security Dads. In kids' worst nightmare, dads roam the halls as alternative security forces, replacing guards or teachers who were notoriously ineffective. We'll put our Iconomoney on an angry dad versus a Crip or a Blood any day of the week.

Primary education today is a swirling maelstrom of tradition clashing with the anticipated needs of the twenty-first century. Determining valedictorians by grades has fallen out of favor, perceived as way too hierarchical and elitist in these days of team building and egalitarianism. In its place is greater recognition of community service performed by students, which lays the seeds for a whole generation of civic-minded adults. School yearbooks are moving closer to extinction, an anachronism for a generation raised on CD-ROMs and Web browsing.

Somewhat paradoxically, however, school uniforms are back in style, with more plaid seen on playgrounds today than on the set of *Braveheart*. Waiting lists for admission to private, preparatory, and Catholic schools are often years long, as many parents seek safe havens for their kids from the nightmare that is often public education. For kids today, *gray matter* is about finding the educational formula that best fits the needs of each child.

iconogasm: cultural climax, marketing opportunity
Leverage consumers' desire to add more matter to their *gray matter* through educational products and services.

Self-Improvement

"Our goal is simple . . . to help you reach yours." —Successories motto

A big chunk o' *gray matter*, of course, revolves around our gaining more knowledge about ourselves. The quest for personal growth is taking interesting twists and turns, embodied in places like Successories, the Noah's Ark of self-help products. With more than ninety retail stores, Successories is tapping into Corporate America's lust for motivationalia. If you're in search of words to live by, Successories is a veritable bible of creeds, inspiring messages, and timeless insights to stir your inner whatever. Its line of motivational decor (do not mention the word "poster" to a Successorian) is designed to help that goal-driven guy or gal down the path of self-discovery and, ultimately, success. According to Successories, "Research indicates motivational wall decor can significantly impact employee performance," no doubt a cost-effective investment in the age of re-engineering. If a lithograph doesn't turn employee Sluggo into Salesperson of the Year, check out Successories' collection of "Attitude Apparel," a line of T-shirts, hats, and sweatshirts stamped with the age-old adage "Attitude is everything." If that doesn't work, Sluggo probably needs something from Successories' Lombardi Collection, a cornucopia of books, plaques, and prints inspired by that Green Bay Packer in the sky. Successories believes that "you become what you think about," challenging the traditional tenet that "you are what you eat" (unless maybe you can become what you think about eating). In any case, Successories is blazing the trail of the new business frontier where inspiration meets perspiration.

iconogasm: cultural climax, marketing opportunity
Jump on the current theology preaching that success is a matter of knowing who you are.

Wisdom

Cruised the aisles of your local bookstore recently? A bona fide wisdomfest has hit the publishing biz as readers look for the answers to the big questions of life. Beside the undisputed heavyweight champion of publishing, the Bible, religion-oriented books have descended upon us like a plague of locusts. Bill Moyers, that font of wisdom, has led the charge with *Genesis: A Living Conversation*, a testament to the power of hope, forgiveness, and redemption. If your tastes lean more to the Founding Fathers rather than the Holy Father, check out Paul M. Zall's *The Wit & Wisdom of the Founding Fathers*. Within its pages, one will find pearly gems written or spoken by George Washington, John Adams, Thomas Jefferson, and Benjamin Franklin.

Wisdom of an entirely different nature is served up by Rachel Naomi Remen in *Kitchen Table Wisdom*, which celebrates the resiliency of the human condition. Remen, an M.D. specializing in psych-oncology, uses stories of healing to demonstrate how people are indelibly connected. Even kids are being looked upon as wise ones. *The 11th Commandment: Wisdom from Our Children* offers wee words of advice ("Try not to get divorced," for example), while *Kids' Book of Wisdom: Quotes from the African-American Tradition* gives children some juicy nuggets to live by. If none of these whets your wisdom whistle, look for *The Wit and Wisdom of the 2000-Year-Old Man in the Year 2000*, a sequel to the classic routine created by Carl Reiner and Mel Brooks. It all means one thing: Wise up!

In search of the secrets of success, Corporate America is more open than ever to alternative approaches to wisdom. One of today's leading gurus is James A. Autry, a former *Fortune* 500 senior vice president turned poet. Autry retired as head of the Meredith Corporation's Magazine Group in 1991 to conduct leadership seminars and write books such as *Life and Work: A Manager's Search for Meaning*. In a later volume, *Confessions of an Accidental Businessman: It Takes a Lifetime to Find Wisdom*, Autry maintains his belief that leaders can learn a lot from poetry. His management philosophy revolves around the ideas that leadership should be a form of stewardship and that inspirational poetry is one way to rally oneself and one's troops.

At the Ehama Institute in the Santa Cruz Mountains, managers skin the wisdom cat a different way. Executives from organizations as diverse as Mattel and the Air Force are heading to the hills to learn from Rainbow Hawk and Wind Eagle, a married Native American couple. In the Institute's tepeed training facility, Mr. Hawk and Ms. Eagle instruct corporate types in ancient Native American teachings for arriving at new methods of holistic problem solving. The highlight of the weekend course is the "council ceremony," during which participants gather around a sixty-foot circle with a fire pit as its center. Wearing special robes and censed with fragrant sage smoke, each member adopts one of eight different perspectives or attitudes in the tradition of Indian councils.

iconogasm: cultural climax, marketing opportunity
Expect ways of wisdom not taught at Harvard Business School to gain cultural legitimacy.

Technology

Technology has redefined the ways we acquire and express knowledge, opening up new channels (literally) of discourse. Products like Web TV give access to the Internet, a portable college in a box, for just a couple of hundred bucks. Having a million- (billion?) dollar library at one's fingertips is, in historical terms, an unprecedented opportunity. As the encyclopedia of the new millennium is indexed, expect the Net to become our primary source of information and communication.

Television has become our new schoolhouse, tapping into our lust to know more about the world we live in (or at least watch). The popularity of cable networks such as Arts & Entertainment, the Discovery Channel, and the History Channel signals the opportunity for us to split up the information pie in an infinite number of slices.

Growing up with computers will inevitably produce a generation of adults who think, speak, and write much differently from their parents. According to *Technology and Learning*, 2 million K–12 students will have access to the Internet by the year 2000, the basis for what is being called "webucation." Seeing the writing on the screen, *Wired* magazine has issued a "Kids' Rights" manifesto for the Net, while *Smartkid* has formed a magazine and website for li'l smartypants. The backpack accessory kids crave most, Virtual Gameboy, has astutely partnered with the National Education Association to action-pack curricula. History homework for kids tonight: to virtually experience Lincoln's Gettysburg Address and then write a two-minute speech on the merits of honesty.

$$4 + 7 \times 10 \div 3 = x$$

the capital of Michigan is...

Microsoft and Apple have jumped into the techno-educational fray by sponsoring school-based learning events for families. Over the course of one academic year, Microsoft held Family Technology Nights in thirty cities, providing free one-hour computer seminars. PTAs organized the seminars, with local geeks demonstrating how the digitally challenged can get online. Microsoft products were made available at discounted prices, and a portion of sales earned free software for participating schools. Apple has tapped into the *gray matter* market by distributing free Family Computing Workshop kits, which provide schools with the necessary materials to hold workshops on their own. These efforts represent exemplary *gray matter* marketing, a truly cooperative alliance among businesses, schools, and consumers.

iconogasm: cultural climax, marketing opportunity
Develop creative ways your company can help schools and at the same time build brand equities.

Arts and Crafts

The very opposite of technology is also at the core of *gray matter*. Arts and crafts are experiencing a renaissance, in part as a backlash against our overcyberized, ultradigitized world. Americans are flocking to learn new skills that help them get in touch with the left sides of their brains. Regret quitting piano when you hit puberty? Many do and are again taking music lessons so they can play the classics. Shostakovich may be out of reach, but in a couple of years you could pick up a Mozart sonata or two.

Language lessons have become *de rigueur* for those sorry they quit French or Italian when they were know-it-all teenagers. Again, fluency may be a stretch, but in just a few weeks one can impress the fois gras out of a date at Chez Shishi.

Writing, too, is back in style as we yearn for what is becoming a lost art. Poetry readings abound at cafés, birthing a new generation of Allen Ginsbergs. Every Generation Xer we know is writing a screenplay destined to knock Robert Redford over at a future Sundance Film Festival. Lawyers are dropping their briefs to write the Great American Novel, trying to follow the same path blazed by John Grisham. Family histories have become an exercise of passion as younger generations record their parents', grandparents', and great-grandparents' stories for future generations. There's extra credit for going back to the Old Country to examine local birth and death records, but keep in mind that you might discover a debtor or ne'er-do-well on the family tree.

iconogasm: cultural climax, marketing opportunity
Help consumers turn their *gray matter* a rainbow of colors through artistic ventures.

sign #2: altered states

Thought the days of mind expansion went out with the Nehru suit? Think again, or, should we say, think *alternatively.* The desire to change one's emotional or psychological state of being, what we called *altered states*, is still very much alive and well. Perhaps more than ever, people are interested in pushing their cognitive brains to turn their fantasies into realities. People are actively seeking ways to adopt alternate identities, to temporarily become, in essence, other people. Why such interest in trying on new forms of consciousness? The legacy of the counterculture has created a climate that encourages experimentation of all kinds, leading to a plethora of tricks we yearn to play on ourselves.

Entertainment

Nose rubbed raw on the grindstone? Escape to the silver screen, whether it's a made-for-cable *Tsunami over Texas* catastrophe, a fifty-nine-cent rent-a-vid romance for your home-entertainment cocoon, or a trip uptown for a Real Butter cine-blockbuster. Whatever the setting, movies send us into full-fledged *altered states* of being. That flat, flickering image is evolving into a full celluloid jacket of 3-D sight, next-generation Dolby or THX sound, and seats that go bump in the dark. Movie theaters and home theaters are battling to win over consumers' film fancies, and *we* are the victors. Sit back and let your mind wander into Jane Austen's nineteenth-century England or the distant galaxies of George Lucas's twenty-fifth century. Congratulations! You just proved Einstein's Theory of Relativity, moving through the dimensions of time and space without even getting up for a snack!

iconogasm: cultural climax, marketing opportunity
Position your products and services as resources for the imagination, the real final frontier.

Travel

People in every society need to have some *altered states* for getting away from it all, and we have plenty. As stress becomes the normal state of being for those unable to pursue simpler ways, opportunities to hop out of the pressure cooker are growing. Destinations of escape include race-car schools and cooking schools in Italy or France, offering the frazzled full immersion in exotic learning experiences. For the most thrilling forty-five seconds of your life (okay, second-most thrilling), hit the Olympic bobsled run at Lake Placid, New York. You'll ride shotgun with a professional sledder so "Rosebud" doesn't become your final gasp. For the man or woman with everything, including a headful o' worries, aeronautic escapes await. Just take a ride on a jet fighter or, for the vertigo-inclined, a 747 flight simulator. Waxing nostalgic for those good times at Camp Runamok? Sign up for adult summer camp; or if you're one of those few good men and women who wants to experience life as a new Marine recruit, sign up for boot camp. An ex-sergeant will make you drop and give him twenty, and you'll be better for it.

Nature, of course, provides us with a hotbed of *altered states*. Western cattle drives await city slickers, and outdoor-survival vacations offer more than skinned knees for those who want to push their abilities to the limit. You'll be dropped off somewhere in deep woods and have to find your way back to civilization. Bark never tasted so good!

iconogasm: cultural climax, marketing opportunity
Change consumers' attitudes by changing their latitudes.

Gender Infidelity

One of the more interesting sites for *altered states* is centered around gender. Seems like every other movie these days has a man wearing a dress, while in TRW (The Real World), transgenders are ready, willing, and able to break out that new, cute Ann Taylor. Mick Jagger and Axel Rose have shown us that a man in a skirt can be more macho than a Hell's Angel. Even the No Fear set (teenage boys) are wearing nail polish to show off their sexual confidence. You know gender infidelity is legitimate when an NBA star can sign autographs in a bridal gown.

With anonymity a major attraction of online culture, both men and women are adopting *altered states* as their better halves. There's even a place in New York City where a woman can be professionally made up to be a "Man For a Day," giving her a glimpse into life with a different set of reproductive organs. We venture to say that the traditional male/female archetype is gradually breaking down as men and women adopt characteristics of the opposite sex. Get ready for a gender-neutral "third sex" to emerge in the first decades of the next century.

iconogasm: cultural climax, marketing opportunity

Tap into the narrowing gap between Venus and Mars as women and men get down to Earth and embrace alternative gender roles.

Spirituality

As any fire-and-brimstoner can (and will) tell you, spirituality has always been a means for achieving *altered states*. As we approach the end of the millennium, however, people are getting that old-time religion in new and different ways. Higher states of consciousness are being realized, for example, at motivation seminars led by charismatic leaders. Attend one of Tony Robbins's harangue-a-thons, and you'll be standing on your seat, yelling, "Yes, I can!" before you can say "Sammy Davis." Make a pilgrimage to a Promise Keepers rally (more on this in chapter 3), and you'll find yourself "fresh with Jesus," chock full of the power and the glory.

A more independent type might make a silent retreat to push the mute button on the end of the twentieth century. Silent retreaters spend some time at monasteries or other spiritual places to listen to themselves think. Even better, make a vision quest to reach a higher plane—expose yourself to the elements for a few days while going without food, water, and sleep, and you'll see God too. The renewed popularity of mind-body techniques such as meditation and yoga is another sign of our interest in visiting different bioemotive states.

iconogasm: cultural climax, marketing opportunity
Play God by raising people's spiritual consciousness.

Pharmacology

When all else fails, there are always drugs. Actually, drugs are a traditional avenue for experiencing alternative realities, rooted in, well, roots and other plant life. Pharmacologically induced states of being are more popular now, however, than when Goldie Hawn wore plastic dresses on *Laugh-In*.

The new generation of mood-control drugs has revolutionized America's collective temperament. Prozac, in fact, is the most prescribed drug at Target Store pharmacies. Legal drugs such as Herbal Ecstacy, Cloud Nine, and Ultimate Euphoria have segued from fringe rave culture to mainstream club culture quite nicely, thank you. Just pop a few all-natural, almost-all-caffeine tabs, and you'll be doing the macarena to techno music, about as scary an *altered state* as we have ever heard. Harder core, illegal drugs like psychedelics and heroin have made a big comeback as rush seekers make a rush for the ultimate high. The less adventurous look to over-the-counter products such as Ginkgold, Kava Kava, or blue green algae, preparations that purportedly help you think more clearly.

A more atmospheric *altered state* approach is to take oxygen hits, an increasingly popular trend we first spotted in Japanese bars some years ago. Just hook yourself up to a tank of O_2 and feel the rush of pure, untainted air. Brace yourself for more added-value air as marketers brand the ultimate commodity. Will Perrier bottle and sell just the bubbles?

iconogasm: cultural climax, marketing opportunity
Tap into our desire to play mind games by defining products and services as providers of *altered states* of consciousness.

sign #3: back to the future

So what lies ahead for the future? The past, of course. History is being used as an active resource, repackaged in infinite combinations to create new products and services. Postmodernists will even tell you that we have no original culture anymore, that everything around us is a pastiche of other times and places. Neo-Freudians will tell you that the past is everything, because the present is fleeting and the future is yet to be. Shakespeare would tell you that the past is prologue, but he's dead. Or is he? In many ways, the Bard is more alive than ever, reaching a bigger audience today than he ever did in sixteenth century England.

As a society, we are steeped in the past because it is safe and known, a warm and fuzzy feeling in the pit of our collective consciousness. Was the *Brady Bunch* that good the first time around? Not really, but reincarnating the happy, shiny family elicits a powerful sense of *déjà vu* all over again. People under a certain age are actually surprised to learn that at one point we didn't feel compelled to reference something from the past, that something was actually *new*. Holy existentialism, Batman!

Memory Marketing

Marketers have caught on to the power of memory, exhuming the bones of the past and wrapping them up in brand-new skins. Fashion marketers constantly reinterpret styles of the past for those too young to remember them. Collecting and wearing vintage *haute couture* have become all the rage as the demand for the real thing exceeds the supply. Many advertisers have given new life to dead icons, providing a steady stream of income to the lucky descendants of such stars. Steve McQueen is pitching Persol sunglasses, Gary Cooper is again cruising around in a Mercedes, and Marlene Dietrich's nasal passages have finally been cleared with the help of Breathe Right strips. Fred Astaire dances with a vacuum cleaner, while the Duke swaggers for Coors beer.

Fragrance marketers are positioning their products around the glamor associated with stars of the past. Want to smell like Marilyn Monroe in her prime, circa 1962? A little dab of Chanel No. 5 behind the ears will do ya. Media is increasingly living in the past through Nick at Night rerun TV and in one of the hottest book genres, memoir. Historic radio programs are coming back, allowing a new generation to listen in the dark and create their own visions. We call all this history mania *memory marketing*, a strategic packaging of the past. *Memory marketing* will become only more effective as aging boomers try to relive the halcyon days of their youth.

iconogasm: cultural climax, marketing opportunity
Take a trip through time and recycle the stuff of our collective past.

American Icons

Nowhere is *back to the future* so evident than in the recycling of classic American culture. While America has become more diverse, traditional icons of national identity are stronger than ever. Those American symbols which we all can agree are rare and precious will only appreciate in value. Consider the return of the American diner, a reminder of a time when things were simpler and food tasted better. Or how about the renewed popularity of shoe brands considered the staples of our collective foot consciousness? Hush Puppies are again soothing our aching dogs, while Converse and Jack Purcell sneakers are *de rigueur* for the properly attired Generation Xer. Fashion marketers such as Ralph Lauren have leveraged their brands' American identity into new products for the home, splashing their packages with warm and fuzzy graphics of flags, front porches, and other Norman Rockwellian images.

If that growling sound in the distance is what we think it is, the motorcycle business is ready to go *back to the future*. Harley-Davidson execs are hearing 1200cc footsteps getting closer; the American motorcycle market dominated by Boss Hog is just too juicy for others not to throw their helmets into the ring. Excelsior-Henderson of Belle Plaine, Minnesota, will be the first chopper out of the blocks when its Super-X heavyweight cruiser rolls off the line in 1998. The Excelsior-Henderson brand was one of the original Big Three American cycle manufacturers, resurrected to recall the romance of pre–World War II motorcycles. E-H will target upscale boomers compelled by biker culture.

Polaris also is going to charge into the motorcycle fray, leveraging its manufacturing and distribution strengths in snowmobiles, personal watercraft, and all-terrain vehicles. Polaris's motorcycle line will be branded "Victory," another reference to the mystique surrounding bikes of yesteryear. With 30 percent gross margins, more than half the North American market share, and a Sturgis-sized waiting list, Harley has become an American success story too irresistible to remain unchallenged. Look for other transportation icons (Packard? Duesenberg? Pierce-Arrow?) to be brought back to life in the years ahead as savvy *memory marketers* package our collective consciousness.

iconogasm: cultural climax, marketing opportunity
Turn icons of American popular, consumer, and material culture into compelling business opportunities.

Health Care

Back to the future can be found even in health care. Ads from the 1930s decorate the walls, a *Collier's* magazine sits on a table, and Benny Goodman blares from a stereo that would require carbon dating to determine its age. No, you're not at an antique store; you're in the Alzheimer's wing at the Jewish Home of Central New York. This 151-bed nursing home is an entire environment of Depression-era America, when most of the septuagenarian and octogenarian patients were young whippersnappers. With many Alzheimer's patients' long-term memory better than their short-term, the therapy is helping them feel calmer and safer by surrounding them with familiar things of the distant past. The nursing home, decorated with vintage furniture found at flea markets and in grandmas' attics (kind of like our houses), also holds the occasional sock hop. This therapy for superseniors is an interesting example of how to recycle the past for use today. Unless a cure is found, more boomers will eventually be struck by Alzheimer's, raising some interesting scenarios of what their re-created primes might look like in thirty years. What will our grandchildren think when they visit us in nursing homes filled with bongs, black-light posters, and the Strawberry Alarm Clock wafting out of the eight-track?

iconogasm: cultural climax, marketing opportunity
Leverage the ability for memories to have a positive effect on our emotional and physical health.

The Arts

The music scene is pulsating memories. One of the truest, most indigenous American art forms, the blues has proven to be an enduring force, convincing new generations of Big Mamas and Big Daddies to get down and get dirty. The pure energy and raw emotion of the blues appeal to our rekindled desire for honesty, simplicity, and hearing it straight from the heart. Without synthesizers to muddy the musical waters, the blues is 150 proof that less can definitely be more in our streamlined times.

Blues clubs, already among the more popular joints in many a town, are getting a jolt of delta energy as the House of Blues chain and syndicated radio programs of soul man Elwood Blues himself, Dan Akroyd, jellyroll across the Mason-Dixon line. Not to be out-bluesed, the king of the blues, B. B. King, is tuning up his own Memphis-based club with branches in New York, L.A., and San Francisco. Expect blues, jazz, and other staples of our musical heritage to outlive any angry rock 'n' roll genre.

The Derby, the Hollywood club made famous in the film *Swingers*, is the definitive world capital of swing, another form of music that is now taking us *back to the future*. The Derby is a veritable feast of retro sights, sounds, and tastes, filled with the hippest icons of American popular culture. Daddies (men) and babies (women) sip frufru drinks in colors that do not occur in nature. We recommend a Cosmopolitan, sort of like an 80-proof Big Gulp. The red, king-sized-bed pool table is more sculpture than sporting equipment, and the private booths simply sing with romance. Be prepared for the occasional waft of Macanudo smoke to envelop you like a three-alarm fire in Cuba. The pizzas, by the way, are a *tour de force* in flour, tomatoes, and lactose. Dress is formally casual (casually formal?), but vintage fabrics with chemical-sounding names are a necessity. Do not wear flannel unless you're Dave Pirner or Eddie Vedder.

And oh, there's the music. Swing jumps from the stage, making one's body do things never done before (in public). Dancers toss one another around like rivets but are sure to follow the clearly posted house rules: NO AERIALS. Wednesday nights are particularly hot, with Big Bad Voodoo Daddy chopping at the woodside. You may run into an actual celebrity, but you're more likely to run into people who've met Heidi Fleiss or Faye Resnick at a party. Music starts around 10:00, so bring a date and don't be late. Pretense and affectation never felt so good.

The theater has gone *back to the future* in a big way by reviving shows of the past and by packaging history in exciting new ways. The recent Broadway musical *Bring in 'Da Noise, Bring in 'Da Funk* is poetry in full-force motion, a potent historical tap-dance timeline from slave ship to gospel, hip hop, and beyond. According to creator/director George C. Wolfe, the show's idea came from his vision of Savion Glover (lead tapper and choreographer) as a living depository of rhythm: "There are these old black tap dancers who were taught by the old black tap dancers, and so on. All of those guys passed on that information to Savion, and it landed in his feet, and his being, and his soul. . . . I wanted to see how we could use tap to convey desires and drives—how it could become a source of delight, intensity, rage, or power." And it does, every heel-and-toe pigeonwing, double-shuffle step of the way. The young cast, all in their twenties, are so passionate as folk-art storytellers—with poetry, photography, video, dance, drumming, song—you can't help but be swept into the historical moment. *Noise*'s critical bravos, four Tonys, and roaring box office demonstrate the power of history when viscerally presented.

 iconogasm: cultural climax, marketing opportunity
Dust off your company's or product's past to bring in 'da biz.

chapter 2: body

Think Gumby—that cute green guy with rubberized limbs. He could b the celebrity spokesperson touting our society's relationship with th body. Americans are stretchflexing their bods, concocting the stranges sometimes dangerous, at all times boundary-bruising ways to put o organs to the test. Some lean and serene Gumbys routinely defy gravit racing their agile buddies up cliffs of granite or kayaking white water eve the Clintons couldn't navigate. Other Gumbys tweak their senses wit exotic snorts, elixirs, and rubs to stimulate desire, relaxation, energy concentration, or healing. This is the age of skin as Play-Doh. Any Gumb unhappy with a flat chest or square chin can easily resculpt his parts c tattoo her tush. Gumby may be an egotist, a risk hog, a hopeful romanti or all in one. Most important, Gumby's main muscle, the heart, is beatin with a renewed rhythm, nurtured by a *joie de vivre* awakening to th purest, simplest joys of life.

sign #4:  carpe diem

Seize the day! Forget about *pushing* the envelope. *Shred it!* This is the attitude advancing an all-out quest for fun, passion, adventure, and guilt-free experiences of the Now. The *carpe diem* headwater is youth culture, but the free-fall, lockjawed, daredevil compulsion to press the body to its limit has also grabbed boomers by their hedonistic balls. *Carpe diem* jettisons the Christian theology of sacrifice and delayed gratification, replacing it with attitudes and actions screaming, "WE WANT TO HEAR, TOUCH, SEE, SMELL, TASTE THE RUSH NOW."

Sports

Anyone for train hopping, road luging, night-vision mountain running, shovel racing, downhill snow biking, speed ice climbing? These are but a few of the next-generation extreme sports stretching the limits of head and limbs. They're not for the faint of heart. It's likely that at any cramponned moment you face a staredown with Mr. Death, but that's part of the shrill thrill. No one lives forever, right?

Capitalizing on the insane sport of it all and the big-money angle, ESPN spun out the Winter X Games. In January 1997, $200,000 of corporate-sponsored booty baited more than 100 athletes to hit the wall. These more-is-more games were a gasp to watch for 20 million viewers in 150 countries, proving the tremendous audience appeal that is growing extreme sports by quantum leaps and bounds. Expect a rapid cloning of extreme dream competitions—Discovery Channel's Eco Challenge Adventure Race ("Before you can win you've got to *survive*")—to capitalize *carpe diem*'s catastrophic edge.

It's said that *carpe diem* devotees are addicted to adrenaline. Intense experiences literally invade your bloodstream. During an adrenaline rush, the body releases dopamine, the same hormone activated by having sex or sniffing cocaine. The euphoric, orgasmic sky-high keeps 'em coming back for more and greater risk rushes. One sport valued for its adrenaline quotient is BASE (Buildings, Antennae, Spans, and Earth) jumping—strapping on a parachute and hurling yourself off a highrise building or other fixed object (gives us a buzz just thinking about it). For BASErs, half the fun comes from stealthing under society's laws prohibiting such foolishness; the other half comes from sheer stomach-somersaulting terror. The Eiffel Tower is BASE jumping's pinnacle *pièce de résistance*. *Vive la France!*

If you're thinking this is a Men's Only Grill, meet Missy "the Missile" Giove and Susan DeMattei. They've made blasting terrain on fat-tire bikes their sport. DeMattei, on her Diamondback, won the bronze in Atlanta's Olympic cross-country mountain-bike racing competition. Missy's claim to fame: She's an in-and-out-of-control wildfire on wheels. She consistently pulls down a reported $300,000 a year from prize purses and corporate endorsers like Reebok. Her *carpe diem* credo: "What really keeps me motivated to keep risking my life is the feeling of hanging it all out, raging on my bike, going as fast as I can. It's a huge rush. And it's a philosophy of life."

You don't always have to sport killer abs to be a *carpe diem* devotee. Killer instincts seize the day (and skin) in ultimate fighting, the latest event to challenge the accepted belief that homo sapiens is the most advanced species on the planet. Called ultimate, extreme, or toughman fighting, this unregulated form of boxing forgoes wimpy gloves and mouthpieces and allows cerebellum-challenged pugilists to attack any part of the body. No training or experience is required, and forget about matching fighters by weight. And oh, there are no rounds or rests. The zero-holds-barred sport is gaining popularity, thanks to the ear-chomping escapades of Mike Tyson. Can you say "Apocalypse now"?

👁 **iconogasm:** cultural climax, marketing opportunity
The rush is on. Think about ways to package and deliver the addictive experience, then *do it.*

The Hero's Journey

Carpe diem is more often than not an individual adventure. Sure, *technically* it may be a group jumping out of a chopper to snorkel-ski the Bugaboos, but it's *your* legs, *your* lungs, *your* life insurance policy on the line. If and when the gene hunters officially identify a high-risk DNA demon, we can hang the credit/blame on body chemistry. Until then, let's attribute the crave for dangerous fun to a modernist's spin on the mythic hero's journey: "[The hero] feels there's something lacking in the normal experiences available or permitted to the members of his society. This person then takes off on a series of adventures beyond the ordinary, either to recover what has been lost or to discover some life giving elixir," writes Joseph Campbell in *The Power of Myth.* Millennial elixir? Adrenaline Shooters.

iconogasm: cultural climax, marketing opportunity
Is there a hero inside your product, service, or self that's itching to break free? Provide the tools for making the journey. 👁

Fans

For bods that can't or don't want to cut the athletic mustard, *carpe diem* attitude is alive and yelling from the sidelines, courtside, and in the bleachers of major-league sports. The birth of super-fandom—those dudes and dudettes decked out in cheese wedge heads and team colors costumes or seen scrawling J-E-T-S on their shirtless bellies—is ferocious fun. Granted, you're not laying your life on the line by acting dingy at a Raiders game, but being caught on camera brandishing your belly is an irresistible thrill. What drives these antics is a need to feel truly alive, to kick decorum in the teeth, to let it all hang loose, and that can be addictive as well.

iconogasm: cultural climax, marketing opportunity
Girls and boys just want to have fun! Amp packaging and promotions to new levels of excitement. 👁

Media

Have BIG MOUTH, will travel. Out there on the absurd edge is a posse of *carpe diem* broncobusters breaking the rules and ratings records of radio. We agree, it is hard to fathom that this new breed of smart, tart-tongued talkers came out of the same closet as Fibber McGee and Molly, but for the big guns—Don Imus, Rush Limbaugh, Howard Stern, Sports Babe Nanci Donnellson, "Dr. Laura" Schlessinger—shooting off their mouths is how they earn the bounty and why they are wildly popular. Each has his or her own unique brand of brash. They have no fear as they kick out all the stops, making a beeline for their callers' jugulars. These airwave wranglers dish out heaping helpings of outrage and hilarity; political, social, and spiritual disdain; sobbing sympathy; and tabloid-style advice. Listeners tune in by the zillions, hungry for an interactive daily dose of emotions from these surrogate snipers. In-your-face radio is a war of words, delivering a *carpe diem* mind rush to callers, listeners, and dj's alike.

iconogasm: cultural climax, marketing opportunity
For marketers not afraid of controversy, the cryptic edge courts a mega audience.

sign #5:  joie de vivre

We're talking pure, unadulterated luuuuuv. It's one of the enduring joys of life, rooted in sensuality, aesthetics, and earthly delights. There's no need to apologize for our French accent as Americans are captivated by *joie de vivre*—the joy of life. This reveling is the naughty big sis of all ages. Boomers are finally taking a breather to smell the roses while those rambunctious Generation Xers are already revved up to take a juicy bite out of it all. And don't forget the feisty seniors, kicking up their heels on golf courses, tennis courts, and in museums all over the world. How does that old luuuv song go? "They asked me how I knew my true love was true / I, of course, replied / something here inside cannot be denied. . . ."

Books

How do I love thee? Let *joie de vivre* count the ways, and for starters, in the itty-bittiest books imaginable. Have you ever spied so many tiny tomes on the joys of living life to the overflowingest? Pop into a local independent bookseller or one of the big chains to see these romantic little cuties. The typical pygmy format fits in your palm, and there is a stunning diversity of titles. For true romanticos there are at least twenty-five declarations of unrequited love, such as *African Love Poems & Proverbs, The Kiss, Motherhood: A Gift of Love,* and *Love Letters,* a 125-page, no-bigger-than-a-minute manuscript of cherished intimacies from Mark Twain, Sir Walter Scott, Virginia Woolf, Napoleon, Mary Todd Lincoln, and that insatiable duo Henry Miller ("To stay with you for one night I would throw away my whole life") and Anaïs Nin ("I am overflowingly, desperately in love with you").

We didn't have enough fingers to count all the angels in flight. Next to Billy Graham's *An Angel a Week,* the wee *Christmas Angels: A Pop-Up Book* was aflutter. Name a favorite hobby, sport, or obsession, and there's a minimonogram of *joie: The Quotable Teddy Bear, A Little Book of Saints, Friends* (killer lines from Rachel, Ross, and the gang), *Sherlock Holmes, Jackie* (Kennedy), *Golf Talk, Oy Vey! Jewish Wit,* and *Country Music's Best and Funniest Lines* ("There ain't no queen in my king-sized bed").

iconogasm: cultural climax, marketing opportunity
Little things say a lot. How about reducing that annual report or corporate mission into a statement of vision and love?

Sensual Products

Joy, of course, is an intrinsic quality of *joie de vivre* products. Consumers are infatuated with the beauty and luxurious textures of sumptuous bath towels, hooded terry robes, and 300-thread-count Egyptian cotton bedsheets. For that reason, it makes remarkably savvy sense for Kmart to jump into the shower with Martha Stewart bath and bed boutiques to mass market joy. Cozy up with your honey in an ultradown comforter or Polar fleece blanket, a steal at less than forty dollars.

While we're exploring sensual subjects, what could be sexier than slinking into the Piggly Wiggly wearing your Marilyn Monroe–brand silk teddy underneath those sweats? Warners is betting the lingerie drawer that women will love to scratch their seven-year itch. Fulfilling our intimate-wear fantasies may garner the Warnaco Group, Marilyn's sugar daddy, as much as $50 million in yearly revenues. All these items may take a tad bigger bite out of the budget, but consumers feel it's a small price for tactile bliss.

iconogasm: cultural climax, marketing opportunity
Snuggle up to consumers with products and services offering ultra comfort.

Little Luxuries

The "I'm worth it!" philosophy continues to drive the affordable-luxury craze. Indulging ourselves is much different today than in the big-ticket spendthrift '80s. The theme is feeling good about our authentic selves rather than trying to impress someone else with an Armani suit or showy set of wheels. Don't get us wrong; luxury goods are selling well, with no abrupt end in sight, but consumers jarred by an ever-downsizing icon-toppling world are giving more thought to how they spend their greenbacks. That's why people are forgoing a sixty-dollar lunch and deriving great glee from a three-dollar latte sipped languidly at a sidewalk café.

Whether you sign on with one of the budding bouquet-of-the-month clubs or shell out four dollars for a bunch of pungent posies at a Safeway or Payless Drug Eurostyle flowermart, blossoms indicate a mainstream infatuation with bringing scent and sensuality into everyday life. Why wait for the weekend when life is to be lived and loved all week through?

For the twenty-ones and over, the quest to quench the *joie de vivre* thirst has retreaded cocktail culture. May we recommend a window seat at Sonsie's, a Boston bistro, where the martini menu beckons with killer concoctions like Ed's Chocolate Martini (Absolut, crème de cacao, and a chocolate-covered almond) or Tom's Manhattan (Makers Mark bourbon, sweet *and* dry vermouth, a dash of bitters, and a cherry)? Guys have all the fun! But wait! Gals do too—they're smoking Escudo Cubanos and hoisting single-barrel bourbon with a vengeance.

iconogasm: cultural climax, marketing opportunity
Present products as accoutrements of the good life.

25

Art

Hoity-toity is out. Egalitarian is in. In the twenty-first century, the arts are for and by everybody. No, we won't be saying *au revoir* to those venerable marble mausoleums built to showcase the masterpieces. In fact, expect their roles to expand by leaps and Lautrecs as museums open their treasure troves to the masses. Mounting supershows hyping an *artiste* as superhero continues to fuel the fascination of a new generation of culture hounds. In the late '90s, museums registered a 10-percent increase in attendance by hawking weeks-in-advance ticket sales that reserved viewer time slots for the "greatest hits" of Picasso, O'Keeffe, and Monet. With the right timing, spin doctoring, and Oprahesque personality revelations—Did Leonardo really view the world through dyslexic glasses?—the masters' momentum has no place to go but grow.

What does presenting art as Super Bowl blockbuster do to art? That's the question Don McNeal, curator of the General Mills modern art collection, talked about with us: "When you have to go to a museum to experience art, there is a real problem: Art doesn't really have anything to do with everyday life. It is something to pay homage to instead of being part of the fabric of life." McNeal seems to lament the day the Brits stole the Elgin Marbles, put them on pedestals, and called them Art. He's not alone. All over the country we see a movement to reconnect dance, painting, sculpture, photography, film, architecture, and myriad new media with the masses.

The momentum taking the arts to the streets springs from a widening reverence for and desire to express our creative selves. Children, recognized by arts administrators as a future lifeline, are being courted with classes, interactive hands-on exhibits, and in many cities their own museums. Currently, there are forty-six American youth museums, with an additional sixty-seven museums planned for the new millennium. Parents, deluged with creativity-expanding magazines, CD-ROMs, television, and institutional programming, feel anxiety pangs if their youngsters prefer Scooby Doo puzzles and the limiting eight-pack of Crayolas.

For the eighteen-to-twenty-four crowd it seems there's hardly a pierced ear who doesn't have a screenplay idea, a poem angsting, or a night gig playing bass. Boomers, never ones to be left out of what's in, are filling painting, sculpting, photography, and creative writing classes, preparing themselves for lucrative (?) second careers. It takes only a cruise through a Lions Club weekend art festival in Tucson or Sanibel to see seniors painting and peddling canvases of sunsets and saguaro cacti. For sure, gawking and hawking art aren't reserved for austere urban galleries or a Sotheby's auction anymore. Every which way you peer . . . art is here.

iconogasm: cultural climax, marketing opportunity
Is there an artist inside your customer? Coax and coddle his creativity.

Music

"The number of 18- to 24-year-old operagoers increased 18 percent between 1982 and 1992—even though that age group's overall population decreased 16 percent," *Time* reports, using figures from the National Endowment for the Arts. All signs are go; opera's on a millennial roll. With American youth cutting their wisdom teeth on *Aida* and *Cosi Fan Tutte*, maybe there's room for more than the Fugees in their repertoire. The figures make sense. The newest fans of "popera" love symbol-lush rock-music videos, and now with the friendly use of subtitles they can get down with the music and lip-synch the storyline too.

Joie de vivre is rekindling a love affair with all genres of music. The appointment of Leonard Slatkin to lead the National Symphony is seen by concert critics as a breakthrough for American composers; Slatkin is known for showcasing the nation's own—Duke Ellington, Leonard Bernstein, and other Yank legends. Music as a universal language comes through crystal clear in the public's embrace of world music's ethnic rhythms. Lately anything with the lilt of a Celtic lass or lassie is flowing like whiskey at an Irish wake. Uillean pipes, dulcimers, tin whistles, fiddles, bones, bodhrans, and accordions all lend their spirits to the haunting lullabies. The megawatt CD hit *River Dance* is a sellout even in children's bookstores.

Spontaneity is an intrinsic element of *joie de vivre* and is being leveraged by savvy marketers. At the Cannes Theater in Seaside, Oregon (population 5,580), we found motion-picture soundtracks wedged between the Junior Mints and Dots. Sophisticated retailers Old Navy, Victoria's Secret, and Starbucks offer their private, very hip CD music collections at irresistible prices, positioned by the register for a quick "I deserve this" buy. Acid jazz from those hepcats at The Pottery Barn has made its way into our Iconocollection, along with *Songs of Love* from V's Secret (Etta James, Michael Bolton, Tony Bennett, Vanessa Williams, and Sheena Easton, all under one cover). Combine that with an electric-blue bustier and even a Sultan's eunuch could get in the mood.

iconogasm: cultural climax, marketing opportunity

Align your brand with the universal, transcendent, passionate experience of music.

sign #6: biomorphing

Perpetual puberty? Today, a scary thought; in the next millennium, a body-bending opportunity. *Biomorphing* is the ability, desire, and technology to shapeshift any part of your anatomy into what you dream it should be. Thanks to science and imagination, the physical self is a *tabula rasa*, an infinitely malleable blank slate. Here's how it's playing itself out from the head to toe. CAUTION: *biomorphing* gets a bit slicey-dicey at times.

Hair

Those nasty telltale signs—dandruff, itchy scalp—and then one innocent April morning (horror of horrors) . . . clumps of hair in the comb . . . "OHMYGOD . . . It's sexy on Jason Alexander, but on *moi?* Ugh!" If you're one of the 22 million women experiencing hair loss, don't panic. Female follicle fallout is out of the closet and promises vigorous business growth, as big or bigger than the care available to their 30 million balding brothers. Hair-care healers are preaching the gospel of thicker, stronger, healthier hair through chemistry, hair-plug implants, and Dolly Parton wigs.

At Regenix Hair Retention System, the biologists are standing by; they "understand your concerns." Touting the latest in fiber-optic intrafollicular microanalysis, their individualized "herbaceutical" treatments promise to fertilize ailing manes. Rest assured that hair specialists are on full-bald-spot alert, ready to fight the hair bandits: micropollutants, impacted sebum, and follicle debris. Call today to schedule lab time at one of the many newly sprouted studios devoted to hair enhancement. Or, if you prefer, Rogaine topical cream is sold over-the-counter. Catch their commercials on MTV . . . yes, MTV!

iconogasm: cultural climax, marketing opportunity
The graying of America means the balding of America. Get head and shoulders over the competition by biomorphing hair-loss therapies.

Face

Born a Scandinavian blondie but yearning for the luscious complexion of yesteryear's pop star Janet Jackson? Soon you'll pop a pill and let the next generation's permutation of sunless tanning creme bronze you from the inside out. For envious Caucasians eager to celebrate Chinese New Year with Asian features, try laser surgery for almond eyes. For a more exotic flare, literally the cat's meow, *biomorph* your pupils into cat's-eyes. Sound like science fiction? Fact is, most of it is already here, with the rest soon to follow.

Putting a good face forward is so easy these days. All it takes to change that Durante schnozz or baggy lids are a real desire, tolerance and time for recovery, and $$$ (insurance usually doesn't foot the bill for "cosmetics"). The options for tweaking nature's cameo are many and playing as close as your plastic surgeon's operating theater. Latest techniques include liposuction; laser resurfacing; chemical peels; and chin, cheek, and jaw implants. An injection of collagen can give you a smooch just like Goldie Hawn's in *The First Wives' Club*. Liposuction, holding out its carrot of the perfecto face and body without the torment of conscientious dieting, is love-handles-down the most performed procedure for face and torso. Of course Zsa Zsas have been going under the knife for decades, but what's changed is how the ease, availability, cost, and sagging baby-boom jowls are romancing a once-upon-a-time vanity operation into a necessity. For anywhere from $2,000 to $6,000 you can save face, joining the family album of the more than 85,000 American liftees since 1994.

iconogasm: cultural climax, marketing opportunity
Watch easy and relatively pain-free laser technology dewrinkle America. It could make laserderm the franchise op of the twenty-first century.

Phallus

Long Dong Silver rides again! Beverly Hills plastic surgeon Brian Nova is offering a product hilariously called Penis Dumbbells. (Ouch! It hurts just writing about it.) The PD is a bell-shaped weight designed to stretch that less-than-big boy an extra ¾ to 1 inch. Just tape the 1- to 2.2-pound stainless steel contraption over your johnson and let the dangling begin. It takes about three months to see results. Best to avoid cold weather and magnets during the treatment.

So long, psychoanalysis! Hello (if the Penis Dumbbells failed), ego operations! For a man embarrassed by an undersized member, a snip of the penis suspensory ligaments can add that same ¾ to 1 inch in length. The relatively simple surgery, close to the common man's budget at $5,000, was first the rage on the California coast. (Why are we not surprised?) Iconobets are that penis tailoring—a nip here, a padding of liposuctioned groin fat there—will *biomorph* a guy off the couch and into the health-club showers with a new sense of *savoir faire*. Look for lengthening to culturally redefine prowess and performance "standards" for esquires everywhere.

For little esquires in the making, we hear of the continual drop in the numbers of American newborn boys being circumcised. Circumcision peaked here in 1971, when 90 percent of Toms, Dicks, and Harrys got their johnnies whacked. That year, however, pediatricians rescinded their recommendation for the procedure, and circumcision since has shrunk, uh, fallen to somewhere between 60 percent and 70 percent. The unkindest cut of all will take a Bobbitt-sized plunge in the years ahead because of the rising population of Asian- and Hispanic-Americans, who tend not to believe in the practice. Medical opinion is conflicting, with one group thinking the small risk of infection, bleeding, and damage is worth the prevention of future health problems. With circumcision no longer standard medical procedure, insurance companies such as Blue Shield of Pennsylvania and Prudential have stopped paying for it. Adding fuel to the fire down below are anticircumcision groups, who feel that filleting the mignon imprints violence in little fellas and creates mistrust between sons and

31

their mothers. (Freud, not surprisingly, believed that circumcision was unconsciously associated with castration.) In groups that consider circumcision optional, the backlash against the procedure has made possession of a foreskin something of a status symbol among the wealthier and higher educated.

iconogasm: cultural climax, marketing opportunity

Reach men where they live through products and services dedicated to the phallus.

Breasts

Too big? Too little? Breast augmentations, reductions, and reconstructions are commonplace on today's *biomorphing* bodyscape. Once silicone gel and now saline implants are routinely inserted to boost the sizes of women's bazooms. Since the '60s, between 1 and 2 million fems have joined the bigger-cup club, with 70 percent of those operations performed solely for cosmetic reasons. Culturally speaking, U.S. men have notoriously been in love with larger orbs, and the recent creation and subsequent push up in Wonderbra sales play to the cleavage obsession.

If a saline baggie isn't in the budget, maybe breast hypnotherapy is. Some hypnotreatments claim that petite teats can grow an average of two inches with positive hypnotic bosom imagery. Let's give it a try. *You are getting very, very sleepy. You are laying topless on the beach. . . . Now, repeat after me. . . . It is okay to have bigger breasts; let your mammaries blossom; your cups runneth over. . . .*

iconogasm: cultural climax, marketing opportunity

Breasts—"the crown jewels of femininity"—are a niche market in need of beauty and health-care marketing support.

Skin

Today *biomorphers* exalt the body as an artist's canvas, and tattooing is the medium of choice. Tattoos, from anklebone dolphins to full-back and -butt panoramas, no longer carry a burly sailor stigma. Despite the always present danger of infections, the daring general public loves the look. There's a rash of new books positioning tattoos as an art form. Likewise, museums and art galleries are mounting highbrow skin shows. All this tattooing is going to make for great people-watching in the years ahead.

Surgical gloves and antiseptic swabs hover above your navel. Ready for one of the ultimate owie personal statements? Certified body-piercing experts have needles poised at Gauntlet piercing boutiques in New York, L.A., and San Fran. Nowadays it seems that an innie is just an innie unless it sports a 14-karat gold ring. Akin to the tattoo rage, nipple rings, cheek chains, studs, and stones are gripping skin in the darnedest places. An eye-opening wound costs as little as twenty-five bucks (jewelry extra). Whether you keep the new hardware hidden— we had an online chat with one piercer who revealed three studs in her labia ("goes great with sex")—or flaunt a nose bow, *biomorphing* leaves its uniquely "me" imprint.

iconogasm: cultural climax, marketing opportunity

Personal branding is here today but probably gone tomorrow. Savvy marketers will anticipate the *biomorph* backlash, creating products to ease or erase the telltale tracks.

Organs

The freedom to sculpt the bod outside and in will lead to hot new business opportunities. Iconoculture predicts *organlegging* will really take off. Body organs will become a major source of trade as boomers' hearts, kidneys, and livers putter out over the next decades. The used-body-parts business has already seeded a lucrative global market. India controls the heftiest slice of the previously owned extremities and organs biz, with eyes (two, whole) going for $5,000, and skin scalped at $20 per square inch (freckles extra?). An arm or leg costs an arm and a leg—$4,000. In Poland $30,000 buys a kidney. In Russia, testicles (one pair, presumably matched) will set a comrade back $4,000. If the worldwide polarity between haves and have-nots continues to widen, cadavers may even emerge as a form of global currency.

iconogasm: cultural climax, marketing opportunity

The future of commercial harvesting is in your hands . . . legs . . . livers . . .

sign #7: synesthesia

"I don't think this banana is quite ripe . . . it tastes a little triangular." Sound bizarre? Not in the new millennium, where sensory blending—tasting shapes, hearing colors, and seeing smells—will be anxiously expected. This fruit-basket upside-down sense switch is technically named *synesthesia,* from the Greek *syn* (together) and *aisthanesthai* (to perceive). It appears naturally in fewer than one in 100,000 people and was first noted in medical literature about 200 years ago. *Synesthesia*, the result of some very odd goings-on in the subcortical or limbic brain, is the notorious brain quirk of many creatives, including William Faulkner, Virginia Woolf, James Joyce, Dylan Thomas, and Rimski-Korsakov.

"We live on the leash of our senses," revels naturalist poet Diane Ackerman. And in the land of the free and home of the brave, it's an inalienable right—and big business—-to be able to tickle and titillate those senses. Could that be why the pursuit of happiness is even guaranteed in the U.S. Constitution? (Ahhh, John Hancock, what a wily futurist.) The young, old, and in-betweeners are yanking at their leashes like never before. The norm now is a full-time preoccupation with scintillating our senses.

Smell

"What have they been sniffing?" That's the reaction we received a few years back when Iconoculture talked of a warm, fragrant chinook sweeping in from Europe and Asia—the megatrend aromatherapy. Now many more folks outside the fragrance biz know the nose bone is connected to the brain bone. Or, as aromatherapy claims, your sense of smell tremendously affects your physical and emotional senses of well-being.

Ian Smith, research chemist and materials scientist writing in the *Aromatherapy Quarterly*, roots aromatherapy in the systems view of life: "This view emphasizes the essential interrelationship and interdependence of all things." The tools of this therapy are essential oils distilled from the multiple parts of plants—stems, bark, flowers, roots, fruits, leaves. The oils (they're called oils but really have a watery consistency) are highly potent, with one drop of essential-oil concentrate able to produce about thirty cups of herbal tea. Supposedly if a fresh garlic clove is rubbed into the sole of the foot at 12:00, by 12:30 you may be reaching for an Altoid to hush garlic breath. For physical health, recipes mixing pungent drops of essential oils are either rubbed on the skin, taken in a tea, or warmed to infuse the air. Aromatherapists prescribe custom scents for almost any ailment from teething to teenage acne, hypertension to sprained ligaments, muscle cramps, allergies, even chronic bad breath.

The future of aromatherapy smells great. Watch it seep into society's pores. One out-there idea: Backlashing against overmedicated children, the more natural approach to correcting hyperactive behaviors of Attention Deficit Disorder might include pumping a soothing, lavender-laced air into classrooms and school buses.

From mercantile to medical, a sniff of *synesthesia* is in the air. Dr. Alan Hirsch, director of the Smell and Taste Treatment Foundation, has his nose to the trail, linking smell and sexuality. He's found that certain odors can increase blood flow to the penis. The smell of cinnamon buns, for example, helps men achieve erections, as do smells of licorice and pumpkin pie (those crazy Pilgrims). The research may be used to treat impotence or, working backward, to quell the appetites of criminal sex offenders. Expect sensatherapy, an offspring of aromatherapy, to be recognized as an accredited medical modality, with diagnosis and treatment channeled through the experience of a patient's vision, taste, smell, hearing, and touch. With multisensory environments as therapy chambers, could Cinnabons be an outpatient clinic in our future?

iconogasm: cultural climax, marketing opportunity
Smell the marketing coffee through aroma-based products and services.

Sight and Sound

Synesthesia is an especially luxurious sign of the times to mine. Mundane products, places, and services are being transformed into multisensory bubble baths, leaving you tingling from earlobe to reflexed big toe. Those mood-altering, whirling-dervish sounds, colors, textures, and scents once reserved for hawking cosmetics at Bloomies will continue to pump up the volume on Main Streets, in classrooms, and in bedrooms from Omaha to Odessa.

Check out The Sharper Image shops and catalogs. They're *synesthesia* toystores, brimming with multisensory gear. The Ultra Heart and Sound Soother is one of the Iconokids' favorites (our dog, Geneva, digs it too). The Soother, with its "Burltech finish," is the essential night-table toy. Switch the dial to California Coast, plump the pillow, and quicker than you can say "Hush, little baby," the *zzzzzs* come calling. Heartbeat, North Woods, White Noise, Summer Night, Tropical Cruise, Ocean, Brook, and Rain Forest are on twenty-four-hour calming call.

iconogasm: cultural climax, marketing opportunity
Create a buzz with new products steeped in the senses.

Taste

The baker, the butcher, and the candlestick maker are recovering from the malling of America (between 1970 and 1990 a new shopping mall opened every seven hours in the U.S.), by cashing in on *synesthesia*.

Breadsmith, a Eurostyle bakery franchise, is leavening the way with its crusty loaves, droolsome aromas, and "would you like to sample our French Peasant?" The Wonder Bread crowd is rediscovering the "real" stuff. In small burgs across the country, European-style loaves and rounds tease the nose, tongue, and imagination with Tuscan rosemary, wild cherry, and chewy pesto-tomato foccacia. The rising mania for a fresh braid, baguette, boule, or challah is definitely a bread awakening that is clearly the twin of the coffee-bean bonanza. Breadsmith bakeries, like candylands and "candles only" shops, hyperize and overlap the senses, plunging us into feeding/spending frenzies.

iconogasm: cultural climax, marketing opportunity
See me. Feel me. Touch me. Hear me. Taste me. Be a *synesthesia* wizard!

Touch

"Have fragrant, healing hands; will travel" is the mantra of Paul Herb, masseur extraordinaire. Herb is a master in melting touch into taste into music into total-body titillation. This massage minstrel strums hamstrings from Hawaii to Minneapolis to New York and back to San Francisco, offering up unique "special body care events." One of the exotic happenings is titled "Los Angeles, The Angels," a delicious ensemble of creamy cremes, soothing strokes, and heavenly melodies. Herb's client commitment is to deliver a total escape from the stress fractures of everyday living. Bets are Disney couldn't package this treat any better.

An elegant invitation entices patrons to "join me in celebrating the divine here on earth through music, touch, fragrance, and imagination." Arriving for your archangel-a-thon, leave your troubles on the doorstep and float into a cumulus cloud. The massage studio has been restaged into a slice of heaven. The total-sensory experience begins when you slip out of your Calvins onto a heated, cushy table (tummyside up, please). Head to tingly toes, you'll be rubbed rosy with Herb's own luxurious concoctions: Milk & Honey Facial Massage Creme, Vanilla-Almond Body Oil, Frankincense & Myrrh Foot Balm. Paul, costumed all in white, glides, caresses, and staccatos synergistically to Jane Siberry and k.d. lang's "Calling All Angels." Follow it up with almond tea and cookies. In the name of trend research, the Iconoheads confirm winged sightings.

iconogasm: cultural climax, marketing opportunity
Reach out and touch consumers through products and services offering the magic of human contact.

sign #7: synesthesia

Dentistry

After a personal visit from the IRS, making a speech, and death, a root canal is ranked right up there with modern humanity's greatest fears. Dentists, lend us your *synesthesia* ear. Lay back in the comfy dentalounger, close your eyes, and enjoy the ride. An undulating mechanical masseuse kneads away shoulder stress, while Baroque music gently massages the right and left lobes of the brain. A gentle spring of chamomile wash gurgles the gums . . . *"Open wide"* . . . the phantom laser drill silently saves the day.

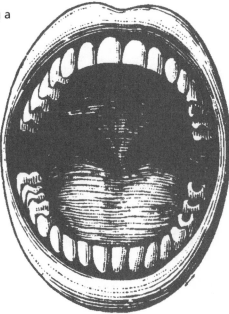

 iconogasm: cultural climax, marketing opportunity
Ease the anxiety by manipulating the sensory mood.

sign #8: healthwatch

To quote Bernard Shaw, "We have not lost faith, but we have transferred it from God to the medical profession." That old, dusty paradigm is being turned on its cranium and shaken from clavicle to sacroiliac. So long to doc as deity; that dead horse is being kicked by managed-health-care providers on one side, alternative and preventative health care on the other. One current turn of fate: HMOs have taken over playing God. The force-fit triage—patient, doctor, insurer—is frankly a pain in the butt to most consumers, who are fed up with the complexity and remoteness of the marketing-driven, cost-cutting system. The Hippocratic Oath is in critical condition, fighting an infectious disease diagnosed as "Show me the money."

Scandals abound. *USA Today* reports, "Medicaid and Medicare will lose an estimated $2.2 billion to fraudulent homecare providers." *Health* asks, "Did Joyce Ching die because her doctor had his eye on his bank account instead of her health chart?" It doesn't take a brain surgeon to see public confidence caving in as America's annual health budget surges past $500 billion. The bottom line: More and more, a skeptical public is looking elsewhere for help, not willing to put all their achy breaky eggs in the traditional institutional basket.

Alternative Health Care

Heal thyself? Clutching at straws? Cough again. This is a Goliath shift, a transformation precipitated by an unmanageable managed-health-care system, our deep-rooted heritage of choice, and an aging tidal wave that levels every inflexible institution in its path. Even five years ago, holistic healing was a stretch for most, but then Bill Moyers's PBS series *Healing and the Mind* expanded our collective consciousness to alternative healers who don't necessarily wear white smocks and stethoscopes. Today, Americans are relying more on themselves, proactively protecting their health with increased exercise, low-fat diets, meditation, yoga, and natural homeopathic remedies—"I'll put on my own leeches, thank you very much." One in three Americans is buying alternative health-care remedies. That's a whopping $14 billion estimated being spent yearly, more than what folks paid out of their own pockets for conventional cures and probably *not* covered by good old Blue Cross/Blue Shield.

iconogasm: cultural climax, marketing opportunity

Put consumers first by giving them a voice in their care regimen through relationship-building programs and products.

Health Insurance

An X ray of the health-care system of 2020 shows convergence care. Societal pressure will force traditional and alternative medical modalities to purge their professional prejudices, and uncanny alliances will emerge. Heart-bypass patients may elect acupuncture as their anesthesia and will expect their insurance to cover both, plus post-op meditation tapes to boot. On the leading edge of convergence care are companies like AT&T. Since January of '97, the self-financed health plan of AT&T has offered acupuncture coverage to management employees. In hopes of tapping into the demand for nontraditional modalities, Oxford Health Plans, a managed-care provider located in Norwalk, Connecticut, is the first (and as we go to press *only*) HMO to include a qualified network of alternative-medical-care professionals as an option. Given the $50 billion market in alternative health care, Oxford's move seems wise.

iconogasm: cultural climax, marketing opportunity

Insurance providers should check their blood pressure. Consumers will demand an expanding spectrum of alternative treatments from hands-on healing to herbal fasting to guided-vision meditations and beyond.

Holistic Hospital

On the horizon, look for convergence care to birth the holistic hospital, uniting the expertise of allopathic and alternative medicines under one roof. In

Minnesota the best in respective fields exist separately. The Mayo Clinic in Rochester, home to 1,839 physicians and scientists, is a world-renowned mecca that combines patient care, advanced research, and medical education. The collective wisdom of state-of-the-art medical knowledge and practice is brought to bear on each diagnosis, offering a torqued comfort factor for sickies lucky enough to land in a Mayo bed.

Eighty miles away in Minneapolis, Pathways health-crisis resource center is a lifeline to individuals responding to life-threatening diseases. The primary patient plus friends and family are invited to take part in an ambitious range of self-healing programs. All Pathway services are free (that immediately removes one big stress) and emphasize exploring new levels of emotional and spiritual healing. The cross-cultural menu of alternative therapies—yoga, therapeutic massage, healing touch, energy balance, dream decoding, talking circles, art, sonoluminescent healing (sound vibrations), auriculotherapy (Chinese system that stimulates points of the ear), meditation, healing laughter—is impressive, each procedure working to integrate mind, body, and spirit. Pathways and the Mayo are magnets for people from all economic, career, and cultural backgrounds. Often their client is the same person, moving back and forth in search of comfort.

iconogasm: cultural climax, marketing opportunity
Build bridges between the two paradigms of health care to give consumers the best of both worlds.

Hospitals and Clinics

"Help with your luggage, sir? The concierge desk is just ahead in the lobby." The typical white-glove check-in at the Marriott? Not! You've just entered what Iconoculture calls the "cooperative care zone" at the medical mall of the future. The new directional darling of health care and hospital planners, a model designed with all the accoutrements of a Four Seasons, promises to deliver high patient-satisfaction marks with its residential ambience and strong philosophy of helping the sick help themselves. Chemotherapy? Angiogram? Hysterectomy? Hemorrhoids? If you can walk, need inpatient care, and have a committed "care partner," welcome! The care partner—spouse, friend, parent—is trained by a nurse to help the ailing pal with meds, baths, and charting progress. Unlike the traditional hospital, there are no interruptions for reading vital signs or choking down pills. Even the harangue of the hospital paging system is out; individual beepers are in. Privacy is paramount. Doors have locks, and Uncle Elmer can visit any hour you please. Sounds kind of adult, dosen't it? And, most important, the butt-hanging-out-the-gown syndrome is nixed as you cozy up in your own jammies. All this comfort isn't just for show. Early test statistics show you'll beat the traditional 40-percent readmission rate by leaving the cooperative-care zone with a better understanding of your medications, diet, and therapy routine.

iconogasm: cultural climax, marketing opportunity
Welcome to Hilton Hospital. Medicine and room service with humanity and style.

Practitioners

Talk to almost any doctor or nurse and it's likely the conversation will eventually drift to the enormous changes in their professions. Issues of secure salary, prestige, patient-practitioner relationship, professional and financial accountability, levels of service, and payment are roller-coasting. The allure of medicine as a safe career track well worth the long years of school and training is now suspect. Med professionals are waking up from the anesthesia, recognizing that their futures are with the HMOs. One chief of staff lamented to us that he thinks that within three years, plumbers will have it better than doctors, with shorter hours, more creative freedom, lower damage insurance, and better bucks. Ouch.

Contemplating med school? If our noodling is right, by the year 2030 one in five Americans will be sixty-five or older. Of course Betty Crocker will still be gnashing her own pearly whites, but guesses are most Iconokids—that's you!—will be sporting dentures or, for hipsters, dental implants. The rigors of an aging population are goosing the demand for specialists in geriatrics.

The Alliance for Aging Research guesstimates that the U.S. will need no fewer than 36,000 geriatricians. That's four times the number presently practicing. Experts at the American Geriatrics Society seriously doubt whether we have a chance of ever quenching the thirst for docs schooled in the bodily un-functions of the rheumatic crowd. Woe is us . . . less than 1 percent of the 16,000 doctors who graduate each year are certified geriatricians, and only 11 of the 125 med schools in this country require courses or clinics in elderly physiology.

The grimmest fact is that there are only two elder-care specialists for every ten thousand Americans who are sixty-five or older. Why so few? Treating the aged is not as sexy as finding heroic cures for younger sickies, plus the salaries trail far behind other specialists. The real rub is *not* with Ben-Gay for arthritic joints. Without trained-especially-for-geezer physicians, older patients will be misdiagnosed, which could lead to mismanagement of their health care and eventual premature nursing home assignment. Might as well quit worrying about your health. It'll go away.

iconogasm cultural climax, marketing opportunity
Go to the gray head of the medical class. Geriatrics is calling.

Over-the-Counter Drugs

Take two hydroxyprol methylcellulose and call me in the morning. Maybe, but not without a complementary dose of 500 mg of vitamin C spiked with echinacea, twenty drops of goldenseal tincture in a cup of steaming water, and a sublingual dose of melatonin to ease tired heads into nighty-nighttime. In ancient times, wisewomen held the secret for headache relief: brewed feverfew tea. Today, feverfew is giving Extra-Strength Tylenol a run for its migraines.

Since 1995, more than $700 million each year is rung up in sales of herbal-elixir fixers, and the category is in the peak of health, with growth of 20 percent a year, much higher than traditional drug sales. You can't pass by a Barnes & Noble or General Nutrition Center without being avalanched by a ton of new books touting the virility-boosting natural enzyme DHEA or the brain-boosting memory supplement ginkgo.

Supplements, natural enzymes, and hormones go in and out of fashion. Melatonin has been crowned one of the miracle messiahs of the '90s. Even the

New York Times's own Jane Brody quipped that if a tiny tab can do what would otherwise require a dietary overhaul, a daily exercise routine, and a stress-management program . . . why not take melatonin? The undrug claims to boost the immune system; act as an industrial-strength antioxidant; fight stress, depression, and jet lag; regulate blood pressure and cholesterol; and ward off or slow cancer, Alzheimer's, AIDS, Parkinson's, ulcers, schizophrenia, PMS, migraine headbashers, Toxic Shock Syndrome, Sudden Infant Death Syndrome, cataracts, pregnancy (with megadoses), and autism. Oh, lest we forget, it also revs up your sex drive and makes you a candidate for Willard Scott's over-100 birthday club. There have been a few red flags on side effects and of course the usual scientific grumping about not enough human-guinea-pig studies.

The hoopla over herbals has energized the FDA to scrutinize natural "cures." Even so, the public's full embrace of alternative remedies is not going unnoticed by the pharmaceutical giants—Schering-Plough, McNeal, Pfizer. *Brandweek*, tracking the herb trail to Pfizer, found research scientists studying herbal extracts coming regularly from Beijing's China Academy of Traditional Chinese Medicine Institute of Basic Theory. The payoff may come from new products of the ilk of Correctol Herbal Tea Laxatives, with their softening sell: "Relief for your body. Comfort for your soul."

iconogasm: cultural climax, marketing opportunity
Join hands with Mother Nature to share in the herbal health glow.

Genes

At the National Institutes of Health, the troops are within sneezing distance of revolutionizing medicine. Not since the Salk vaccine has a new technology promised such a giant leap for humankind. The superhero? Gene therapy.

In a nutshell, almost every illness arises in part because one or more genes is not working correctly. Genes give rise to proteins (the worker bees of cells), and defective genes cause disease when they instruct cells to make the wrong amount or a weird type of protein. To correct the bad gene, doctors extract blood with tainted DNA, insert a healthy copy of a gene into a patient's cells, and return the good guys to the bloodstream. The healthy, disease-correcting gene kicks in and kicks butt. So far only a few hundred patients have been treated, but we expect gene therapy to be as common as knee surgery in the third millennium.

At the current rate of discovery, the mapping of the Human Genome Project is announcing almost daily that little girls and boys are more than sugar 'n' spice and puppy-dog tails. Someday soon individuals will be able to purchase their very own Rand McNally gene map, highlighting key biological points of interest, cellular potholes, and major roadblocks—the physiological detours on life's superhighway. How will this play itself out? "Patty, do you take Derrick, with a diabetes, rheumatoid-arthritis, obesity genetic propensity, to be your lawful, wedded husband?" It's a privacy invasion! Expect that little will be left to chance as premarital counseling will include a prenuptial evaluation of the happy couple's genetic codes. Looks like that crazy thing called love may well hinge on the right body chemistry after all.

iconogasm: cultural climax, marketing opportunity

Genetic mapping has infinite happy and scary possibilities. Think small as health care shrinks to the genetic level.

Telemedicine

Singing those redeye, lead-eyed blues? Join the club. At any given moment there are some 17 million Americans experiencing depression. The National Institute of Mental Health guesstimates that 80 to 90 percent can be helped out of the full-funk doldrums, if diagnosed and treated for two to six weeks. It might be easier to tap-dance in quicksand, you say? Not so.

Lee Baer, associate professor of psychology in the Department of Psychiatry at Massachusetts General Hospital, has twisted voicemail technology into an automatic depression-screening system. It allows folks to call from the privacy and anonymity of their own couches, punch in responses to twenty statements ("I have crying spells if I feel like it; I am restless and cannot sleep; I feel others would be better off if I were dead"), and at the end of a ten-minute electronic conversation, get a "mild, marked, or extreme" score for depression, with a suggested course of action. This Freudphone program is in testing at several major universities and is online for faculty and staff (how about students?) at Harvard. Digital Equipment and Southern California Edison are in the dial-a-doc camp. It only makes dollars and sense, considering that in 1990 (and with numbers only rising) the *Journal of Clinical Psychiatry* reported that depression resulted in $43.7 billion in lost productivity, absenteeism, and health-care costs. What's next? A ring-a-ding screen for whatever ails you—eating disorders to substance abuse to diabetes to impotency. Isn't it mind-boggling the trust our culture is placing in prepackaged, computer-driven diagnoses?

iconogasm: cultural climax, marketing opportunity
Put costly service calls on hold with phone diagnostics, but back it up with a human touch.

Ethics

With all this convergence, emergence, and divergence in the health and medical fields, a relatively new field is monitoring the front line of change—bioethics. Hoping to frame the discourse, the University of Pennsylvania School of Medicine created the Center for Bioethics in July 1994. The Center is head-butting with bioethical beasts from organ transplants to doctor-assisted suicide. With more than 900 genetic-disease genes already isolated by the NIH's Human Genome Project, the bioethical questions are beginning to quake Mr. Rogers's neighborhood. Should children be gene-mapped for incurable diseases? Can researchers refuse to share test results with Mom and Dad? Or do parents have the inalienable right to know when their little Travis scores proof-positive for Alzheimer's disease? And here's the most explosive Q: Should the kid be told? These are scary, loaded moral issues of self-esteem, fear, despair . . . real-life monsters coming out of the scientific-advancement closet. Almost as scary: To what degree will the insurance industry demand to read the genetic handwriting on the wall?

iconogasm: cultural climax, marketing opportunity
WANTED: Bioethicist. So many ethical questions, so few to lead the debate.

chapter 3: spirit

Let the spirit move you. And it is. Call it the zenning of America. Call
voluntary simplicity. Call it the new New Age. Call it co-creation. Call
soul rejuvenation. Whatever the guise, there's no doubt whatsoever tha
this nation is awakening to the spiritual height, width, and depth of lif
Our dizzy lifestyles keep us off-kilter, like wobbling tops at the end of th
spin. Help! is on the way. For the Chicago Bulls it comes courtesy
zencoach Phil Jackson's spiritual lessons on how to be a team of wiene
by taming the hot dog within. Fly cross-country on Northwest and anxiou
airphobes can quiet their nerves (and palms) with a soap called Calmin
At Salvation Armies the mountains of cast-off clothes and one-tin
household treasures landmark the all-unconsuming simplicity surg
Marriage—man to woman, woman to man, man to man, woman t
woman—is back by popular demand, torqued to new levels
connectedness. In every way, this is a spiritual wake-up call. Don't blir
or even think of hitting the snooze button; it's no time to sleep.

sign #9:  chi

It's too late now for import quotas. Eastern culture is invading the West, thriving and enlivening the American concept of what's really important in life. *Chi* is the ancient/modern Chinese concept of tapping into your body's energy flow for health and contented well-being. Iconoculture defines the *chi* trend as a symbol of all the alternative spiritual approaches wafting across the American landscape. Key to the *chi* trend is the Eastern philosophy of balance—balance in every cell of the body, every thought generated, every interaction with life's temporal and spiritual planes.

Lifestyle

Shhhhhh . . . Listen to the quiet tinkling, the meditative murmurs. It's the whispers of wind chimes, portable ponds, and desktop waterfalls bringing good health, fortune, and vitality to home and office. The *feng shui*-ing of America is in a full Eastern bow. This eons-old Chinese theory that placement and color empower every aspect of life is captivating architects, city planners, interior designers, and, yes, even the common guy on the street. *Feng shui* believers are adamant about zooping up the energy in their environments. They have a growing fascination with minute details that B.F.S. (before *feng shui*) were merely innate objects. Now even where you hang the bathroom mirror is significant. Building your *feng shui* dream digs? No detail, from how a home is sited to the shape of the roof to the room colors, is left to chance. "Pink is best for the master bedroom. . . . If a single man or woman seeks the opportunity to get married or wants to find a girlfriend or boyfriend, paint the bedroom peach or pink," counsels *Master Lin Yun's Guide to Feng Shui and the Art of Color.*

Furnishings and fabrics, trees, flowers, and shrubs must harmonize to enhance moods; stimulate thinking; and boost health, morality, and good luck.

iconogasm: cultural climax, marketing opportunity

Make *feng shui* your fortune cookie. It may be the differentiator you've been searching for.

Wealth

In the new millennium, look for the *chi* trend to redefine personal wealth. Bragging about your robust mutual-fund portfolio and last month's luxury-laden vacation will be inconsequential, even gauche. Instead, you'll be sharing techniques on how to get in touch with your inner self to maximize your personal strengths. Acquiring wealth will be a tangible perk of putting your intuitive side to work. Libraries of *Get Rich Quick* and *Think and Grow Fabulously Filthy Rich* tomes have been bestsellers for the last three decades. What's happening now is the publication of a new breed of success books. Business how-tos will be patterned after monster bestsellers like Deepak Chopra's *Creating Affluence: Wealth Consciousness in the Field of All Possibilities* and *The Seven Spiritual Laws: A Practical Guide to the Fulfillment of Your Dreams.* These A-to-Z prosperity plans from the timeless mind, ageless body himself advise us to think "E"—"expectancy determines outcome"—in place of a buy low, sell high, Louis Rukeiseresque tack. Expect the millionaire's messenger, and you too will be in the moolah.

For workaholics (like we used to be) *The Seven Laws of Money*, authored by MasterCard creator Michael Phillips, is worth its weight in gold. Lest we forget the accountant types out there, there's *The Abundance Book,* with its "40-Day Prosperity Plan." The result is results, or so goes the testimonial: "On the 30th day of the 40-Day Prosperity Plan my husband was offered a promotion and a sizable increase in salary. On the 40th day an old bill that we never expected to receive payment on was paid in full. We're so excited we're going through the plan a second time." With all of us buying get-rich-and-spiritually-fit-too books, guess who's paying their Visa bill on time?

iconogasm: cultural climax, marketing opportunity
Make consumers healthy, wealthy, and wise by facilitating "inner prosperity."

Work

With *chi* it is okay to keep your nose to the grindstone, providing it's the "right" grindstone. The concept of right livelihood is gaining momentum at community colleges and adult-education centers across the country. Pick up a class bulletin and chances are there's a course or two or three in the do-what-you-love-and-the-money-will-follow vernacular. These classes fire up thousands of downsized, displaced/replaced workers to get a pulse on their *chi*. Of course this value on purposeful work is being focused by the insecurities of long-term corporate commitment to employees, the mobility and flexibility of the laptop computer age, and the erosion of confidence in our traditional bedrock foundations: family, work, school, church, City Hall. These uncertainties will follow us into twenty-first century life, turning a nation inward to find and act upon a purpose-centered lifestyle. Author/lecturer Marsha Sinetar, an avid advocate of this new mindset, points the way: "The individual [in balance with life] feels that the work is part of something universal, special, sacred."

iconogasm: cultural climax, marketing opportunity
Purposeful work is no longer a fringe benefit. The best job description brings money and personal satisfaction into alignment.

Sensuality

America's manifest destiny in 2002 will be less a land rush and more a mind rush, a pervasive search for balance and centeredness. From the personal perspective—and, of course, everything *chi* is personal—understanding the ebb and flow of the body tides will be essential.

Take tantra. This form of Eastern-wisdom-turned-New-Age-spirituality is blossoming in the secret garden, providing its growing number of practitioners an alternative to the West's do-or-be-done approach to sex. Derived from the Sanskrit *tanoti* (to expand) and *trayati* (to liberate), tantra launches sensuality into a higher orbit of "self-actualization, well-being, transcendence." Tantra offers a useful view of life and sex (is there a difference?), teaching its followers to celebrate the senses, revere the now, and see life and sex as ceremonies of sharing. Tantra retreats are convening regularly in the Manzano Mountains of New Mexico. Makes us wonder if the Poconos can be far behind.

iconogasm: cultural climax, marketing opportunity

The door is open to elevating the mundane realities of daily life to a higher level of consciousness.

Health

A healthy bod is a healthy mind is a healthy *chi*. Have you had your annual *chi* check-up? Family members of all ages and, crazy enough, even the family Airedale and tabby are being treated with Eastern wellness modalities. Tennis elbow? Migraines? Fur ball? For many, Excedrin isn't the answer. Both acupressure (applying hand or finger pressure to energy points) and acupuncture (the science of tapping into the body's energy meridians by pricking the skin with tiny needles) are Eastern pain-relief techniques designed to keep the body's *chi* system surging. The belief that blocked *chi* is the root of disease is being flirted with by the open-minded, if not yet fully embraced by the mainstream.

Not to be left in the rickshaw dust, Americans are breaking ground in the development of alternative pain-relief therapies. Upledger Institute, founded by osteopathic physician John Upledger and with more than 10,000 alumni worldwide, is a headwater for many wellness methodologies, including CranioSacral Therapy. Oh, how to describe CranioSacral . . . Ever had a fairy tap-dance on your face? That's how this healing touch feels. With all the raw power of a gang of Lilliputians, this gentle-pressure technique is gaining a reputation for relieving a bevy of body aches and ills—chronic back pain, migraine headaches, TMJ/jaw grinding, dyslexia, hearing problems, ear infections, ADD, depression, and anxiety.

So how does this miracle nondrug therapy spell relief? In a healthy bod the cranial fluid flows freely with a rhythmic pulse through the brain and spinal cord. Sickies have a weak or irregular pulse that needs to be revved up ever so gently. Simply by cradling the skull, neck, spinal column, and face while pressing on specific points and manipulating the fascia (the connective tissue that holds us together), a patient's ebb and flow will flourish. A small but growing cadre of physical therapists, psychologists, massage therapists, chiropractors, and other health pros are skilled in CranioSacral nuances.

iconogasm: cultural climax, marketing opportunity
Key into CranioSacral and other no-pill Prozacs as they gain mainstream attention, opening pocketbooks and attitudes to *chi* health care.

Diagnostics

Pioneering the marriage of mind/body are Dr. Norman Shealy, neurosurgeon, and Caroline Myss, a medical intuitive. Though they live 1,200 miles apart, Dr. Shealy phones Myss for help in diagnosing the condition of a new female patient. Except for the patient's name and birthdate, Myss knows nothing of the woman's health history, aches, or pains. Focusing her intuition, Myss reads the energy of the life force within the patient's body and queries: "Did you check her for TMJ syndrome? Her jaw is so tight. She has a rigid smile because it hurts. She has fear of inadequacy despite many accomplishments. There is much tension in her abdomen, and this is because of her feeling of inadequate power. She is out of balance and reaching for what she needs there. She also has pain in her right hip. Treat her temporomandibular joint, and teach her about issues of personal power which are contributing to her problem." Later, a by-the-book medical exam confirms the TMJ trouble.

No, we're not tuned to *Star Trek: The Next Generation*. This is the real-life manifestation of the somersaulting medical paradigm. Claiming that Myss has a 93-percent success rate, Shealy depends on her insights into the emotional, psychological, and spiritual stresses which they both believe are causative factors in physical disease. Their *chi* credo: Our emotional anatomy is as real and organized as our physical anatomy, and when you understand the human energy system, you can create health at the most fundamental level. Simply put, you are what you think. . . . So, what do you think?

iconogasm: cultural climax, marketing opportunity

It is time to think holistically as Western culture shifts from a mind vs. body paradigm to an Eastern view of a unified, harmonious self.

Fitness

Chi is mirrored in a new body consciousness in which barbells and full-sweat step aerobics are being usurped by gentle-on-the-joints *tai chi*, Pilates, and YogaRhythmics. East is definitely meeting West at the nation's newest user-friendly fitness centers. At the Mindful Body in San Francisco, for example, members are taking classes in Bikran Basics, Somatic Exploration, and Creative Visualization up the yin yang. Chicagoans at Zen Fitness work out in a "friendship circle" as incense wafts through the air, while New Yorkers at Equinox enjoy Rolfing and Visceral Manipulation. In addition to this holistic-a-gogo, fitness centers are adding additional health services to their mix. Between relaxation classes at the Downtown Athletic Club in Eugene, Oregon, members get flu shots and their cholesterol screened. The Chelsea Piers Sports and Entertainment Complex in New York offers pre- and post-natal care, while Lynn Brick's Women's Health and Fitness Club in Baltimore has an entire Breast Wellness Center. Wellness is rearing its healthy head in some truly novel ways, like at Fitnosis in San Francisco, where members can cook up a sweat without moving a pec through a forty-five-minute visualization workout. If that's still too much effort, head down Highway 1 to Malibu Health for a "therapeutic" view of the ocean.

The key to *chi* fitness is holism—you can't really be healthy and fit unless your emotional, intellectual, spiritual, and physical dimensions are in sync with one another and the world around you. It is the sense of fluid wholeness gained by exercise, nutrition, stress control, and relaxation that keeps disease from your temple door.

iconogasm: cultural climax, marketing opportunity

Recognize people's desire to find a personal sense of equilibrium by facilitating opportunities for them to bring the spiritual and physical into balance.

sign #10:  unplugged

Unplug yourself? What . . . consume less? It's not as strange or distant an idea as you might surmise. In fact, multitudes are singing the joys of an acoustic lifestyle. Simplifying, paring down, disengaging, cutting back, tuning out, streamlining—these are the verbs that cloak the *unplugged* values shift in process. For some, the decision to slough possessions, positions, relationships, and out-of-reach/out-of-whack goals is a voluntary tack. For others—literally tens of thousands—corporate downsizing is the catalyst for them to reinvent their lives. Whatever the push, it has come to shove.

Simplicity

The *unplugged* movement is driven by aging boomers who want to grab their piece of the pie before all their teeth fall out. After two decades of job stress and dissatisfaction, boomers are wondering what the '80s got them besides a big mortgage and a thirty-six-month lease on a Lexus. Their yearnings for time to relish the delicious little morsels of life—planting a garden, tinkering, reading a trashy novel, playing softball with the kids, seeing Spot run—are giving rise to a library-cartful of bailout books. Bestseller lists are bristling with how-tos on creating high-value, low-maintenance lifestyles. Elaine St. James's *Simplify Your Life* and Sarah Ban Breathnach's *Simple Abundance: A Daybook of Comfort and Joy* are less-is-more manifestoes that resonate with women especially. What strikes home as you page through each of these books is the straightforward ease and grace with which the ideas are shared. No motivational hype, twelve steps, hokey empowerment jive; just *unplugged* common sense. "Make peace with the knowledge that you can't have everything you want," we read in *Simple Abundance*. "Why? Because it's more important for us to get everything we need. Like infants, we feel contentment when our essential needs are met." Simple, eh?

Another cheerleader for the *unplugged* pilgrimage is *Adbusters*, that vexing lens and self-proclaimed "Journal of the Mental Environment." Perpetual champions of unclutter, *Adbusters* is blown away by the "quantitative shift" from a gotta-have-it-all, spend, spend, spend mindset to an enthusiastic global buy-in to the Media Foundation's Buy Nothing Day, held annually on November 29 at the zenith of the $eason. Could *unplugged* or at the very least the spirited discussions of antimaterialism and self-sustainable living "mark the beginning of the end of the biggest consumption binge in history"? (Expect a mass shredding of Discover, Visa, Amex, and MasterCard? No way. Plastic is here to stay.)

Nipping the consummate consumer in the bud is the mission of Cornell University's Center for Religion, Ethics and Social Policy. Their Seeds of Simplicity children's program works to instill the virtues of not blowing allowances on unnecessary plastic stuff. Learning early that the road to happiness is not paved with Tickle Me Elmos is a seed, they feel, that can't be planted soon enough.

iconogasm: cultural climax, marketing opportunity
Unplug your brands by positioning them as vehicles of personal independence and freedom.

Furnishings

Maybe it's a backlash against the opulence of the '80s, or maybe it's a reality check on a roller-coaster job scene, or maybe people are just de-stressing and re-dressing their lives in a simpler, uncluttered style. Whatever. Less is more is in. Open The Pottery Barn's catalog and kick back. There's reverence for R-E-L-A-X at every turn of the page—pine farmer's tables, sisal rugs, distressed-wood beds and chests, loose livin' slipcovers, organic-cotton terry towels (white-white of course), all designed to chuck formality and wingbacks out the window. There are coffee-table books—*Shabby Chic, Chic Simple Home*—flush with slouch decorating 1-2-3's. Kick-back lounge style is about living life as an onion, peeling away the layers of hype, stress, stiffness, imitation, ostentation, excess. At the core is the heart seed of what really counts—more time with pals and pets.

iconogasm: cultural climax, marketing opportunity
Remember that home is where the heart (and the action) is.

Work

"[M]en labor under a mistake. The better part of the man is soon plowed into the soil for compost." —Henry David Thoreau, *Walden*

Thoreau saw the writing on the wall more than a century ago, and now Americans are jumping into his pond like lemmings. There's a full-scale voluntary-simplicity movement quaking this country's wingtips. Whether given a little push off the plank of U.S.S. *Corporate America* or if the leap was purely by design, many of us are "opting out" and creating "exit strategies" for gentler, simpler lives. The numbers of the full-time employed are falling like a rock, as number crunchers and paper pushers eagerly accept departure packages offered by cellulite-trimming companies. Lawyers, bankers, and financial chiefs are trading in their white collars for blue denim, getting out of the rat race and carving out new identities in our postaffluent society. Walk into your local bookstore or café any weekday and you'll see them, lattes and newspapers in tow, planning their next nonstrategy. Heeding Mick's warning that time waits for no one and it won't wait for me or you, middle-aged slackers are dead serious about reclaiming control over their days.

The end of the traditional American work ethic as we know it represents the crumbling of another pillar of postwar society, no less significant than the tearing down of the Berlin Wall and end of the Cold War. The movement is directly connected to the new populist tenet that the American Dream is over or, at least, no longer relevant in a nation being clearly split into the haves and the have-nots.

As *unplugging* spreads from the margins to the mainstream, support groups like Seattle's New Road Map Foundation are springing up around the country to help those looking to trade in their ties for tie-dyes. The groups help exiters get through the tough transitional period of giving up traditional measures of success like income or job status for new measures like happiness and fulfillment. In direct contrast to the terms of the 1980s' fast-track contract, the 1990s' slow track prescribes quitting your job and re-creating yourself within the emerging freelance economy grounded in information technology.

iconogasm: cultural climax, marketing opportunity
As the simplicity movement continues to ooze, look for ways to help your workforce get back to the basics of life.

Hometown

Smalltown America, once on the endangered-species list, is on the way back. More of us are *unplugging* our Williams Sonoma toasters, abandoning our urban nests, and staking a claim on the new frontier, an enduring theme in the American experience. New pockets of communities are developing in rural America, with common interests such as religion, art, or industry at their cores. As Americans move to the country or small towns to escape crime and other social ills associated with big-city life, an authentic geography quake is jeopardizing the growth of metropolitan areas for the first time in our history.

Americans are going back to the hills in significant numbers, says Joel Kotkin of *The Washington Post*. The populations in rural areas are growing three times as fast as in the 1980s, with a net increase of some 1.1 million between 1990 and 1994. Edge cities (suburbs of suburbs) and small cities are growing even faster, creating a mass migration not seen since the Joads hit the dusty trail for Paradise. What's driving this exodus of biblical proportions? Middle-class, older, predominantly white people are retreating from inner cities as Latin Americans, Asians, and Middle Easterners change the culture of urban neighborhoods. Walden wannabes seek to reduce the complexities of life by searching for the idyllic, imaginary past.

Corporate America is also packing up and leaving town, seduced by lower operating costs, less regulation, and cheaper housing for employees. The wonder of late-twentieth-century technology is also contributing to the revival of small towns as "Have modem, will travel" becomes the mantra of the new millennium. As cyberspace conquers many of the constraints of real space, more of us will live and work outside of major cities. Smalltown life will thrive in the years ahead as more cities become nice-places-to-visit-but-I-wouldn't-want-to-live-theres, and a cultural chasm between urban and rural America like that of antebellum days will gradually cleave the country in two.

iconogasm: cultural climax, marketing opportunity
Take the road less traveled by anticipating the smalltown revival.

Sexuality

Gay culture, historically rooted in big cities, is beginning to thrive in smaller cities, towns, and rural areas. As the gay rights movement spreads from urban America to small towns, more gays and lesbians are remaining country folk. Just as big-time marketers are speaking directly to the gay market, nightclubs, bookstores, and other retailers on Main Street are catering to gays and lesbians. Gay farmers and lesbian ranchers are coming out of the silo, more willing than ever to pronounce their sexual preferences to family, friends, and neighbors. This shift in smalltown culture is, not surprisingly, ruffling a few feathers, principally those of the Christian Right, who point to the Bible to argue that homosexuality is fundamentally immoral. Gays are fighting back by forming advocacy groups and by pushing for antidiscrimination laws in local communities. Watch for small towns to become havens for gays and lesbians as they continue to gain political and economic clout.

iconogasm: cultural climax, marketing opportunity
Smalltown values—whether real or mythic—are a magnetic pull. Want a unique point of difference? Position your college, corporation, or community with the images of a smalltown utopia.

Food

If you want to experience *unplugged* pleasures firsthand, take a jaunt off the interstate in search of Main Street. Granted, the Subwaying of America is daunting, but there are goodies galore within a tongue's lick of the insane lane. As we trek the farm-to-market routes chewin' the fat with locals and poring over the love-of-the-simpler-life zines—*Midwest Living, Country, Sunset*—one cultural cue is as crisp and clear as the country air: Regional food is a wellspring of civic pride. In Gustavus, Alaska, it's Dungeness crab potato salad and nagoonberries that keep them on the map. The Pacific Way Cafe in Gearhart, Oregon, serves the traditional north coast marionberry pie. What's Cape Ann, Massachusetts, minus its Yankee Anadama Bread, or Clarksville, Arkansas, sans peach cobbler? Scratch is in, with homemade jams, breads, salsas, sausages, corn-fed prime, cheeses, backyard-smoked lake trout, kitchen and medicinal cure herbs, and organic veggies and bedding plants a big hit at hometown festivals and farmers' markets. What we're tasting in Smalltown U.S.A. is a celebration of traditional roots and regional ethnic cuisine (a high-falutin' term for just plain good eating off the land).

LOCALLY GROWN

OREGON'S FINEST

1st place

Every food package is an *unplugged* billboard. Even Girl Scout cookies have the nutritional breakdown on the box. Scrutinizing saturated fat grams, cholesterol, and sodium content has become the game of choice for health-conscious shoppers. The food industry has been forced to communicate in lowest-common-denominator terms, and in the process they're driving home in a shopping cart that you are what you eat. Another round of Hostess Ho Hos for the Iconokids!

iconogasm: cultural climax, marketing opportunity
Pump up food sales with un-pumped, *real* ingredients.

Language

If you're like us, dealing with postscientific-jargon trauma, not able to define or even come close to pronouncing bedeviling behemoths like "transhydrogenase reaction," relax . . . even science is simplifying! *Nature*, one of the globe's more prestigious scientific journals, is spearheading a campaign for plain talk. Why? Isn't talking and writing in unintelligible syllables a prerequisite for being scientific? Funny enough, *Nature* discovered that even their more learned readers got stuck in the jargon. Time to *unplug,* because recognizing and remedying the lexicon problem will undoubtedly help attract the whole wide anisotropic world to the wonders of science. Huh?

Our sentimental favorite example of how ideas, language, and even taboos are being *unplugged* is the children's book series My Body Science. Big people and little people alike can't resist the titles—*Everyone Poops; The Gas We Pass: The Story of Farts; The Holes in Your Nose; Contemplating Your Bellybutton;* and *The Soles of Your Feet.* Kane/Miller imports these strictly "educational" bodily-function exposés from Japan offering such fascinating tidbits as "a healthy person releases almost half a cup of gas in a single fart (about 3½ oz.)." Ahhh, the mysteries of life; how (even when poop's the scoop) refreshing!

iconogasm: cultural climax, marketing opportunity
Cut the jargon, red tape, hierarchy, and professional smokescreens. Learn to walk the path of straight talk and you'll never walk alone.

Sabbaticals

Time out for adults. Feeling burned out, dried up, done in? Maybe you're ready to take some real time off from work, more than those mile-a-minute weekends and overcooked-turkey holidays. More companies are willing to let employees take sabbaticals or extended leave without pay as an alternative, win-win means of downsizing. Companies are becoming aware that offering employees time off will likely work to their own advantages over the long term. Legions of fortysomethings are taking sabbaticals to let their creative soil lay fallow for a bit, reemerging after six months or a year with rejuvenated body, mind, and spirit.

Estimates are that one-third of all U.S. companies, in fact, offer some sort of sabbatical program to employees or plan to over the next few years. As additional ammo when you walk into your boss' office, keep in mind that smartypants like Tom Peters and Eric Utne have put their day jobs on hold to recharge their brainy batteries. Sabbaticals have long been a tradition for college professors, who sporadically take a year off from teaching to pursue research or write books. The less erudite typically use the time for more earthly matters like fixing the leaky roof or getting to know their kids. More and more baby boomers are using sabbaticals to yank the plug on reality and fulfill their lifelong dreams of learning to play the piano, sketching at the Louvre, or hiking through the Andes. Employees usually return to their jobs happier, more focused, and more productive . . . and there's a lot less time lost whining around the water cooler.

 iconogasm: cultural climax, marketing opportunity
Hit up your boss for some quality time with yourself. Tell her Iconoculture sent you!

sign #11:  soul searching

Soul searching is all about the "R" word: RELATIONSHIPS. Relationships with your self—yoo-hoo, anybody in there? Relationships with higher consciousness—God, Buddha, angels. Relationships with soul mates—"I need someone to love, to hold, to tickle, to boogie down the highway with. . . ." The quest for spiritual and warm body love, commitment, and companionship seems to be reaching a fevered pitch as the acquisition quest—grabbing for the gold rings, gold faucets, trophy spouses, big houses—loses luster. Don't get us wrong; *soul searching* is *not* about rejecting or diminishing the lifestyles of the rich and famous. It *is* about finding contentment whether renting a wreck or a Rolls.

Inner Search

Is your self struggling with the universal queries? "What is it, in my heart, that I must do, be, have? And why?" Consider James Hillman's acorn theory, eloquently unfurled in *The Soul's Code: In Search of Character and Calling*: "[E]ach person bears a uniqueness that asks to be lived and that is already present before it can be lived." Each of us comes into this big, hairy, scary world with character and calling. Don't be frightened, Hillman calms. Each of us is given a soul mate or companion—called by Christians a guardian angel and by the Greeks a daimon. The daimon will protect you. Whether you are seeking answers or more questions, this read is not to be dismissed.

It takes only a scan of the bestseller lists to see there's a crowd at the station buying tickets to ride the soul train. Titles abound. At the opposite, slightly Ozarkian end of the spectrum from *Soul's Code,* you'll find a steaming-hot cauldron of *Chicken Soup for the Soul* books bubbling (recipes by Jack Canfield and Mark Hansen). The vast mainstream popularity of these easy-to-slurp soul journals can be credited to the right pinch of poignant passages and epiphanies spiced with a smidgen of healing humor. By now, we suspect, you all have devoured the New Age soul jungle safari, *The Celestine Prophecy,* and its soul sister, *The Tenth Insight.* It's a hip read on college campuses and with senior book clubs, too. What's the trendwind fanning this fire? Soul guru Thomas Moore says: "The great malady of the Twentieth Century, implicated in all our troubles and affecting us individually and socially, is 'loss of soul.' When the soul is neglected, it doesn't just go away; it appears symptomatically in obsessions, addictions, violence, and loss of meaning."

If one reads into what's being read, *soul searching* is a compelling hunt for genuineness, deep satisfaction, and meaning in life. Locking into a definition of what or where the soul hangs out is like chasing the silky confetti exploding from a milkweed pod. Yet soulfulness, Moore contends, is "tied to life in all its particulars—good food, satisfying conversation, genuine friends, and experiences that stay in the memory and touch the heart." At the margins of our society, it may be this need to fill the emptiness with soulfulness that is the glue of gangs. Hey, soul's where you find it.

iconogasm: cultural climax, marketing opportunity
It doesn't take a rocket scientist or a theologian to recognize that products, ideas, services, advertising sell best when they feed the soul.

Religion

"Hurting? 1-800-4PRAYER" —Bumper sticker for Assembly of God's National Prayer Center

Want to increase the chances that your prayers will reach those busy ears of God? Surrogate prayer centers, managed by Christian organizations, are flourishing as Americans look for ways to get their prayers voiced and heard. According to *USA Today*, calls, letters, and electronic messages are flooding into churches, denominations, and ministries, where "prayer warriors" relay them to the big problem solver in the sky. The Peale Center in Pawling, New York, gets 2,000 letters, 450 phone calls, and 175 Internet prayer requests each week. The

Upper Room Living Prayer Center of Nashville gets more than 100,000 pleas for prayers each year, while the Silent Unity prayer ministry of Kansas City gets 3,300 calls a day.

What's driving the prayer-a-thon? Supporters say that praying for others is simply in the Christian tradition, while critics suggest it's just a way to build mailing lists for fund appeals. Money must be coming from somewhere, because it costs $9.5 million a year to run Silent Unity's prayer central. Prayer representatives code requests into thirty-six different problems (celestial pigeonholing?) and then distribute them to the warriors (volunteers or paid employees) who do the actual praying. After each prayer, the request is marked "Prayed For" and then is shredded.

iconogasm: cultural climax, marketing opportunity
Bow down to the marketing gods by satisfying America's insatiable thirst for religion.

Events

From prayers to promises and back is the path hundreds of thousands of *soul searching* men are taking. They're finding religion and community by joining the ranks of the Promise Keepers, a for-profit Christian company based in Boulder, Colorado. Men of every age, from backslapping Harley bikers to high-fiving bankers, are joining the PK evangelical army founded and generaled by former University of Colorado football coach Bill McCartney. The collective goal is to return "integrity" to the American lifestyle by exalting followers to reclaim their "rightful" biblical role as the head of the family.

At mammoth rallies across the U.S., men are instructed on how to reassert their manliness. The happenings—typically 50,000 or more rally for the fifty-five-dollar fire-and-brimstone, loaves-and-fishes-included weekends—are strictly a guy thing, held in football stadiums and complete with

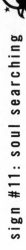

sermons, music, and the book *Seven Promises of a Promise Keeper* (their addendum to the Bible) instructing on how to take back the home-front reins. Pastor Tony Evans writes, "The first thing you do is sit down with your wife and say something like this, 'Honey, I've made a terrible mistake. I've given you my role. I gave up leading this family, and I forced you to take my place. Now I must reclaim that role.' Don't misunderstand what I'm saying here. I'm not suggesting that you ask for your role back. I'm urging you to take it back."

In postrevival news interviews with Promise Keeper wives, the comments have been overwhelmingly positive (although NOW—the National Organization for Women—is less than pleased). Give the movement some time to "realign"; the domestic-bliss vote is still out. We'll be keeping our eyes glued to the cultural Richter scale—this could be the "big one."

iconogasm: cultural climax, marketing opportunity
Pat men on their butts by giving them renewed purpose and meaning in their lives.

Diversity

America's religious diversity is quaking our national boots as both traditional and alternative forms of spirituality continue to flourish. Aspects of Jewish culture, for example, are spreading across our country like lox on a bialy, with renewed interest in such things as kosher foods and Kabbalah (Jewish mysticism).

In danger of going the way of Latin, Yiddish, the practiced language of European Jews, also appears to be making a comeback. Many of the nation's leading universities, including Harvard, Berkeley, UCLA, Michigan, and Texas, are adding more Yiddish courses to their curriculums. At a recent Association of Jewish Studies conference, sessions were held on modern

Yiddish and Hassidic literature, another sign of the times that the academic community has gone *meshugena* over the language. But don't get too *verklempt* over this surge in Yiddishalia. Yiddish takes three or four years to master, with knowledge of Polish, German, or Russian a prerequisite. More *yenta*s may be on the way, however, with the launching of Yiddish into cyberspace. Dial up Mendele, the Yiddish chat group on the Internet (named after the first modern Yiddish writer, Mendele Mokher Sforim).

The growing number of branches of the Kabbalah Learning Centre signals there is a whole-hog—oops—Carnegie-Deli-reuben-sized embracing of other traditional forms of Jewish culture. Kabbalah ("receiving," in Hebrew) is sacred, secret lessons of Jewish mysticism, limited to Orthodox scholars until only recently. The KLC opens the hidden passage, teaching the more spiritual side of Judaism to anyone interested. Jews, like everyone, are starving for answers to the big questions of life and are studying Kabbalah because it addresses topics outside traditional Judaism, such as reincarnation, astrology, angels, hell, and meditation. Kabbalah thus may keep in the fold some Jews who otherwise might look to alternative forms of spirituality. Kabbalah has been off-limits to so many for so long because it has always been considered potentially dangerous stuff—capable of making you crazy if applied the wrong way. But Kabbalah is increasingly becoming part of Jewish services, courses, healing rituals, and meditation programs, revealing the mystic soul to the masses.

iconogasm: cultural climax, marketing opportunity

Get that old-time religion by reviving ancient, traditional expressions of spirituality.

Retail

Spiritual—*ka-ching, ka-ching*—awakening? It's divine. Cash registers are ringing up sales faster than you can exclaim *hal . . . le . . . lu . . . jah!* The search for infinite wisdom is on, report the country's largest independent Christian book chains—Family Bookstores (184 stores), Joshua's, Borean Christian Stores, and Baptist Bookstores (63 stores). Christian retailing reaps $3 billion annually. But Christian booksellers don't live on book bread alone: Inspirational clothes, framed art, videos, and spiritual doodads drive big sales. Take time out to visit some of the stores, and you'll be impressed by what savvy marketers these folks are. The Living Vine, Family Bookstores's 30,000-square-foot superstore in Irving, Texas, reflects a lifestyle experience. Value-laden manna is every which way you stroll. The kids' section is awesome, and rightly so, since children will inherit the Earth and are thus a very strong growth market for these retailers. Parable parenting gets a boost from kid-video series like the live-action-animation *McGee and Me!* and *Last Chance Detectives* (think Hardy Boys meet the virtue police). A cruise through the music department is an enlightening experience. The literally thousands of titles are testament to Christian music, born again and again and again, with annual sales of $550 million.

All this action in the Christian category doesn't necessarily mean that America is becoming more religious. Church attendance isn't up, but experts in tune with this slice of life say that a "parallel universe" exists. This is a culture that is both not reflected in mainstream media and not searching for wisdom in the icons of pop culture. To get in touch with the power and the glory of this lifestyle you'll have to meet them on their own turf—concerts, talk radio, bookstores, church.

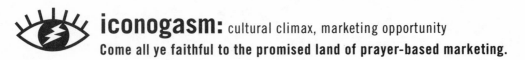

iconogasm: cultural climax, marketing opportunity
Come all ye faithful to the promised land of prayer-based marketing.

Music

Enlightening has struck. Meet Point of Grace. These amazing Gracies, graduates of Ouachita Baptist University in Arkedelphia, Arkansas, are one of the hot acts on a contemporary Christian music scene that brings in nearly $1 billion a year. The beauty bevy—Denise Jones, Shelley Phillips, Heather Floyd, Terry Long—are what you would get if you crossed a Tanya Tucker twang with four Shirley Temple wannabes. Backroad, rural churches are their gig; the altar their stage. Audiences are jampacked with teenage Puritans writhing to chastity in synthesized rhythms. Jesus is in their hearts and throats, while they sing His

praises as their salvation from drugs, premarital sex, and other temptations. Point of Grace's persona is that of the girls next door—innocent, feminine, honest, true blue, and (without a doubt) virginal. Their vow, to remain "pure" until marriage, draws idolizing cheers from fans. Amen.

Chant music is selling like Gregorian hotcakes these days. The leader of the hooded pack is of course the Benedictine Monks of Santo Domingo de Silos, with their mega hits *Chant (I),* and a *II,* and a *III.* Other religions, sniffing the sweet smell of secular success, are also chanting. *Chants Mystique: Hidden Treasures of a Living Tradition* is a collection of Hebrew liturgical music culled from centuries of history. Jewish chant, possibly the oldest form of the genre still practiced, took on different forms as Jews wandered across the Mideast and Europe. Influences of Roman Catholic, Latin, and Islamic cultures make *Chants Mystique* a multicultural matzah for the ears. Pass the musical soup!

iconogasm: cultural climax, marketing opportunity
Hear the angels sing and harmonize through spiritual forms of music.

Soul Mates

For those looking for long-lost pals, the *AARP News Bulletin* suggests checking out the Old Friends Information Service. Founded by Michael Franks when he had difficulty finding his own long-losts, Old Friends is the tool of choice when telephone books and genealogical services fail to come up with the goods. The matchmaker has brought together some 2,000 old friends and old flames, achieving an overall success rate of 68 percent. Employees scour electronic databases and directories, using only public information. When a long-lost is located, Old Friends sends a letter notifying the searchee of the searcher. Once permission is received, information is released to the searcher. Most clients are more than fifty years old, many of them veterans looking for old Army and Navy soul mates. Old sweethearts also come to Old Friends, some of them still pining for lost loves after forty years.

iconogasm: cultural climax, marketing opportunity
Friends of all ages want to stay in touch. Package products and services as ways to connect.

Office Mates

Want to come over and see my Daytimer? Office romances, long considered a potentially volatile combination, are rapidly becoming kissin' cousins. Companies are encouraging couples to get together by providing opportunities for socializing, dating, and mate finding. Until recently employees were often scorned for having on-the-job relationships and occasionally were accused of favoritism and security breaches. In reengineered Corporate America, however, human resources departments have determined that a happy, fulfilled worker is a productive, competent one. With 75 percent of women in the workforce and everyone working longer hours, it's no wonder more sparks are flying over the water cooler. In fact, 33 percent of all romances start at work, in part because, well, when two people work for the same company, they already have something in common. Companies like Xerox are going out of their way to act as *Fortune* 500 cupids, transferring wayward lovebirds and holding social events for employees, where the hormones can take over. Johnson Wax offers theater and travel clubs, intramural sports, a pool, tennis courts, a gym, and—get this—a seventeen-cottage lake resort. Where do we sign up?

iconogasm: cultural climax, marketing opportunity
Let love and business flourish. Invite cupid into the office.

sign #12:  the other side

One of Western culture's biggest bugaboos—death—is finally being confronted head on. Just as we are creating new ways of living as we approach the new millennium, so we are redefining the way we die. Part of the sea change in our attitudes about death stems from our greater interest in Eastern and Native American cultures, which offer interpretations of the big good-bye that differ from the West's see-ya-in-heaven-or-hell paradigm.

Death is also at the intersection of a number of today's more passionate of passion points: There are few among us who have not been touched by AIDS in some way; the abortion debate rages on; and Dr. Kevorkian has made physician-assisted suicide an issue impossible to ignore. Finally, empowerment-crazed Americans are trying to rationalize the Big Mystery in the belief that if they understand it, they will have more control over it. Expect the lines between life and death to become less clear as we look to *the other side* for answers.

Death as Therapy

It should not be too surprising that a generation raised on psychotherapy is using death for therapeutic purposes. Cardinal Joseph Bernadin's decision to die a public death in 1996 helped us vent some of our own demons, while Julia Sweeney's one-woman show, *God Said, "Ha!,"* put her experience with her brother's death (and her own bout with cancer) right on Broadway (and humorously, too). Sweeney turned death on its hollow head, recasting a tragic story into one about family love.

Funerals have become exercises in therapy rather than the theological rituals they were. Families today play a much greater role in funerals, less accepting of a generic going-over of the gospel. The Christian tradition that views death as a punishment inflicted on us by God for Adam's "original sin" is itself going to the big hotel in the sky. Marking a death is as important as it ever was, but *how* a loved one's death should be marked is in radical flux. Even the order of the journey of death—home vigil to church service to cemetery burial—is being reversed. Many mourners now want to begin at the cemetery and then proceed to a memorial service, changing the focus from the sorrow of death to the joy of life.

iconogasm: cultural climax, marketing opportunity
Expect death to be recast as an integral, even positive, part of life's experience.

Death Marketing

With growing interest in *the other side*, death is becoming a tidy little business, thank you very much. Angel fever was sparked in part by the comfortable idea that the divine can appear in anthropomorphic form, in turn making death a friendlier proposition. Books about death are hotter than, well, hell, as authors take dying and the dying process out of our cultural closet. Dr. Sherwin Nuland's *How We Die* told readers what the final moments of life will be like, while *Final Exit* showed readers how to take their own lives if they so choose. In addition to the many conferences held to discuss how we can die more humanely, there's an entire magazine dedicated to helping with the mourning process. *Bereavement, A Magazine of Hope and Healing* publishes articles about the grief experience as well as "poems, tributes, stories, and photos from the bereaved." These all are examples of what we call *death marketing*, the launching of products and services centered around the canoe trip of canoe trips.

iconogasm: cultural climax, marketing opportunity
Look to *death marketing* as a smart undertaking.

Grief

"Death is un-American." —Arnold Toynbee

Grief is in a state of transition as we close the book on the twentieth century. *American Health* speaks of a new age in understanding, appreciating, and managing the grieving process. Americans are typically unprepared for the loss of a loved one, not equipped to deal with the psychological, physical, and social pressures associated with bereavement. Catherine Sanders, author of *Surviving Grief—and Learning to Live Again*, suggests that Jackie Kennedy has served as our principal role model of grief, an unfair standard for us mortals. Because we have shifted the site of death from homes to hospitals and are often geographically separate from family, American mourners suffer from unusually high levels of anger, guilt, anxiety, despair, and depression. That is changing, however, as a vast array of resources are made available to those experiencing grief. AARP's Widowed Persons Service, for example, connects widows and widowers with information and support programs, while The Compassionate Friends provides a similar service for bereaved parents and siblings. Grief Recovery Helpline offers counseling during business hours, and National Self-Help Clearinghouse provides names of a wide variety of bereavement support groups.

Cybermourning is a relatively new avenue for grieving. Web page memorials and links to friends and message boards allow cybergrievers to mourn online. Newsgroup memorials are a new twist on the eternal effort to make sense out of what is sometimes nonsensible. People affected by national tragedies like the Oklahoma City bombing have a place to share their loss, connecting with one another on the Internet through a website created by Families and Survivors United. Expect the Internet to emerge as a primary communal gathering place to grieve.

iconogasm: cultural climax, marketing opportunity

Look for grieving to become a full-fledged industry as the first wave of boomers heads toward the final third of their lives.

Death Fingerprinting

Ashes to ashes, dust to . . . golf bag? New life is breathed into death as the funeral industry *fingerprints* (see sign #18) via custom-designed funeral urns. The selection is awesome. Enshrine your family Shriner in a ten-inch molded fez. If Pop's first love was putting, may we recommend the "wood cultured" brown-tone golf bag model? It's the perfect resting place, a real hole in one. Oh, but you say his passion was hunting? The sitting duck on the pond is one of the top sellers (with no doubts that this one has gone on its last migration). Or for the horse lover, "what could be more fitting," assures funeral director Dennis McNulty, "than the cowboy boots?" For Mr. McNulty, a veteran embalmer and sales manager at Kelco Funeral Supply Company, the cremation market is hot. The Cremation Society of North America estimates that one in five people opts to go up in smoke, with that number to double by the year 2010. *Business Week* attributes the trend to its lower cost, a shortage of space, and the ease it affords an increasingly transient society. It could also be a spinoff of growing environmental concerns. What's for sure is that in a land that prizes personal freedom and individuality, the upscale urns are the ultimate celebration of lifestyle or, more accurately, deathstyle, proving once again to marketers that you really *can* reinvent the wheel. Available for about $550 at fine funeral parlors everywhere.

iconogasm: cultural climax, marketing opportunity

Two things are certain: taxes and personal expressions of death.

Proactive Dying

"Death is anything but a failure. It is a critical chapter in human biography. For some, the last days are the crowning completion and the most precious jewels of an entire life." —Therese Schroeder-Sheker, founder, Chalice of Repose Project

As our culture comes to terms with *the other side*, there is a parallel effort to make the passage a positive and peaceful one. Hospices, residences for the terminally ill, are spreading as many choose alternatives to impersonal hospitals as places to die. There are even hospices for children with progressive, life-threatening illnesses which offer families emotional and spiritual support. Hospices will undoubtedly flourish in the years ahead, as will the decision to die at home, surrounded by loved ones.

The angels are singing at St. Patrick Hospital in Missoula, Montana, through the Chalice of Repose Project. When a patient is terminally ill with a life-expectancy of anywhere from six months to a few hours, support for "conscious dying" is made available through the Project's "musical-sacramental-midwifery." Using only voice and harp, teams of two or more midwives gather at bedside to immerse the patient in the soothing vibrational tones of Gregorian chant. Based on the belief that dying is a spiritual process and an opportunity for growth, the musical vigil is designed as a "healing without curing" for the patient, family members, and health-care providers. The sole focus is to help the dying person move toward completion and to break away from anything—especially pain and the fear of pain—that prevents a tranquil passage. Project midwives believe that the musical vibrations are absorbed by the entire surface of the skin, helping patients drift into a deep, peaceful sleep.

The Project is unique in the world and gaining international recognition for its pioneering discipline of music thanatology, a milestone in medical and spiritual partnership. Missoula is furthering its reputation as the world capital of *the other side* through the Missoula Demonstration Project, a long-term study of how community residents face their own deaths and the deaths of loved ones.

iconogasm: cultural climax, marketing opportunity
Recognize the growing belief that deathing, like birthing, is a blessed event.

Death-Defying Acts

It seems like you haven't really lived these days until you've died. You can hardly flip a channel, cruise a zine, or bring up a homepage without having a near-death experience, that is, a personal glimpse into *the other side*. More than 7 million of us have tales of out-of-body (OOB) trips, typified by a "beyond Technicolor," unconditionally loving light at the end of a dark tunnel. Sometimes OOBs are accompanied by celestial guides who lead welcome-home parties of long-gone loved ones.

Skeptical empiricists dispel the visions as neural light shows exhilarated by an endorphin rush. In years of interviews with the living dead, however, there is astounding similarity, clarity, and purpose to such experiences. Earthbound angels return with orders from the Big Cheese for us to love one another and to be kind, tolerant, and generous. Whatever the explanation, there is a powerful pull on our culture to connect with our spiritual side by literally taking leave of our senses. For more on taking a walk on the wild side, pick up Betty Eadie's seminal work on OOBs, *Embraced By the Light*.

Despite all the evidence to the contrary, some people are even denying the existence of death, sure that the postlife experience is simply a change in venue. Elisabeth Kubler-Ross, one of the original leaders of the hospice movement, has become a spokesperson for this idea, as outlined in her book *On Life After Death*. Life after death, according to Kubler-Ross, is one big adventure filled with peace, unconditional love, and, in her words, "dancing with angels." Heaven sounds a lot like Woodstock!

iconogasm: cultural climax, marketing opportunity

Count on lots more peeks into *the other side* as boomers hit the mortality wall.

chapter 4: experience

As the second millennium draws to a close, we are combining mind, body and spirit to form an authentic culture of experience. Mid-life boomers, suddenly aware that they actually may die, are pushing their experiential envelopes to new dimensions. Seniors are active in ways their parents never could or would be, while Generation Xers are putting their *carpe diem* money where their twentysomething mouths are. Marketers able to translate products and services into experiential terms will benefit most from this megatrend to "just do it."

sign #13: vice versing

Huh? Vice in these days of AIDS, MADD, AA, the AMA? Sure there's vice; you just have to look for it or, more precisely, know it when you see it. Today's vice, a version we like to call "nice vice," is much different from yesterday's vice. *Vice versing* subscribes to the belief that sensory pleasures are to be relished, not repressed. In the early 1990s we rejected wholesale the hedonistic lifestyle of the 1980s, exchanging it for one that denied many of life's pleasures. As we end the decade, however, we have happily found ways to accommodate vice and still remember what we did the night before and how we got home. We have accepted that hedonism in moderation is natural and even healthy, a legacy of boomers' perpetual desire for some form of indulgence.

Smoking

Today you'll find many people who smoke but few who will admit they are smokers. What's up with that? This is called *social* smoking, a definition that says a cancer stick on the lips and a drink in the hand when out with friends just doesn't qualify you as a smoker. You're not really damaging your lungs; you're just being friendly. Yeah, and we're related to British royalty. In any case, smoking is hugely popular again, despite the demise of that phallic ship of the desert, Joe Camel.

The resurgence in smoking is also fueled by new products that make smoking a more interesting, even exotic experience. American Spirit has for the past few years been the brand of choice for Generation X, liked for its Native American image and being more "natural" than your basic coffin nail. Cigarettes from India called beedies, however, have displaced American Spirits as the butt to see and be seen with. Beedies (from the Hindi *bidi*) are roughly half the diameter of regular cigarettes and are hand-rolled in *tendu,* or ebony, leaves. Don't be fooled by their Tiparillo appearance, however. Beedies contain up to 8 percent nicotine, four to eight times your average American cig. Beedies come in flavors like clove, menthol, and strawberry, and cost around three bucks a pack, about the same the Marlboro Man charges. Although they are known as "the poor man's cigarette" in India, cool cats in the States like 'em 'cause they look like joints and do indeed pack a buzz. Ask for them by name—popular brands are Mangalore Ganesh and Kailas—but don't say Iconoculture sent you.

Other smokes popular with the hip set are "single-serve" cigarettes, expensive, imported products purchased one at a time at bars and cafés. No need to invest in an expensive pack (or again, admit to yourself you're actually one of *them*) when you can buy a yummy Dunhill for a buck. The big cigarette companies are going to school on the success in microbrews by marketing "microsmokes," added-value, niche-oriented, beautifully packaged packs o' tobackey. The Moonlight line of microsmokes from R.J. Reynolds includes brands Sedome, Politix, and Planet, while Philip Morris tests out microbrands Dave's and Player's Navy.

And then there's the cigar movement, which we hold entirely responsible for our elevated dry-cleaning bills. Cigars roll out a perfect form of *vice versing*, representing sophistication, possessing intense flavor, and opening the door to an entire subculture of smoking jackets and cravats.

 iconogasm: cultural climax, marketing opportunity
Position products and services as forms of *nice vice*, which deliver intense but safe physical pleasure.

Eating

Eating too has been *vice versed*, an opportunity for moderate indulgence. Now that we know fat to be the work of the devil (or devil's food), most of us have cut down on the red meat we eat. When the beast within calls and nothing but a steak will do, however, we're likely to get the biggest, best darned hunk of beef this side of Omaha. Steakhouses are flourishing in every major city in this country, an irony in this age of medical wisdom and rising concern about health care. Whole Foods, this country's biggest co-op chain, sells chickens raised by Amish farmers, triumphantly taking the foul out of fowl.

Bread boutiques have hopped onto the *vice versing* wagon, popping out gorgeous loaves of spinach-infused, cheese-engorged, chocolate-laced beauties. Sure it costs twice as much as the sliced and diced not-so-Wonder Bread, but it's worth the extra two bucks. Very few of us have $50,000 for a Jag, but almost all of us can splurge on the occasional filet mignon or pumpkin-walnut sourdough.

iconogasm: cultural climax, marketing opportunity
Create "affordable luxuries" or "exotic commodities" to make consumers feel like kings and queens for a day.

Drinking

Man and woman do not live by baked goods alone! Dunk that biscotti in a double au lait or triple espresso, and we're talking major *vice versing*. The Starbucking of America has left us all bright-eyed and bushy-tailed, hopped up on good old caffeine and ready to take on whatever life dishes out. Tea and more recently chai also ride the coffee trend, perceived as kinder and gentler than that supercharged cup o' joe.

Just as our consumption of red meat has dropped, we're also no longer knocking back pitchers of beer like we did in college days. When we do feel like having a beer, however, only a rich and chewy brewski will do. Hence the microbrew movement, which has made a fair-sized dent in the humongous beer industry. Indeed, society's addiction to being entertained has given marketers permission to concoct mythical, folkloric personalities for even the most basic of life's necessities (like beer). On a recent trend trek along the Mississippi, we ambled into Ole's Maiden Rock, a classic Wisconsin bar. "What'll ya have?" wasn't even out of the barman's mouth when a shout from near the dartboard came through loud and clear . . . "BIG BUTT HERE!" Those words might have crassly offended lesser trendspotters, but not us. "BIG BUTT HERE"? we inquired. This bar call double bock beauty, we learned, rages through the Midwest every autumn, a short seasonal brew with genius branding and solid taste. From Miller's little brewery, Leinenkugel's, the classy bottle logo tells the whole story—two muscular, curly-horned rams head-butting. There's actually a lot to learn from Big Butt about brand building in a saturated marketplace. The name, package, ingredients (Mt. Hood and Cluster hops from the Yakima Valley), and smoky taste deliver on a promise of fermented fun. Lest we forget, the legend is stamped on every bottle: "Handcrafted in small batches since 1876 in Chippewa Falls." Take a load off, settle in . . . BIG BUTT HERE!

If Big Butt is, well, a little out of your league, there are always single malt scotches, pure grain bourbons, and small batch tequilas and mezcals. A common thread throughout *vice versing* is the desire for a clear, distinct, uncompromised flavor or experience, not blended or cut in any way. A Macanudo should be all Macanudo, a cup of Kona coffee should be all Kona, and a Glenfiddich should be pure and straight from the Scottish Highlands. Hard cider is another beverage that has been promoted to the status of nice vice. Apple vineyards in the Northwest are taking the craft of fermenting apple juice to a new level, creating drinks of biblical temptation.

Juice culture on the West Coast is positively frothing at the mouth. Get Juiced, a Phoenix juice bar, sells smoothies made with stuff like bee pollen, wheat grass, ginseng, spirulina algae, and aloe vera, the latter supposedly helpful in keeping things on the straight and narrow in the body's southern hemisphere. Scottsdale's Surf City Squeeze is partial to proline, a collagen-building amino acid. Their "Thinker Squeeze" concoction allegedly creates "performance transmitters" that improve thinking and reduce stress.

Despite the medicine-show claims, juice bars are rapidly becoming big business. There are already well more than a hundred Surf City Squeeze outlets and counting, and more than twenty-five Jamba Juice bars in San Francisco alone. With people like Howard Schultz, big kahuna at Starbucks, sitting on the Jamba board of directors, look for *vice versing* juice bars to roll across the country like James's giant peach.

Finally, where would we be as a culture without martinis? Like cigars, martinis are mostly about staging and appearance (fueling a parallel increase in the cufflinks industry). As a prop, martinis take us back to a time when a man was a man, a woman was a woman, and a drink was shaken, not stirred. Sure they taste like rat poison, but pour a berry infused vodka and throw in a few chunks of pineapple, and they're actually palatable.

iconogasm: cultural climax, marketing opportunity
Leverage the trend toward authenticity and purity by positioning brands as socially responsible forms of hedonism and fun.

Sex

Puffing, munching, and sipping ain't the only vices around, you know. Sex has also been *vice versed*, a function of AIDS and a more conservative sexual climate. Oddly, various permutations of sex previously considered perverse or kinky are now mainstream because they are, in fact, safer than actual intercourse. Take S&M (sadism and masochism), no longer considered the stuff of disturbed sexual deviants. Handcuffs are displayed openly in gift shops, and even that wholesome couple the Petries (Mary Tyler Moore and Dick Van Dyke) have posed in *Vanity Fair* in full S&M regalia. Big cities across the country have thriving S&M club subcultures, where leatherboys and leatherettes gather to abuse one another.

Voyeurism is no longer grounds for permanent incarceration. Those who prefer watching to doing have turned voyeurism into an art form, equipped with high-tech binoculars and telescopes. The next time you're snuggling, you might keep in mind that someone out there is using night-vision goggles in a way the military never intended.

Why the outing of such interesting dimensions of human sexuality? As acts of the mind rather than the body, neither S&M nor voyeurism involves exposing oneself, so to speak, to the dangers involved in having sex . . . all the fun without any of the risks. Check out the back pages of any alternative weekly newspaper and you'll begin to realize how big the phone sex industry is. Men remain hugely interested in having sex with strangers; it's just that now they can let their fingers do the walking.

Cybersex is a way the hot and bothered are getting it on without that inconvenience of having someone else in the room. The Internet is a virtual lover's paradise, a love connection between you and the rest of the known universe. No bites, but plenty of bits and bytes! Upscale strip clubs are another avenue for people to look-but-don't-touch, a classy way for men to be bad boys yet still live up to their marriage vows. (God didn't mention anything to Moses about lap dances when he delivered the Ten Commandments, ya know.) Engaging in public sex is something couples are doing to keep monogamy fun and exciting. A risque rendezvous in the minivan might be just the thing to bring back the magic to some couples' married lives.

iconogasm: cultural climax, marketing opportunity
Create permissible outlets for consumers to let the monster out of the box.

Recreation

Feel like you deserve a reward for being such a goody-goody during the week? Many do and are rewarding themselves with various forms of recreation. Gambling—or gaming, to be politically correct—is a vice that somehow got versed. Whether at one of the many casinos around the country, online, through a lottery, or in a sports betting pool, Americans are passionate about gambling. Despite the odds stacked against us, the chance to get rich or just richer for what is usually a small investment is an irresistible idea. Once associated with criminals and banned by religious groups, gambling has become a legitimate, socially acceptable vice. Visit Las Vegas today, and you're more likely to see strollers than hookers, a clear sign that gaming has gone straight.

Another way people are pursuing socially responsible irresponsibility is through vice shopping, a remnant of the 1980s born-to-shop ethos. No, you don't really need another pair of black shoes, but one lives only once, *n'est-ce pas*? (As many as 6 percent of Americans are compulsive shoppers, however, suggesting that easy credit may be too much of a good thing.)

Last, taking a vacation to an exotic locale can be a form of contained vice. Indulge yourself by laying on a lava beach, eating great food, and calling the cabana boy for more piña coladas from your cushy chaise longue. That ecotravel tour to the Bering Straits by cargo ship can wait until next year.

iconogasm: cultural climax, marketing opportunity
Market products and services that offer experiences as get-away-from-it-all, you-deserve-it-all kicks.

Health and Beauty

Mmm, lay back and let your touch therapist's fingers do their magic. Many of us are turning vice into positive energy through massages and a plethora of other delicious services offered at spas and salons. Get that sea kelp body wrap, that mud facial, that hurts-so-good dermabrasion—you deserve it! New Age Dr. Kelloggs have brilliantly packaged physical pleasure as guilt-free, even healthy, experiences. Cosmetic surgery is another acceptable form of vice—unnecessary, expensive, but also a practical investment in oneself. Men on the back side of fifty are jumping into the nip 'n' tuck pool like sagging lemmings, trying to maintain their boyish good looks to keep both career and that twentysomething trophy wife in tow. American men spend $700 million a year on treating baldness alone. Necessary? No. Worth a few grand? Absolutely.

iconogasm: cultural climax, marketing opportunity
Blend one-half self-indulgence with one-half self-improvement to make the perfect *vice versing* cocktail.

sign #14: merit badges

So what does one do for an encore after having it all (or at least a good chunk of it)? Unlike the 1980s' race to collect more things, the late-1990s are about collecting more experiences. Baby boomers are driving the experiential train, trying to scramble up Maslow's hierarchy toward self-actualization. Affluent boomers are in a postmaterialistic phase of their lives, recognizing that their complete set of Calphalon sure is nice but is not an end in itself. Social status has not gone away, of course; it has just been recast from what one *owns* to what one *does*. Four-wheel-drive sport-utility vehicles, for example, are symbols of high social status because they suggest their owners are going somewhere interesting in them (although they're probably just taking the kids to soccer practice). Within this paradigm, status, or *merit badges*, are rewarded to those who rack up the most challenging and exotic experiences.

Travel

What to do when you've been there, done that, and got the T-shirt? Take a "collectible" vacation that will blow the doors off your neighbor's slide show of that oversized mouse and his goofy pals. Combine learning with travel at a Young Presidents Organization (YPO) seminar in Australia, or take an ecotravel trip to the rain forest, where you'll have to forage for your own food. *Merit badgers* are in search of must-in-a-lifetime experiences, like bagging wild animals on an African camera safari or biking through Vietnam. Hitting the dusty trail of Death Valley by horse is another 120-degree experience sure to produce some interesting Kodak moments. "Micro-niche" travels, unique trips to places way off the beaten path, are also increasingly recognized as the way to spend some truly quality time. Have a Bat Flight Breakfast in a cave, visit Sweden's Ice Hotel, or investigate remote civilizations like the Asmats of Indonesia. You're bound to be the hit of your next rotating dinner.

Traveling in order to collect experiences is ground zero of *merit badges*. Thrill seekers travel thousands of miles to take rides on the biggest and best roller-coasters scattered around the world, adding to their collections of adrenaline rushes. Interestingly, we are in the midst of a roller-coaster renaissance, with more rides being built now than any time since the freewheelin' 1920s. In these times of sense and sensibility, many find that tampering with the laws of gravity is apparently a means of getting grounded.

Bird-watching is another way Americans collect experiences. The American Birding Association reports that close to 25 million oglers take at least one trip a year solely to watch birds, spending $7.5 million on their feathered adventures. When it comes to impressing your friends, a confirmed sighting of a yellow-bellied sapsucker beats a BMW in the driveway any day.

iconogasm: cultural climax, marketing opportunity
Create opportunities for consumers to add to their "experiential portfolios."

Fantasies

Da plane! Da plane! Americans are heading off to fantasy islands every chance they get. You don't have to be Ricardo Montálban to understand that many of us want to know what it feels like to fly a plane at warp speed or just to have a job that doesn't involve spreadsheets. People want *merit badges* not awarded by Harvard Business School, like for surviving two weeks of boot camp. That's right . . . sir! These green recruits come back to real life tougher, more disciplined, and in the best physical shape of their lives.

For those who lack interest in a jungle-foraging ecotravel tour, there are alternative *merit badges*. Schools where you can drive cars in ways not recommended by the highway patrol are becoming particularly popular in these airbaggy days. At car-racing schools, NASCAR wannabes learn what 200 miles per hour in a Porsche feels like. Just going for a spin without a car seat is a big thrill for some of these Daddy-are-we-there-yet types. Other motor enthusiasts are crossing the big pond to attend the Land Rover Driving School in the U.K., while those with some definite aggression to vent are joining the Terminator III Racing Team.

Terminator III offers classes in driving car-crushing monster trucks for fun or competition. At the one-day fantasy camp, you will learn everything you need to know about squashing automobiles with a 1,400 horsepower Ford truck, which makes a Hummer look like a Yugo. The Terminator III stands 11'9" tall, is 12'8" wide, and weighs 11,000 pounds. The tires alone are taller than your average NBA guard. If you've ever dreamed about what it might be like to drive a three-bedroom colonial, here's your chance. Training in traversing obstacle courses is, naturally, included in the price, as are safety tips designed to keep you from becoming the crushee rather than the crusher. All systems are go after putting on your Nomex driving suit, Simpson full-face helmet, five-point safety harness, and neck brace. Flip the ignition and fuel-on switches, push the start button, and feel 500 cubic inches of big-block engine under your seat. Proceed to squash girlycars like the puny ants they are.

iconogasm: cultural climax, marketing opportunity
Position products and services as opportunities to pursue dreams rather than as symbols of consumption.

Extreme Sports

Feeling a little too safe and secure in your cocoon? Spread your wings and hit the slopes, waves, or pavement. Participation in extreme sports is a way that many of us feel we rightfully earned our *merit badge*, not to mention that huge gash on our left shin. Go vert by heli-skiing or tractor skiing, achieving multiple-peak ascents all the way. Hit a high-altitude workout station after a morning of downhill snowbiking, speed ice climbing, or supermodified shovel racing. Better yet, let the huskies do all the work by dogsledding through the Alaskan Rockies. If water and terra firma are more your media, try catamarans, in-line hockey, or fat-tire racing.

Extreme sports may have been invented by teenage thrashers, but that doesn't mean they get to have all the fun. Putting life and limb at risk or just challenging the rules of nature is *merit badges* in its most visceral form. Just watch out for road rash and freezer burn! (For you homebodies, that's what's left of one's skin after a disagreeable confrontation with the road or ice.)

iconogasm: cultural climax, marketing opportunity
Offer consumers the opportunity to earn *merit badges* by pursuing high-altitude, monster-depth-charged, frostbitten experiences.

Expertise

With *merit badges* centered around experience, expensive things have become less signs of wealth than symbols of expertise. Having a collection of fine wines, for example, suggests today that the owner is an oenophile, not that he or she is necessarily rich. Demonstrating expertise and good taste through things is an essential way to show off *merit badges*. Cranking up that top-of-the-line laptop while flying first class is a relatively graceful form of elitism, as is working out with a personal trainer or not eating a crumb without first consulting a personal nutritionist.

Possessions are clues we read to evaluate others' personalities. A briefcase from a spy store suggests the owner is doing secretive (and thus important) work, while a $1,000 Mont Blanc pen or Cuban cigar is a symbol that shouts that its owner cares a great deal about what she writes with or smokes. Titanium golf clubs (set of irons starting at $2,000) and Mercedes-Benz mountain bikes ($3,300) are indeed costly but are purchased to show off your passion, not your wealth.

iconogasm: cultural climax, marketing opportunity
Allow consumers to flaunt their *merit badges* by defining products and services as symbols of expertise.

sign #15:  roadtripping

Want to hear the heartbeat of America? Get out there on the highway and take a long, loose *roadtrip*. Exit the interstates and cruise the backroad bluelines; that's where the mainstream flows. As we put another 100,000 miles a year on our Iconovan, we're seeing lots of easyriders like us who regularly feel the need to hit the road. While virtual travel can give you a sense of what a place is like, there is simply no substitute for the sights, sounds, smells, and tastes unique to every corner of the Earth. "True adventure requires losing sight of the shoreline," someone once said, giving credence to today's trend toward meaningful, purposeful travel. Here are some ways Americans are earning their saddle sores.

Getaways

Sky-high airfares and time-crunched careers are working together to encourage a whole new love affair with the weekend trip and overnight getaway. The proliferation of comfortable driving machines—sport-utility vehicles, minivans, RV's—makes it cheap and easy to scratch that itch to be someplace else. A new generation of road warriors, in passionate pursuit of what remains of authentic America, are putting pedal to the metal for the reward of experiencing the real thing.

That covers just about any venue with a menu that celebrates local, traditional roots. Festivals celebrating just about any fruit or vegetable you can think of (the Sorghum Festival?) are calling jaded urbanites home. Whatever tickles a fancy, there's a festival glorifying it—bluegrass, salmon, ice, sweet peas, jazz, storytelling, sausage making, opera, basket weaving, local lore, corn on the cob, rodeos, ribs, poetry, winemaking, crabbing 'n' crawdaddies, apple picking, chili making . . . Besides pumping personality and a lot of money into the local landscape, these gatherings keep American regionality from being franchised into extinction.

iconogasm: cultural climax, marketing opportunity
Appeal to our need for constant renewal and growth by building *roadtripping* into your marketing mix.

Cruises

With some 159 cruise ships representing more than fifty cruise lines departing from American ports, consumers have a smorgasbord of cruises to choose from, many of them geared around feasting the various senses. Adventure cruises are gaining knots over the traditional gorge-yourself-on-goodies-twenty-four-hours-a-day plan. Travelers insatiable in their quests for learning and experience are setting sail with crews of trained biologists, naturalists, and ecologists as onboard seminar leaders and onland cultural guides. These experts are definitely more the ilk of the professor on *Gilligan's Island* than Julie McCoy on *The Love Boat*. Cruising for the decadent fun of it will always fill the captain's table, but leaving the tux at home currently rides a giant swell.

Cruising, of course, isn't limited to eco-enthusiasts. Carnival, Norwegian, and Royal Caribbean cruise lines all offer family-style cruises, but it's the Big Red Boat that caters best to little sailors. The line's two boats o' fun run Disney films nightly and, for a few extra bucks, will even have a Looney Tunes character tuck in the wee skipper or skippette at beddy-bye time. Best of all, the giant crimson tubs offer in-port supervised child care and all-night group baby-sitting, so Mommy and Daddy can get reacquainted. The Big Red Boat won the National Parenting Center seal of approval, so it must be doing something right. As Disney's own cruise line sets sail in 1998, get ready for Mickey, Minnie, and the rest of the gang to rule the waves.

iconogasm: cultural climax, marketing opportunity
Spread the word that the family that *roadtrips* together stays together.

Experiential

The most compelling *roadtrips* are those that allow travelers to take on alternative lifestyles. A canal tour through the United Kingdom, for example, stops at all the local pubs so you get a flavor of working-class Brit culture. Absolutely fabulous! Here in the States you can visit an organic farm or even spend a couple of days working a real farm. City slickers get in touch with their rural sides by milking cows, picking fruit, and trying not to get winnowed by threshers. A company called Déjà Vu Tours even offers "healing vacations," spiritual trips that enable that reincarnated *roadtripper* to relive past-life adventures. Yikes! What would a postcard from one of those excursions look like?

The point is that opportunities for experiential *roadtripping* are boundless. Travel and tourism marketers should consider offering roadtrips that push the experiential envelope. Give those corn-fed Midwesterners a chance to go clammin' and crabbin' on the shaw. How about a minor-league-baseball bus tour for those who can't get enough of the *unplugged* version of the national pastime? Or how about a "Roots Tour" through ethnic neighborhoods of cities to trace our Irish-, German-, Italian-, African-, Jewish-, or whatever-American heritage? With history more alive than ever, memory marketers should package tours to famous sites of 1930s' gangster hits, 1950s' beatnik hangouts, and 1960s' counterculture protests.

iconogasm: cultural climax, marketing opportunity
Take consumers on a magic-carpet ride of experiential travel.

Shrines

Another compelling kind of *roadtrip* takes us to shrines—places known for their spiritual power. Almost all societies designate certain places as special cultural destinations that resonate with powers of healing or an especially strong sense of community. As public life in America continues to decline, shrines are endowed with even greater purpose and mission.

Today New Age health centers such as The Marsh in Minnetonka, Minnesota, are considered epicenters of well-being, oases of our time and place that restore the juices of physical and emotional health. Spas like Canyon Ranch of Arizona serve the same purpose: shrines to the wonder that is the human body.

More conventional shrines are, well, conventions—communal gatherings of those with shared professional or personal interests. Visit a *Star Trek* or *Mystery Science Theater 3000* convention or the Harley-Davidson bike-o-rama in Sturgis, South Dakota, and you'll gain a sense of the power of shrines.

Church pilgrimages have, of course, served as the traditional shrine-a-thon. As alternative spirituality becomes a greater part of American life, people are *roadtripping* to new shrines that draw upon Eastern and Native American theologies.

Lynn Andrews, author of *Dark Sister* and founder of the Center for Shamanic Arts and Training, has become master of her domain by tapping into the power of Indian shrines. Based in Petaluma, California, the center teaches students from all over the world such skills as shape shifting (the ability to side-trip out-of-body into the cosmic consciousness). Finding an inner, enlightened relationship with yourself and using that knowledge to help heal the Earth is the focus of her curriculum. Twice a year, students come together to drum for four days and four nights at Joshua Tree in the high desert above Palm Desert, California, and in Sedona, Arizona. Gathering in the shadows of the giant saguaro cacti, the student sorcerers invoke ancient Native American rituals (Andrews believes the saguaro are the desert shamans, keepers of memories and medicine powers). *Roadtrips* to places such as the Center for Shamanic Arts and Training are tapping into the *gaia* trend (see sign #28), the deep desire to connect with the Earth.

iconogasm: cultural climax, marketing opportunity
As Eastern and Native American spiritualities continue to shape Western culture, tap into the power of Earth-friendly shrines.

sign #16:  themeparking

Just fell madly in love over a burger at Boogies while on a shopping excursion to the Mall of America? Are you in luck! The Chapel of Love, a full-service wedding chapel at this mother of all malls, takes walk-ins. For $295 to $595, lovestruck shoppers can get hitched between shoe shopping at Nordstrom's and riding the flume at Camp Snoopy. The reception? *¡No problemo!* Who needs to book a reception months in advance when the food court's Laotian Bar-B-Q, Hot Wings, and Cookies R Us are just steps away?

You have just entered the *themeparking* zone, where every experience—shopping for sneakers, vacationing, eating, getting a haircut—is turned into a Disneyesque adventure. Entertainment has encroached into virtually all aspects of everyday life, especially retail environments. The big winners of the next millennium will be those who make *themeparking* their main mantra.

Shopping

Entertainment is well on the way to dominating the retail landscape as marketers entice consumers into supercharged environments. Master *themeparkers* Warner Bros. and Niketown know that most Americans feel right at home browsing for two or three hours among Tweety Bird and Porky Pig sweats or high-fiving local celeb sports heroes who just happen to tie on Air Jordans. Urban Outfitters, Old Navy, and Oshman's are a few other retailers who have turned their stores into interactive themeparks offering added-value shopping experiences.

iconogasm: cultural climax, marketing opportunity

Go to school on marketers who have defined shopping as something to *do* rather than something to *buy*.

Eatertainment

Eating is now eatertainment. What you put in your mouth is being usurped-burped by the *themepark* in which you choose to pig out. The corner café is giving way to the total-concept eatery, with dining morphed into a theatrical experience of Broadway proportions. The success of Planet Hollywood is living proof that you've never really munched onion rings until you've done so under Mae West's garters or Elvis' britches. The block-long lines at the Hard Rock Cafe, the Motown Cafe, the All Star Restaurant, the Fashion Cafe, and Jekyll and Hyde are testaments that the *idea* of eating has become more important than the food.

Hankering for home cookin'? Cracker Barrel Old Country Store is one of the more compelling fantasies *du jour*. Cracker Barrel is leaving a winding trail of buttermilk-biscuit crumbs through the hometowns of America. You can pick up the scent in Paducah, Kentucky; Elkhart, Indiana; Murfreesboro, Tennessee; or a couple dozen other locations, with the promise of "scratch biscuits" hot outta the oven. Cracker Barrel's romantic vision—"There's nothin' like finishin' the mornin' chores an settin' down to breakfast in the country"—is an offer few can refuse. A dozen cane-backed rockers welcome hungry travelers at the front porch door. Inside is a warm and cozy country store chock full of the best of bygone days: cast-iron cookware, barrels of candy, smoked hams, private-label preserves, and apple butter. Give the morning menu Grade A Fancy rating for everything from the hash brown casserole with Grade A russet potatoes, Grade A Fancy fruit toppings, Grade A extra-thick-cut bacon, 100 percent Grade A pure maple syrup, and 100 percent Grade A Florida oranges. Was Aunt Della's cooking ever so scrumptious? Shucks, who cares? This homespun homage has more than 60 million folks stoppin' in every year for chicken and biscuits.

Yippee-ki-ay! Next time you're in the city so nice they named it twice, mosey on down to a *themepark* of Western proportions, the Cowgirl Hall of Fame restaurant. The Cowgirl Hall of Fame, at Tenth and Hudson in Greenwich Village, has been serving up real chuckwagon chow since 1989, giving city folk a taste of authentic cowgirl cookin' like Frito pie ($4.25) and eggplant fritters ($4.95). What's more, the restaurant was founded to support the National Cowgirl Hall of Fame and Western Heritage Center in Ft. Worth, Texas, a "real, live museum dedicated to illustrating the lives of women of the West, past and present." A portion of all sales goes to support the museum, which honors a different cowgirl every quarter. In case you were wondering, cowgirlness is measured by relative skill in rodeoing, ranching, hat making, music making, and, most important, "for living and being the true spirit of the West." The Cowgirl Hall of Fame restaurant is a bronco-bustin' buffet of down-home cooking and cause marketing, a *themepark* of good food and good intentions.

iconogasm: cultural climax, marketing opportunity
Saddle up to opportunity by riding the gravy train of eatertainment.

Tourism

Even garbage has been *themeparked*. If you've already been to all the tourist traps in Manhattan, stray from the beaten path toward the Rodney Dangerfield of New York City boroughs, Staten Island—home of the Fresh Kills landfill. Fresh Kills is the world's largest garbage dump, 2,200 acres of New York's finest trash. For forty-eight years, as much as 16,000 tons of garbage have been arriving at Fresh Kills by truck and barge. Not about to miss an opportunity, the city's street-smart Department of Sanitation offers tours of this malodorous field of dreams, and *voilà!* People have come!

Camera-wielding Japanese are, not surprisingly, a particularly avid group of Dumpster funsters. The DOS is positioning the landfill as a living museum that offers an educational experience to anyone interested in how a culture manages its waste. A construction trailer functions as the visitors' center, where trashoholics enjoy an eleven-minute video on the history and workings of the dump. Guests also get to climb Trash Mountain and take in an unforgettable combination of sights (lunar-type module vehicles), sounds (more gulls here than in an Alfred

Hitchcock movie), and smells (methane and pine). Hats, T-shirts, and umbrellas are planned, although the city wisely nixed the DOS's serious proposal to sell framed garbage. Even New York City knows when trash can be in bad taste.

 iconogasm: cultural climax, marketing opportunity
Themepark the stuff of everyday life into alternative forms of ecotourism.

The Mall of America

Your adventure is about to begin. Please check in at the elephant."
—Seating call at the Rainforest Cafe

The themepark of themeparks is the Mall of America in Bloomington, Minnesota. Old Walt is probably spinning in his grave as he watches the Mall of America take over as reigning themepark and assume the rightful claim as the happiest place on Earth. Like Disney worlds, the Mall is actually a mega-themepark composed of hundreds of mini-themeparks, each trying to offer the entertainment value of a robotic Abraham Lincoln. The result: the Mall each year fields an estimated 40 million visitors—more than Disney World, Graceland, and the Grand Canyon combined—and powers up $1.5 billion in economic activity.

If kids are in tow, stop in at Enchanted Tales, a magic kingdom of stuffed animals. Then hop on over to the Warner Bros. store and get a Polaroid of the little mall rats with the Tasmanian Devil and his lovely wife. Have lunch at the Rainforest Cafe, which astutely skirts serving mediocre food by turning dining into a Pirates of the Caribbean experience. Work off that Amazon Burger ($7.95, thunder, lightning, and precipitation included) at the Lego Imagination Center for hours of hands-on, plasticized fun. After a short nap at your within-spitting-distance motel, go for the big kahuna of themeparks, Knott's Camp Snoopy. Bet you don't have a flume ride at your strip mall. The Mall of America has brilliantly blurred the lines where entertainment ends and shopping begins, creating a new paradigm of retail as recreation.

 **iconogasm:** cultural climax, marketing opportunity
Put magic slippers on your customers' feet by *themeparking* your products and services.

sign #17:  stealthing

How do you beat the system from within the system? Through *stealthing*, flying beneath society's radar through a conscious decision to fold, spindle, and mutilate the rules. More and more, consumers are lying in the reeds, confident that they now have the advantage in the marketplace. *Stealthing* is played out through "guerrilla consumerism," hide-and-attack tactics designed to get the biggest bang for the consumer buck.

   Stealthing first emerged on the American scene a generation or so ago, when baby boomers began to reject the values of their parents' conformist society. Technology has since fueled the rise of *stealthlike* behavior, as has the breakdown of traditional media and distribution outlets. As more of us recognize the power of remaining invisible, marketers need to adopt their own *stealthing* tactics to survive the skirmishes of the next century.

Technology

Online culture is the undisputed capital of *stealthing*, the perfect environment in which to remain anonymous or assume an alternative identity at whim.

Cybercrackers represent the more villainous side of *stealthing*, breaking into institutional databases for both fun and profit. Most Net surfers display some elements of *stealthing*, however, routinely breaking the established, traditional rules of communication, shopping, investing, and even dating.

Sullen wallflowers, for example, are known online as lurkers. Lurkers hang around silently in otherwise noisy chat rooms, eavesreading other people's conversations for vicarious fun. For those who do "talk" online, E-speak has literally rewritten the English language, creating a new form of discourse that has crept even into f-2-f communication. Online shopping empowers consumers by giving them access to the global marketplace, making the entire idea of geography irrelevant in one fell cyberswoop.

Investing has become a much different animal because of the virtually unlimited amount of information that is now available. Online investor groups such as Motley Fool (see more in sign #31) offer subscribers a competitive edge, effectively leveling the playing field between smaller and larger investors.

Romance, too, has gone underground, carried out over modems instead of in the backseats of Chevrolets. More than one Romeo was surprised to learn that his digital Juliet was a balding, middle-aged man instead of the Julia Roberts lookalike she/he described.

iconogasm: cultural climax, marketing opportunity
Marketers can tap *stealthing* instincts by appealing to Net surfers' desires to be invisible online.

Retail

That Old World maxim—"Never pay retail"—has spread beyond New York's Lower East Side. With more purchase options than ever before in history, the stealth shopper can pick and choose how and where to buy based on the best value. Discount stores have evolved into warehouse superstores, outlet stores into outlet malls. Sure, that two-gallon mother of all jars of mayo is a bit on the large size, but what savings! Car shoppers, now aware of dealers' list prices, can dictate what to pay or simply go to a competitor. Within a paradigm of *stealth* shopping, retail will inevitably split into two paths, one headed toward low price, the other around interactive entertainment (*themeparking*). Retailers will have to choose which path to take or get stuck in the retail purgatory of not offering consumers price value or added value.

All consumers have developed *stealth*-shopping habits by now, but how *stealthing* is expressed varies by generation. Seniors living on fixed incomes are master *stealthers*. They know where the cheapest greens fees are and are perfectly happy to eat dinner an hour earlier if it saves them a buck or two. Baby boomers, the first generation raised as a target audience from birth, have

embraced *stealthing* as a means to streamline and simplify their lives. Generation Xers are often *stealthers* by necessity, known to pay for seven-layer burritos with change from their car floors.

iconogasm: cultural climax, marketing opportunity

Cross-target audience demographics through the common denominator of guerrilla consumerism.

Alternativism

As *value vertigo* (sign #23) shakes America in its cowboy boots, there will continue to be dramatic rises in the rejection of mainstream institutions and in the acceptance of alternative ones. With the decline of public education, for example, alternative educational methods (home schools, charter schools, etc.) have gained significant ground. Similarly, the failure of Western medicine to effectively treat everyday health problems has allowed alternative therapies to flourish. The inability to find a store tomato that does not taste like the crate it was shipped in has led to an entire biodiversity movement. In sports, major-league greed opened the door for more affordable, populist sports like minor-league baseball and bowling. You name the category; there has probably been a serious challenge to the mainstream by once-marginal, now perfectly legitimate alternatives.

So how does the rise of alternativism relate to *stealthing*? As mainstream culture loses status and alternative culture gains status, we are becoming a society that endorses *stealth* attitudes and behavior. More outlets to vent antisocial, iconoclastic feelings are forming, some of them perfectly healthy, others not so. The popularity of vintage clothes or found art, for example, is a sign of increasing awareness and dissatisfaction with our disposable society. Similarly, the incredible number of zines (personal magazines) is an indication of the individual's need to be heard over the din of the mainstream media. Now there are even alternatives to alternatives, such as the Slamdance Film Festival, an antiestablishment response to the once-alternative now-mainstream Sundance Film Festival (and don't forget the alternatives to alternatives to alternatives, such as the Slumdance Film Festival).

The legacy of baby boomers' countercultural revolution has much to do with the ascendency of *stealthing*, as does the alienation many Generation Xers feel toward society. Expect alternative culture to continue to expand, and with it the desire to have one foot outside societal norms.

iconogasm: cultural climax, marketing opportunity

Create opportunities for consumers to declare their independence and freedom from mainstream values.

Just who do you think you are? Don't panic! This isn't an essay exam; it's multiple-choice question, and most of your fellow citizens aim to answ

chapter 5: identity

d) all of the above. The cult of the individual has an expanded identity the peripheral personality. Think of the self as a laptop computer wi ports for multiple identities. For just one simple Simon there are eas ports for career, fashion, family, sports, genealogy, birth orders, urban a getaway lifestyle, social conscience . . . that plugs in but a few. T overlapped, connecting identity cords get tangled but not enough to ke the majority from wanting to plug in more. Instead of being forced choose the one perfect persona, we crisscross ethnic, cultural, even gend boundaries. The backlash, quite naturally, is the simplicity moveme which peels away materialism and activity layer by layer to find a tru essence of life. There's a rekindled passion for nostalgia; going to t source to find authentic products, people, foods, and mythic lifestyles emulate. Most inspiring, everywhere we travel and at all ages, individu are listening to an inner call to follow their integrity, giving a hand needy people and a needy environment. That takes us back to the co question: Who do you think you are?

sign #18:  fingerprinting

Baaaaaa. Baaaaaa. Dolly's been cloned, and someday so will we. Or so it seems. The next step on the road to being one big herd? Don't bet the alfalfa farm on it. We still want and need to be *me*. The quest for individuality intensifies with every plastic lawn chair, black Gap turtleneck, and box of Cheerios cookie-cut for the consumer marketplace. In this consumption-based society, our authentic *fingerprint* is expressed through each person's consumer portfolio. Building that portfolio drives the economy. What's wacko is how we're copycats, all buying a lot of the same stuff—clothes, furniture, food, mutual funds, cars. What singles us out from the rest of our Dollymates is how we uniquely strut the same stuff. Is this self deception perception or reality? In a backhand way, this sheds light on why the unisex fragrance CK One is the most shoplifted product. Doesn't body chemistry "guarantee" it will smell unique on every crook? *Fingerprinting* aims to affirm that old identity axiom "They threw away the mold when they made me!"

Services

Me-focused shoppers deserve a little TLC. Those merchants and manufacturers creatively coddling their customers are way ahead in brand loyalty. No matter how hackneyed it sounds, the personal touch touches and keeps 'em coming back for more.

It doesn't take a lot of capital expenditure to connect viscerally with a customer. In the Atlanta area they're proving that a little empathy goes a long way. In parking lots of Publix chain shopping centers and supermarkets, giant wooden storks reserve a few front-door spaces for expectant moms. If you shop J. Crew you know how their salespeople take time to jot a note of thanks for buying those oatmeal cords—"They looked fab on you"—or to warn of a new shipment arriving Tuesday—"Come take a look." Why wouldn't you be a

103

regular? They understand your signature style.

Large retailers could learn much from the J. Crew crew. Retail service, once a prized selling point of the big department stores and a gimmee in the good old days of free tailoring, is in sad shape now. The *New York Times* reports on a 1996 survey of 4,000 consumers conducted by the market research firm Yankelovich Partners, in which department and discount stores scored only a 25 percent "very good to excellent" rating for service. That's 12 percent *less* than most everyone's perennial service grumble, the U.S. Postal Service. Rated the worst were automobile dealerships. The blame at most stores falls on lean sales-training budgets, cutbacks on floor personnel, and stretched-too-thin floor management. Slim margins don't include smiles or extra helping hands?

iconogasm: cultural climax, marketing opportunity

A little service is a lot when none is what you've got.

Products

Fingerprinting crowns the consumer king by taking the "mass" out of "mass market." Products and services that forge honest relationships and expectations with their customers earn the right to ring up sales at higher price points. Bought a pair of jeans lately? The correct butt-hugging fit is crucial, and when image is everything, a pair of custom-fit Levis is well worth the price.

"Have you been Colorprinted?" In women's cosmetics, Prescriptives is the mastercraft Colorprinter of custom makeup, touting more than 100 choice shades of facial foundation to enhance each individual's lip, cheek, and eye tone. Being Colorprinted is a gas for younger and older women, who put their faces on deck to take advantage of "free" appointments with Prescriptives color stylists. All this lavish attention makes it near impossible to exit without purchasing some or all of "your" custom color cache. The same *fingerprinting* principle of empowering the customer is alive and moisturizing at The Body Shop. Shoppers are encouraged to customize lotions by autographing an unfragranced base with a drop of their favorite scent.

Après ski in Aspen, belly up to the Fragrance Bar on East Durant Avenue. Its design is reminiscent of an old apothecary, with a wall of glass bottles holding precious cargo—jasmine, tea rose attar, ginger, lavender. The "bartender" is an alchemist, trained to tempt patrons to create their personal perfumes. This fancy *fingerprinting* is a pampering both men and women enjoy. Designing an olfactory calling card is an event that allows the consumer to create his own personal brand. The scent, worn regularly, marks his territory, communicates distinct brand personality, and over time may even become an icon, announcing his presence even before he walks through the door. Hershey's smells distinctively like Hershey's, Noxema like only Noxema, and—ta-da! Harry smells only like Eau de Harry.

iconogasm: cultural climax, marketing opportunity
Take the "mass" out of "mass market" by allowing consumers to write their unique signatures with your product.

Pharmacy

We are becoming a nation of know-it-alls, thanks to a shopping-bagful of home-health I-spy kits, and the variety is growing almost as quickly as bacilli in a petri dish. Consumers seem right at home taking their blood pressures or monitoring their glucose levels. In fact, blood pressures may  rise when it comes to making a buying decision—one Iconoshopper reported six different brands of pressure kits in one pharmacy alone. Ready to relieve or confirm your worst nightmare? Over-the-counter test kits for HIV; osteoporosis; and cervical, bladder, and breast cancers put control in the hands of the individual, bypassing medical-lab expenses and slowpoke turnaround times. *Fingerprinting* what's happening in your body without letting anyone else in on the secret is very appealing to worry-wart consumers. A recent survey by the U.S. Centers for Disease Control found that 42 percent of those at risk for HIV say they would be likely to use an anonymous home test. The Home Access Express HIV test, manufactured by Home Access Health Corporation, sells for $44.95 and sends results in three business days—cheap and easy when peace of mind or your life is on the line.

iconogasm: cultural climax, marketing opportunity

The more we know about our health, the more we want to know. Do we have chronic bad breath? Hyperthyroidism? Low sperm count? Make it your business to let us know.

Food

Hungry for profits? Check out the grocery industry. It's a leader when it comes to understanding their customers—hungry folks in a hurry. They need to have their favorite eats ready to eat, *now*. Grocery stores are no longer just in the ingredients business; today they compete with fast-food restaurants for the take-home-meal dollar. Who has time to roast a chicken, chop the slaw, shuck the corn? Harried consumers, more than at any other time, opt to swing by Safeway's deli, snarfing up hot goodies, hurrying home to park in front of *Mad About You,* where Helen and Paul are probably eating take-out too. To the food industry this is the monster *fingerprinting* trend—$25 billion spent yearly—they call home meal replacement (HMR), and it leaves grocers, packaged-goods marketers, and restaurateurs shaking in their aprons.

Brandweek prepared the full-meal deal with side dishes of facts, figures, and future scenarios. Digest this: More than 40 percent of consumers have no idea at 4:00 P.M. what they will eat for dinner; Americans eat an average of 4.1 commercially prepared meals per week; by 2005 the meals-on-wheels lifestyle is projected to boil up a $100 billion industry (and who knows how many megatons of mashed potatoes). If you've got the hungries and are lucky, HMR may be as close as your local grocery store. In the Midwest, the Byerly's chain is an orgasmatron of take-out cuisines. They seem to devote at least 15 percent of store space to a bodacious buffet of ready-to-heat-and-eat entrees, yummy veggies, pastas, and desserts. Byerly's has a magic recipe for comforting the starving hoards: If you can't sate your appetite at the deli, take a number at the in-store Asia Grille, Caribou Coffee, or Wolfgang Puck's pizza kitchen.

Expect strong growth in partnerships among traditional grocers, local restaurants, and national franchisers. America's tummy is growling. It's time to heat up the kid's take-home meal of macaroni and cheese, then your take-home plateful of Penne Romano (uppity mac 'n' cheese).

iconogasm: cultural climax, marketing opportunity
Keep an eye on evolving lifestyle choices. Be ready to *fingerprint* life to make it easier, faster, better.

Body Image

Dinnnng! Microwave done. Dish up that KFC order of extra crispy, wedge yourself in a nice, cushy wingback, turn down the tube. Let's chat about how all this fast food is teaming with minimal exercise (too much driving/too little walking), and the death of manual labor as our leaner forefathers knew it, to turn us into a nation of fatty-fatty-two-by-fours. The *fingerprint* of this country is the fat, fatter, fattest it has ever been in history. The Centers for Disease Control calipers that 34.9 percent of the general population is carrying way too much weight. In America, 300,000 citizens qualify as obese. Retired Surgeon General C. Everett Koop claims fat and all its bad health complications is the number-two killer, behind heart disease. How can this be in the land of nonfat everything, personal nutritionists, personal trainers, and pudgeless role models? 16"... 24"... 32"... 72"... whatever the belt size, the national stats support the proposition that Americans have an obsession with body image. Eighty percent of U.S. women are on some incarnation of a diet. In fact, flogging fat is a national pastime and a $36 billion industry. The saddest statistic: Four percent of our high school and college women binge and purge, afflicted with anorexia and/or bulimia. And the lose-it drug, Redux, is being prescribed to tens of thousands of fatties since hitting the pharmacy in early '96.

If it's not enough to be forever fighting the battle of the bulge, think about all the psychological hits an overweight human has to handle. The taunts and teases have created a body-image ache that's feeding a new social cause called fat activism. All this bad-body badmouthing has spawned a plethora of zines, music, and comics that celebrate rather than insult XLs. Their missions are to put an end to discrimination against the behemoth *fingerprint* and, of course, provide good self-esteem vibes for our bigger friends. Check out *Big Beautiful Woman, Big Ad, Living Large,* and *Fat Girl* ("A zine for fat dykes and the women who want them"). These publications remind us that big doesn't have to be better, just *as good.*

iconogasm: cultural climax, marketing opportunity

Showcasing XXL can bring a measure of reality back into advertising and will viscerally connect with the larger-than-life general public.

Ancestors

Want to find out if you're the sap in your family tree? Many do, according to the National Genealogical Society in Arlington, Virginia. The NGS tells us that genealogy is the nation's third most popular hobby and that genealogical classes, clubs, and tours are booming. The ten-part PBS television series celebrating the significance of family history, and its excellent companion book, *Ancestors,* by chief *fingerprinters* and cohosts Jim and Terry Willard, are testaments to the new national passion. Rootless Americans concerned that they were left on the doorstep by gypsies or are extraterrestrials with the bloodlines of alien pods are flocking to the NGS to trace their ancestries through a free lending library, computer bulletin board, and directory of professional search firms.

Another place to pick up the trail of one's great-great-greats is the Louisiana Heritage Center in Baton Rouge, where one can bayou through more than 500 million names. If Grandma's and Grandpa's scents are still elusive, take a pilgrimage to the Family History Library in Salt Lake City, where those Latter Day Saints take tracking earlier days religiously.

The interest in genealogy is all about finding identity and a sense of place in our increasingly polyglot society. Adventure is also part of the experience, mixing travel to the Old Country and detective work, often through cemeteries and musty records. Boomers have a special interest in genealogy, because learning how one's ancestors died—breast cancer? heart attack?—may help prevent a premature carving on the family tree. Occasionally, however, sleuths find a few surprises, like old Granddad's granddad was the town drunk, village idiot, or a dirty rotten scoundrel. Still, everyone from genealogical search franchises to software marketers are reaping the benefits of telling the uprooted who begot whom.

iconogasm: cultural climax, marketing opportunity
There's plenty of room in the name game to make a mark in genealogy.

DNA

For those people not planning on resurrection, there's still a reasonable chance for immortality: Preserve your DNA! That unique *fingerprinting* gene pool fills every pore and cell. Just rub your finger on a gauze pad, then ask your favorite biochemist to extract the gene print from the skin cells. Before you can say "Jurassic Park 3," you have your very own genetic sample which, with proper care, will survive way longer than the rest of you. Given the current alternative for a shot at perpetual life after death—having one's head lopped off and frozen like a twenty-pound pork chop—we say, DNA take me away!

Kary Mullis, winner of a Nobel prize in chemistry, is blazing the trail in genepreneuring. A few years ago, through his company StarGene, Mullis developed trading cards with holographic reproductions of the DNA strands of celebrities. Working from a lock of our favorite hound dog's hair, Mullis also has embedded teeny drops of Elvis's DNA into artificial gems. Certainly brings new meaning to the ecumenical phrase "The King is risen." The word is Mullis has the hair rights to a bevy of famous dead guys and gals, including Abe Lincoln, James Dean, Geronimo, and the original bad-hair-day dude, Albert Einstein. Better living—and dying—through chemistry!

iconogasm: cultural climax, marketing opportunity
Appeal to consumers' desires for immortality with products and services that give a glimpse into eternity.

Mating

Is that you we hear, John Harvard, somersaulting in your grave? Obviously he just flipped through *Harvard Magazine*, spotted those big, bold letters— **PERSONALS**—wedged coyly in the classifieds, and his crimson curiosity got the best of him. Us, too! "Date someone in your own league." So here's where the highbrows browse for educated, cultured, cuddly companionship. Let's see who fits the Ivy League *fingerprint*. More than fifty ads pump up the virtues of sparking with grads, faculty, alums, and academics of the Ivies and Seven Sisters. (Hmmm, guess that leaves out the single Hawkeyes in the crowd.) They're a learned lot: "Nifty Smithy," "Cambridge male," "eye-catching art historian," "spirited female physician," "Harvard poetess," "literate ex-Catholic," "kind, lithe Renaissance woman (arts, medicine, humanities)." And they know just what they're craving: "magnanimous, fit, nonsmoking, diversely interested, worldly gentleman, 55–65, of sound judgment and integrity, academic/diplomatic/ business executive, to love and compliment, not compete with..." Love knows no bounds? As long as the *fingerprints* match.

iconogasm: cultural climax, marketing opportunity
Be true to your school. Common experiences equal common values equal unequaled networking.

sign #19:  cultural infidelity

"Best Espresso in Iowa City . . . Dim Sum Served Sundays"

Huh? This street sign of the times is very clear: cultural crisscrossing ahead. *Cultural infidelity*, the magnetic merging of polar opposites—north/south, east/west, traditional/alternative, highbrow/lowbrow—is breach-birthing a nation of cultural hybrids. The Great American Melting Pot is empty. It bubbled over in the 1990s with the greatest immigration since the storming of Ellis Island. But unlike the foreigners of yesteryear, new citizens in the twenty-first century will be valued for, instead of stripped of, their unique cultural identities.

Immigration

Immigration, a staple of the American experience, continues to be a passion point as we head farther into our final decade of the century. The *New York Times* reported some startling findings based on a new reading of the 1990 U.S. census, revealing the huge impact immigration is having on America's demographic and cultural landscapes. Minority immigrants are replacing whites in the nation's larger cities on an unprecedented scale, making the white flight of the 1950s and 1960s seem like a walk around the mall. Betcha didn't know that during the 1980s more immigrants entered this country than in any other decade in American history, more than 80 percent of them Latin American and Asian. Ten million legal and illegal immigrants came to the United States on Reagan's and Bush's watches, a million *more* than reached American shores in the first decade of the century. Rather than settling in all parts of the country, however, more than 75 percent of this tidal wave splashed down in the urban areas of just six states, specifically ports of entry in the Southwest (from Houston to San Francisco), the Northeast corridor, and in the historically ethnic cities of Chicago and Miami. What's most surprising is that these new immigrants did not simply add to these communities' populations but rather displaced white residents, who left for more Anglo destinations. For every ten minority immigrants who came to one of these communities in the 1980s, in fact, nine whites promptly fled for a paler part of the country. Rich whites, who are not economically threatened by new immigrants, are not leaving the cities; it's lower-middle-class and underclass whites who are heading for the Caucasian hills.

The result of this cultural exchange program is, naturally, a much more Balkanized America, with cities and the country as a whole essentially split into two distinct types of regions. Urban communities are increasingly segregated by race, ethnicity, and class as less educated and less affluent whites in big cities call Century 21, leaving highly stratified neighborhoods and schools made up of wealthy whites and a minority underclass. With America's larger cities starting to resemble multicultural versions of eighteenth century Paris, marketers need to address these major shifts in our cultural plates in every aspect of their business.

iconogasm: cultural climax, marketing opportunity
Jump out of the melting pot and into the salad bowl as Americans choose to segregate themselves.

Population

A *cultural infidelity* quake is rumbling across this nation's fault line, changing the way America looks and acts. Seismic readings show African-, Latin-, and Asian-Americans are rapidly becoming significantly larger percentages of the population, with "minorities" to outnumber the Euro-American "majority" by the year 2015. As America becomes more colorful, Euro-American dominance will recede and a much more diverse cultural palette will emerge. Some of your more savvy marketers are already jumping on the *cultural infidelity* welcome wagon as we become a jambalaya of races, ethnicities, and religions.

What's the future of our wildly morphing culture? More languages are being spoken and taught, creating an ethnic life akin to that a century ago when huge waves of huddled masses came to our shores. American cuisine will be truly globalized, with "two all-tofu patties on a sesame seed pita" a common verse. As Corporate America starts to look more like a Benetton's ad than an old, pale boys' club, economic and political clout will gradually be redistributed along color lines. *¡Muy bueno!*

iconogasm: cultural climax, marketing opportunity

Be true to our national motto, *e pluribus unum* (out of many, one), by recognizing and respecting diversity.

Fitness

Chin up. Butt tucked. *Cultural infidelity* is stretching the fitness scene. It's out of Africa and into an aerobics studio: Afrocentric exercise is what's shakin' and sweatin' with women of color. Fitness classes billed "Afrobics," "slammin' jammin'," and "rap aerobics" combine body-shaping moves from the motherland with hip hop, funk, and tribal folk beats. Free-form grooving is replacing the typical technoblast of predominantly whitey aerobics. Culturally inspired perspiring is the hot new ticket in gyms across the country. In San Fran Club One, "street jam" and Latin-American salsa classes are heart-pumping niche markets. New York's Crunch fitness clubs are attracting a wild bunch for their New Step City funk-a-thon workouts. And sisterly love is alive and jiving at Philadelphia's Market West Athletic Club, where strut-your-Afro-stuff "aerofunk" classes celebrate heavy-breathing diversity. Yes, the growing popularity of ethnicizing exercise is yet another gyration of successful multicultural marketing.

iconogasm: cultural climax, marketing opportunity

As the nation continues to reject an antiquated one-size-fits-all mentality, expect *cultural infidelity* to warp speed ahead.

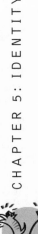

Foods and Beverages

The food and beverage industries were the first to birth *cultural infidelity*. Frenzied flavors like hot-pepper passion-fruit cola, Jamaican jerk pot roast, and ginger-spiked garlic mashed sweet potatoes turned the common man's turnip *haute* haughty. Millennial tastebuds will quiver as tongue-twister combos emerge. The globe is one simmering mulligatawny stew pot, where native cuisines unabashedly intermarry. Lusty Italia is a culinary gigolo, romancing tantalizing tastes from Cuba to Patagonia. Never fear, American diner food is the one purist holdout: two eggs sunny side up, hash browns, bacon, Wonder Bread toast slathered with Concord grape jelly, please!

It's fruit basket/veggie cart upside down: This Bud Berry is for you! A baba ganoush spritzer? Yikes.

iconogasm: cultural climax, marketing opportunity
Don't be shy! Court infidel-flavor behaviors the consumer is willing and ready to eat and drink up.

Education

The schoolhouse is no longer a commercial-free zone. Business and education are doing their homework together. Already 40 percent of the nation's secondary classrooms are jump-started each day by news and ads pumped in from Channel One. With kids ages six to nineteen spending $485 billion each year, what tuned-in marketer should or could resist going back to school? So far only Seattle and Colorado Springs school districts are riding the commercial yellow bus, selling their hallowed hallways as ad space and bus panels in middle and high schools for product logos. We expect full-fledged capitalism to turn Thomas Jefferson's dream of every child guaranteed a public education into a Reeboked reality. Mountain Dew, among others, is ready to quench students' thirst for knowledge and help out the budget-broke ed system at the same time. With close to 46 million children off to school each day, that's a mighty big thirst. Gulp.

iconogasm: cultural climax, marketing opportunity
Invest in the future by supporting public-education programs.

Tourism

Time Out, the definitive guide to goings-on in NYC, reported how *cultural infidelity* is having rippling effects on tourism. Every Sunday morning, droves of European sightseers flock to Harlem's Baptist churches in search of an America untainted by anthropomorphic rodents. Organized by the tour groups Musical Feast of Harlem and Harlem Spirituals, Inc., these gospel-a-gogos offer Europeans a chance to witness a version of Christianity much different from their own. German, French, and Austrian visitors are amazed at the energy and emotion of the services, especially at congregation members' levels of involvement and sheer volume. (Call-and-response is hardly a staple of the European Christian tradition, much less electric guitars and Marshall amps.) At five clams a Eurohead, this *themeparked* divinity has been a financial windfall for churches like Mount Nebo and Mount Calvary, even creating a turf war of sorts among Harlem's holy rollers. Although some major ethical issues are perhaps at stake here, any opportunity to see how the other lives is likely to have a positive effect on global race relations.

iconogasm: cultural climax, marketing opportunity
Look for sites of diversity to convert into marketing opportunities.

sign #20: zentrepreneurism

Before continuing, please take time to brew yourself a cup of tea. Take a little more time to ponder . . . Are you living life sip by sip or gulp by gulp? The first *zentrepreneurs*, the founders of the specialty company The Republic of Tea, steeped into full flavor the Z concept of making business a force for positive

social change on the planet, to actualize a life in which "what you do" is one with "who you are." The fusion of one's personal vision with one's professional mission, grounded in activism and a holistic philosophy, will hallmark the next 1,000 years. *Zentrepreneurism* is surfacing across a wide spectrum of successful, purposeful businesses.

Media

From curbside to park bench, out of alleyways and subways, under boardwalks and highways, the homeless journalist is reporting. Articles communicating a street-level perspective, ripe with humor, irony, and empathy, are the backbone of New York City's *Street News*. It is one of many urban journals, funded in part by private donations, that publish and sell copies to homeless vendors, who hope to use their resale profits to get back on their feet. The newspaper makes its bucks by selling ad space to altruistic/image-conscious corporations. A win/win/win—newspaper, homeless, advertisers—for all sides.

iconogasm: cultural climax, marketing opportunity

Look for the seed of opportunity in the social cause. Helping people where they live beats a handout any day.

Gen X

If you think *zentrepreneuring* is only for the disenfranchised and old hippies gone to seed, think again. An aging Generation X will carry proudly the do-unto-others-as-you-would-have-them-do-unto-you torch into the future. During their college years, they short-circuit their slacker image by volunteering *en masse* to help those less fortunate. From coast to ivy-covered coast, college students log as many as ten to twelve hours per week tutoring, manning rape and suicide hotlines, teaching English, serving up dinner at homeless shelters, or being buddies to the physically or mentally challenged.

Sonya Tinsley is a prime example of youth putting their *zentrepreneurial* zeal where their hearts and mouths are. Tinsley, twenty-six, founded Atlanta's Serious Fun Community Music Project, bringing musicians and young fans together to create a forum for discussing issues (homophobia, abortion, race relations) in students' lives. "The most rewarding thing about Serious Fun," exudes Tinsley in the humanitarian zine *Hope*, "is the opportunity to create a project that involves the two things I'm most passionate about: making music and making change." The do-gooding experience coupled with the *zentrepreneuristic* mood of the millennium will have far-reaching political, social, and economic implications.

iconogasm: cultural climax, marketing opportunity
It's time to pass the baton. Generation X is in training to change the world.

Workplace

It all sounds so boring. Cooperation, not competition. Meaningful work, not big bucks. Sharing in the decision making, not being bossed around. At the Burley Design Co-op, ninety people call the shots because ninety people own the company store. This may be a new-millennium model for American business. How novel—healthy growth as the full-time focus of everyone in the workplace. By the way, Burley builds the essential baby accoutrement: those bright-colored buggies that safely trailer little ones behind the folks' bikes. You might expect a company that produces such a creative product to spawn an enlightened model for building a business. In a time when thousands are experiencing post-downsizing shock syndrome, this employee-owned co-op structure may be a light at the end of the corporate tunnel. According to general manager Bruce Creps, "There's also a second paycheck that people are after here. Many have tried different things and are looking for meaning from their work."

Pride in ownership translates to low absenteeism, low worker turnover (one or two per year), and sky-high productivity. One of the principles of the cooperative is to enhance the workplace and the community where they live. This little *zentrepreneurial* company is known for walking its talk. For sure the Burley team won't be sending jobs overseas to save on labor costs or be forever stressing out over the whims of an all-powerful board of directors.

iconogasm: cultural climax, marketing opportunity
Stakeholders hold the future of business in their hands. Give away a piece of the action to put everyone on the same team.

Beauty

Who cares if it's not your shade? Pucker up for a good cause. Two legends of beauty, Aveda and RuPaul, are using lipstick sales to promote kiss 'n' care campaigns. Aveda, a leader in aromatherapy beauty care, has partnered with the South American Yawanawa tribe of Indians, native to the Amazon rain forest of western Brazil. The tribe cultivates and harvests an indigenous prickly pod called uruku, which they sell to the North American tribe to make three shades of lipstick, called (what else?) Uruku. Both tribes are happily boosting each other's economy.

In out-the-door lines wherever MAC cosmetics are hawked, you'll get an altruistic bonus if you purchase a tube of RuPaul's fav lip flavor, Viva Glam. As the company's saucy ads proclaim, they and their customers are doing much more than paying lip service to fighting a deadly scourge: "Every cent of the retail selling price of MAC Viva Glam Lipstick is donated to the fight against AIDS. Thanks to our customers and staff, over $5.5 million have been raised so far."

iconogasm: cultural climax, marketing opportunity
What a lovely couple! Help consumers save the world *and* look good.

Investing

What to do, what to do with that sorry thing you call your life savings… Our best advice: Put your money where your heart is. There are some forty-two mutual funds that invest only in companies that are morally, politically, and environmentally correct. Although these funds typically do not return as well as sinful funds, you will sleep better at night knowing your money is not being invested in tobacco, alcohol, gambling, or military equipment. The Women's Equity Mutual Fund bills itself as one such "pro-conscience" animal: It invests only in public companies that have a proven track record of advancing the social and economic status of women in the workplace.

There's definitely a fund for every thought-style. If your politics lean distinctly right, you will definitely be interested in the Timothy Plan, a fund comprised of traditionally conservative companies. As boomers plan for retirement and inherit gobs of money, expect to see a gazillion special-investment opportunities with a *zentrepreneurial* twist.

iconogasm: cultural climax, marketing opportunity
Create heartfelt investment opportunities to help consumers do more with their money.

Trade

Thinking twice before buying clothes because of all the talk about worker exploitation in developing countries? There's a way to make sure you're not part of the problem. Alternative trading groups, nonprofit organizations that provide workers with a living wage and safe, clean environments, are increasing in number and power. These groups work directly with producers (almost exclusively women) in Latin America, South America, Asia, Indonesia, and Africa, from product design through shipping. Ethnic apparel, crafts, and food are then marketed at retail or in mail-order catalogs like MarketPlace: Handiwork of India and Self-Help Crafts of the World, offering consumers the opportunity to "trade with a difference."

Alternative trading groups give producers and consumers a forum for discussing issues related to social responsibility, creating a "global dialogue" not limited to the plot line of *Baywatch* or other such American exports. Organizations like Oxfam America, Pueblo to People, and SERVV are ultimately providing workers with sustainable business skills and giving them more control over their lives and communities.

iconogasm: cultural climax, marketing opportunity

Marketers of all shapes, sizes, and colors could explore ventures with alternative trading groups to *zentrepreneurize* their brands while doing the right thing.

Transportation

Who said capitalism and social service make poor bedfellows? On virtually every level of the global economy you bump into the *zentrepreneur* spirit. Greyhound, that dinosaur of public transportation, is doing great works from which more profitable companies can learn. When Greyhound bought out Trailways in 1987, it inherited the latter's program of offering free transportation home for runaways. "Our buses are going in those directions anyway . . . [and] aren't all full," says Tom Schad, manager of Greyhound public relations.

What's really remarkable about the program is that Greyhound goes much further than providing free trips home. The company will, if necessary, negotiate the terms of the return, set up conference calls, and even provide counseling for the runaways and their families. Greyhound has hooked up with the National Recovery Switchboard (NRS), an organization providing crisis-intervention and referral services. Bringing social-service agencies into the loop allows kids to work out the logistics of getting home without intervention from the police, who are typically perceived as the bad guys by runaways. Since partnering with NRS, Greyhound's ticket giveaway has tripled, with the company bringing home 150 runaways between winter 1995 and spring 1996.

iconogasm: cultural climax, marketing opportunity

Marketers should brainstorm ways their products or services can help solve social problems at little or no cost . . . and then do a little more.

sign #21:  artisan

So what are some of the hottest things in this digitized, cyberized, bits-and-bytes world of ours? Anything made by an actual human being which recalls a time when artisanship, rather than technology, was the ultimate form of knowledge. Arts and crafts are experiencing a renaissance of medieval proportions as fair knights and maidens look to aesthetics as a way to express their personal senses of style. *Artisan* is the antithesis of Wal-Marted, mass-produced, plastic-extruded goods. *Artisan* invites booboos, idiosyncrasies, creativity, even coloring a teensy bit outside the lines. For to err is human, and human is *artisan*.

Home Resource

The best treatise on the cultural significance of the *artisan* is Louis Sagar's *Zona Home: Essential Designs for Living*. This eloquent outgrowth of Sagar's SoHo store provides an invaluable perusal of all things *artisan*. First he whets an appetite for collecting a well-turned porcelain pitcher or carved drawer pull or Pueblo pottery. Then he teases the mind and eye into a renewed relationship with our own authenticity: "Creating atmosphere at home can enable you to communicate something about your heritage, your passion for collecting, your love of family—something specifically about you."

Sick of those cookie-cutter homes, the staple of American suburbia? Contract out for a timber-log home, or better yet, build it yourself from a mail-order kit. Abe Lincoln would be so proud! Now furnish that cozy nest not with Space Age chrome and vinyl furniture but with twig and Adirondack chairs and accessories. Neorustic, preweathered artifacts bring nature back into our lives, reminding us that the real world is organic, not plastic or electronic. Stir up the topsoil in your backyard with a rake from Smith & Hawken, and presto! You're a real country gentleperson no matter where you live. Go ahead, gobble up the seemingly bottomless advice of Martha Stewart and Bob Vila, and the American Dream is yours.

iconogasm: cultural climax, marketing opportunity
Accentuate the historical, artistic, and original to find the inner *artisan*.

Products

The trend toward *artisanship* can be found in just about every product category, with no signs of losing steam. The guitar *du jour* is a 1950s-style Fender Stratocaster or Gibson Les Paul, way hipper than anything produced after the age of disco. When you're not e-mailing, write a personal note with a Mont Blanc fountain pen. Forgo that ninja, made-overseas motorcycle for a Harley hog produced and assembled by real American hands. Put down that mega-batch Budweiser for a handcrafted beer made from a pre-Prohibition recipe.

Some sixty years after the Machine Age, the arts of woodworking and metalsmithing are back in vogue. Art is even being worn these days, stuck to our bodies as symbols of our good taste. Architects have achieved celebrity status, recognized for their ability to build things real, beautiful, and enduring as well as create trademark designs for tea kettles, furniture, and dinnerware. As cyber technology becomes our dominant form of discourse, expect the *artisan* touch to be an everlasting means of staying connected to the material world.

iconogasm: cultural climax, marketing opportunity
Make your product an authentic touchstone, positioned to enrich the consumers' lives.

Bookery

A paperless society? Bah, humbug. Not when there are still businesses like the Monastery Hill Bindery of Chicago. Monastery Hill has been making and restoring books for 128 years, giving new life to heirloom Bibles and the great works. Five generations of Chicagoans have come to Monastery Hill to preserve Grandma's

cookbook with her handwritten notes or Great-granddad's favorite hymnal with his personal inscription. Binders there, not surprisingly, work the old-fashioned way, edge guilding and lettering by hand with some 10,000 different tools. Using anachronistic materials like type slugs, 23-karat gold leaf, and tanned goatskin, Monastery Hill can give another century of life to Shakespeare (always brown leather) or Dickens (always green). Repairing that nineteenth century storybook or physician's journal starts at $85, while making an original classic will set you back a minimum of $150. Libraries come to Monastery Hill with their tired and poor volumes yearning for new spines, as do booksellers like Encyclopaedia Brittanica, World Book, and Rand McNally. Monastery Hill is a prime example of our enduring need for *artisanship* and craft in this age of digital information.

iconogasm: cultural climax, marketing opportunity
Satisfy our craving for the real thing by mining our renewed interest in the tactile and palpable.

Food

Weirded out over the overprocessed, irradiated, chemically coiffed fruits and veggies, consumers are seeking out the *artisans* of food—purveyors of all-natural, old-fashioned, flavorful provisions. Spice hounds will go to the ends of the world for authentic Indian curries, French tarragon, or Tellicherry black pepper. Fresh-from-the-souk spicings are the trademark of Penzey's, Ltd. Spice House in Waukesha, Wisconsin. Their catalog resembles a trek with Marco Polo and is the source for (among many other taste spikes) sanaam, dundicut, tien tsin, ancho, chipolte, and jalapeño peppers.

When's the last time you bit into a too-juicy peach? Can't recall? Better call for "the old world flavor of succulent white peaches," the specialty of the fuzzynaveled *artisans* at Nunes Farms. Fruits, vegetables, and beverages by mail are flourishing, livening up the best of potlucks and turning them into *artisan* festivals of flavor.

iconogasm: cultural climax, marketing opportunity
Feast from the horn of plenty that is nature's authentic best.

Collectibles

Dollies on doilies, cute teddies to cuddle, melodious music boxes, plates for the wall (*not* for pot roast)—these are a few of our favorite things. Collectibles are hotter than hot. *Gifts and Decorative Accessories* industry newsmagazine projects a $13.5 billion market by the magic millennium 2000. Who buys this adorable junk? Collecting is the passion of folks ages forty-five to sixty-four who have extra bucks and penchants to fill their booty nooks with limited-edition Barbies and hand-painted porcelain Kit Carsons. Each item, no matter how trite or worthless it appears to one person, can make another's heart sing high soprano. Collectibles have an *artisan* halo, maybe because they're revered as one (or 2,001) of a kind.

Not to be left out in the rain, snow, or sleet, the U.S. Postal Service has thrown its treasure chest of sticky-licky-backed American icons into overdrive. They've launched the first of a possible chain of Postmark America collectibles stores at the Mall of America. Billed as a "unique postal event," the store is a trip down memory lane, when folks waved daily to Frank the mailman (now called letter carriers in these genderless days). Brands and product lines are built around those fearless letter soldiers of yesteryear. Pony Express, Postal Blue, and Airmail are touted as real-life American heroes, and you can buy their original historic-design buckskin-fringed leather bomber jackets, canvas cargo bags, blue serge peacoats, insignia sweatshirts, and baseball caps. (Original historic design, you say? Could this be mail fraud? Who cares? It's great stuff!) And by the way, the coolest stamps from Hollywood legends Marilyn Monroe and James Dean to Civil War muckety-mucks to Paul Bunyan, Pecos Bill, and reams more all are there, baiting you into this newest chapter of cultural history. This sign of the times definitely wears the dual stamp of *artisan* and *back to the future*.

iconogasm: cultural climax, marketing opportunity
Stake a claim on the border of craft and memory.

Antiquing

"AN AMERICAN CLASSIC," the G.K.S. Bush, Inc., seraph script ad began. "A compact Massachusetts Chippendale blockfront chest of drawers in plum pudding mahogany with a warm amber color. Completely original including the spurred bracket feet, central drop pendant and large willow brasses. Circa 1760–1780." What is the allure of this rare beauty? The wood? The shiny brass pulls? No way! The magic is in the aura of the object. The spirit and soul of master cabinetmaker Thomas Chippendale is in each drawer, curvaceous curve, and the rich patina. It's hard to resist. Well, at that price, maybe not.

We would be playing with oxymorons if we billed antiquing as "new." The angle that's new is the passion and vigorous growth of this sleuthing industry. From weekend big-game safaris to country auctions to a demure deal-sealing nose twitch at Christie's, antiquing has gotten into our bloodstreams big time. The search (oftentimes more fun than the find) for the real thing—cherry highboy, a rare Philadelphia lolling, a pair of brass jamb hooks, signed Jacob Sargeant tall clock, original Curtis photograph, scrimshaw powderhorn, intricate Zuni bracelet, whatever that real thing might be—is the hobby soup-to-hand-smithied-nuts *du jour*.

The magnetic *artisan* element is our relationships with the objects of desire. We see ourselves reflected in these precious, inanimate icons. They are much, much more than mere objects; they are the human handprints of history.

iconogasm: cultural climax, marketing opportunity
Raid Grandma's (or Sotheby's) attic for stuff that ain't made like that anymore.

Self-Artisan

More individuals are celebrating the *artisan* philosophy of using the hands and heart to coax the best out of indigenous material—clay, fabrics, wood, stone, metal, glass—by taking up the crafts themselves. Storefront ceramics studios with

names like Color By You sell patrons chances to get in touch with their Picasso potential. Entire families think it's cool to create original one-of-a-kind dishware, that special vase for Grandma Irene, or a customized doggy water bowl for Spot—each piece truly a poetic, personal statement.

How about a beer? Sniff the yeast in the air? Home-brewing stores are bootlegging all the essential ingredients and equipment to turn the avid hop head into a brewmeister supreme. And home sewing is zigzagging with patterning, pinking shears, and computerized sewing machines. The American Sewing Association claims home sewing is back by popular demand, with more than 30 million women ages twenty-four to fifty-four in stitches. (Wow, just think how many straight pins they use—or swallow—each year.) These women enjoy sewing as a stress relaxer and creative release, and please note they are not sewing to scrimp money. They are button-holing proud of their handcrafted clothes and fashions for the homestead—curtains, slipcovers, pillow shams, quilts.

The *artisan* craze is turning us into a nation of three-year-olds: "I want to do it myself, Dad!" Community classes are full of eager student wannabe plumbers, carpenters, glass crafters, and stonemasons. It may still be too soon to revive the craft guilds, but for certain the next-generation Tiffany or Wright is already waiting in the wings.

iconogasm: cultural climax, marketing opportunity
Watch out as amateur *artisans* turn the professional art world on its pointy little head.

sign #22: wisewoman

When in ancient times an industrial-strength problem needed to be resolved, the elder *wisewomen* of the village were consulted, sharing all their wisdom—intuitive, poetic, pragmatic. Somewhere along the historical timeline these feminine fonts were ground into silence by society. Much has been chronicled about the feminist reemergence, and women are once again gaining *wisewoman* roles as the trendwinds blow with favor and force in their direction.

Health

Finally the attention—research, products, therapies—is coming. With women making up more than half the population, it's none too soon. Women's health is one of the white-hot categories in the medical-products field today, and will be well into the new century. After all, none of us is getting any younger, and like men with their prostate prognosis, aging women's bodyscapes harbor deadly land mines—one in eight risk breast cancer, one in three osteoporosis.

Many feel these scourges birthmark the stress fractures of the mom/career-juggling superwoman. For women it's scary; for capitalists it's a huge opportunity. *Fortune* magazine named women's health one of the most promising industries for 1997, medical products representing a $120 billion business. They hailed pharmaceutical giant Merck's bone-density drug Fosomax as ringing up $1 billion in sales by 2000. Other hot corps focused on making women healthier: American Home Products; Biopsys Medical, with their new mammotomy, a less invasive breast biopsy procedure; and Conceptus, whose wonder catheters are forecast to boost pregnancy rates by 125 percent, giving new hope to infertility sufferers. All of this is very good news for the future of women's health herstory.

iconogasm: cultural climax, marketing opportunity

Segment health into gender-, age-, and disease-specific medicines, clinics, and diagnostic tools.

Menopause

In ancient modern times—1950–1992 B.G.S. (before Gail Sheehy)—the word "menopause" was kept safely wrapped in brown paper, tucked behind the maxipads. Today, bookstores are flush with hot-flash books, while women's clinics, newsletters, art soirees, and symposiums exalt the midlife change. All this openness around the previously tabooed passage is making women baby boomers a particularly attractive target market for feminine-hygiene products, hormone-replacement therapies, bone-strengthening supplements, and weight-bearing exercise programs.

Let's give osteoporosis closer scrutiny. The bone density point of difference is easy to understand: Brittle bones, a result of estrogen deficiencies in postmenopausal women, break easier. Bye-bye, bones. What can we say? It really hurts! The facts aren't pretty, especially if a dowager's hump isn't your image. You can almost hear the cracking of America: 200,000 wrists and 300,000 hips KOed annually by the disease, and researchers warn that 40 percent of all American women will endure vertebral fractures. Smoking, drinking coffee and booze, and a sedentary lifestyle are said to escalate the calcium meltdown. The rush to fortify everything from instant rice to Wonder Bread to oj makes us ponder if maybe the best thing about waking up might be a calcium hit in your cup.

And talk about waking up, how about kick boxing the fitness industry into high gear? With 10 million females each year facing the 'pause that does everything to a body but refreshes, shouldn't weight lifting be promoted with a bone-to-barbell positioning? Don't leave out the pre-'pausers. Researchers say prevention is the best medicine for healthy bones.

iconogasm: cultural climax, marketing opportunity

If women are your market, bone density may be your socket.

Office

That bastion of common sense, *The Christian Science Monitor,* squeezed out the skinny on Sanvita, a unique program making a vocation out of lactation. Sanvita, part of Medela, Inc., makers of breast pumps, helps companies create lactation programs for current and potential breast-feeding employees. Sanvita sets up "pump sites" for current feeders and provides prenatal education to feeders-to-be, removing the obstacles and taboos associated with breast feeding in Corporate America. Breast feeders hit the pump room three times a day for ten to fifteen minutes a pop, storing breast milk for the papooses' later use. The benefits of nursing-friendly companies include lower health-care costs (breast-fed babies are often healthier than formula-fed babies), lower absenteeism, a reduction in turnover, and improved morale. The cost to companies is about five hundred dollars per participant for the eighteen-month program, a bargain considering the cost of health care alone. More than twenty-five companies in the U.S. have gone on tap with Sanvita, including AT&T, Amoco, and Fannie Mae. Best of all, Sanvita is targeting all strata of the corporate bedrock, making breast feeding a less exclusively upper-income practice, ultimately leading to healthier and happier babies. Sanvita's program is niche marketing at its very best.

iconogasm: cultural climax, marketing opportunity
Think about how your company can reduce the bottom line while putting more humanity in human resources.

Glass Ceiling

Hi-ho, hi-ho, it's off to work they go. The workforce is home to 75 percent of all U.S. women, but their wages are still dwarfed by their gender opposites. The good news: Congress bumped up the minimum wage. The bad news: Sixty percent of the minimum-wage earners are women, and as *Ms.* magazine blunts, "Let's face it, $5.15 an hour doesn't pay the rent—or buy food or clothing." And about that glass ceiling? *Working Woman* aired an Emily's List census of *Fortune* 500 boards of directors, which found in 1995 that 81 percent of corporations include one woman at the head table. That sounds promising until you read further: Fewer than one-tenth of the *Fortune* 500's 6,274 seats are home to female fannies; ninety-six companies are Men's Room Only. Here are ten in dire need of estrogen-replacement therapy: Dow Corning; Fruit of the Loom; Kelly Services; La-Z-Boy; Microsoft; Northwest Airlines; Safeway; Sunbeam-Oster; Tyco Toys; Viacom.

In the entertainment industry the shards of glass are flying. These women are inspirations and heroines to all going for breakthroughs. *The Hollywood Reporter* 1997 annual "Women in Entertainment Power 50" highlighted the *crème de la crèmey crème* entertainment execs. Of the fifty, twenty-two were in the film ranks, twelve in broadcast TV, seven in cable TV, five each in agenting and music, and one in home video. Many of those named worked across several categories. Most of the names gracing the list are not mainstream familiar, but their titles demand a respectful nod—President, Disney/ABC Cable Networks; Chairwoman, Paramount Pictures motion picture group; Executive VP, Sony Music Entertainment; MTV President; President, Warner Bros. TV; President, United Artists; Senior VP, William Morris Agency; Executive Producer, "Friends." The bottom line represents bazillions. Ranked number three, Oprah Winfrey, Chairwoman of Harpo Entertainment, beat out Steven Spielberg on the '95–'96 *Forbes* list as the highest paid U.S. entertainer—$171 million. Ranked number fifty (but just a rookie on the talk-show trail) is Rosie O'Donnell, reportedly earning a wimpy $5 mil a year. That'll change.

iconogasm: cultural climax, marketing opportunity

Don't get cut by flying glass. Commit to pay equity and put women on the board.

Toys

Sugar and spice and everything nice. That's not all these little girls—Tenko and the Guardian of the Magic, Princess Gwenevere and the Jewel Riders, Sailor Moon, Warrior Princess Xena, Kenya, Sky Dancers, Baby-sitters, Abby Abelskeever, Barbie (for sure!)—are made of. It's a virtual babefest for toys, programs, and products that show off feminine valor, smarts, muscles, and moxie. The superpopularity of those pink and yellow Mighty Morphin Power Rangers slam-bammed open the dollhouse door for girl superheroines. Sky Dancers, the creation of Abrams Gentile Entertainment and Lewis Goluv Toys, was the numero uno girl's action toy in the U.S. in '96. And we suspect that more than G.I. Joe's heart is throbbing for these winged gossamer beauties. Boy toys have long dominated children's TV and the toy aisle, but expect a shake-up in kid entertainment's status quo. Traditional fashion dolls are all primped out. Here to save the playday is Sailor Moon, "a teenage girl who struggles to maintain peace among the evil forces threatening her world." Little gals in Japan and Asia love, love, love Sailor Moon and her five girl scouts. She launched stateside with sixty-five thirty-minute galactic-guarding episodes and 200+ accessories (whoa—another body blow to the Seeds of Simplicity conscientious kid consumer movement). Empowered, intelligent, confident she-characters are Gloria Steinemizing the toy market. Listen up. Hear them singing? "We are wee women . . . hear us roar!"

Here I come to save the day!

iconogasm: cultural climax, marketing opportunity

Before they're *wisewomen*, they're wee women. Offer products and services to help little ones find their power.

131

Youth Media

Are teen dreams really made of this: PROM? "It's just the hugest event of your life, so far!!!" No date? No problemo. "Don't be bummed; go with a bud," counsels the *YM* special prom edition. It's May; it's May, the party-hardy month of May, the time when every frosh, soph, junior, and sizzling senior concentrates on corsages, cummerbunds, and pouf dresses. Teen zines have all the buzz with headlines at *YM, Your Prom* from *Modern Bride, Seventeen,* and *Teen* promising the inside skinny on what guys really want, mega makeovers, and dresses that'll melt him. These issues are flirty, fun, feminine dream books for the promstruck. Each magazine is a teen-tuned headquarters for advertising—Maybelline, Coke, Neutrogena, Gillette Sensor for Women, Hanes, Unionbay, Playtex, Sears, Salon Selectives, Sea Breeze, Tabu Perfume, Sweet Tarts, Nail Fetish, Buf-Puf, Reebok, milk, Noxema.

Now for a taste of the flip side of teen media, let's talk *New Moon: The Magazine for Girls and Their Dreams*. You'll find no page upon glossy page of ads here. This is a "magazine for every girl who wants her voice heard and her dreams taken seriously." *New Moon's* editorial board of girls ages eight to fourteen keeps it on track with original prose celebrating girldom and womanhood. Articles are a refreshing, enlightened break from the boy-centric breed. The hair, the clothes, the makeup, plus how to score a dream date, are replaced with thinking-girl questions such as "Where would you like to go in space and time?" This alternative voice for young women is echoing; *New Moon* rises in more than 7,000 bookstores in the U.S and Canada, with 22,000 subscribers—"any country you name, we've got subscribers."

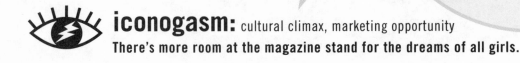

iconogasm: cultural climax, marketing opportunity
There's more room at the magazine stand for the dreams of all girls.

Goddess

The wise working woman keeps a copy of Zsuzsanna Budapest's witchcraft primer, *The Goddess in the Office*, tucked into her briefcase. Budapest is a "founding mother" of contemporary women's spirituality and a leader of the feminist megatrend to get in touch with the Wild Woman within. "I'm now a crone, you know," she shares, "so my book is *Summoning the Fates: A Woman's Guide to Destiny*." The new prose springs from Z's psychic work, and with it she hopes to help "smooth out some of the bumps" of aging. Budapest writes of Chiron, the half-man, half-horse, wounded-healer spiritual teacher who helps us shift into the 50s gear, often with a jarring bone break or emotional slap—all with good cosmic intention, she assures.

Growing into her power as goddess, witch, herbalist, and feminist, this priestess elder has also grown a huge following among women all over the globe (her mailing list is 30,000+ names). The biannual International Goddess Festival is of Z's design and covens 300 fems in the redwood forest of California. This weekend is legendary for its concerts (percussionists Gaia's Heart and Gwen Jones on dulcimer perform), dance, political and social scholarship, and magical rituals. Participating goddesses pledge it to be profound, each leaving the inner sanctum of the tall trees with an uplifted sense of sisterhood.

The goddess movement is not to be discounted by mainstream marketers. Women are recognizing and honoring their connection to Mother Earth in a massive grassroots awakening. Witness the tremendous success of Dr. Clarissa Pinkola Éstes' *Women Who Run with the Wolves*, now in its seventh printing. The goddess calls upon her native intelligence, fecund creativity, and wild unbridled lust for living. She is an animal not to be domesticated.

iconogasm: cultural climax, marketing opportunity
Knowledge of the goddess movement, its elements of spirituality, environmentalism, and feminism, can bring deeper perspective to products and services for and by women.

Crones

"The desert was dressed in its finest. Cactus, mesquite, Palo verde . . . women wore lovely skirts varied in color . . . bells clanged and jewelry flashed as they moved . . . on the altar lay the three crowns." —Ruth Gardner, *Crone Chronicles: A Journal of Conscious Aging*

A natural extension of the female coming of age in the period after periods is a ritual called croning. Reports are beginning to surface in the mainstream press of small covens of fifty or more fems gathering together to mark passage into their *wisewoman* phase of life. Ceremonies honor the three archetypes of woman—maiden, lover/mother, wise elder—as the crone embraces a new birth of creativity, inner and outer beauty, and is crowned with a commitment to sharing the fruits of her wisdom. Bet on the 40 million to 50 million babe-a-licious boomers heading into aging to pay homage to croning with an added-value perspective on wrinkles. Check out *Crone Chronicles: A Journal of Conscious Aging* and *Sage Woman: Celebrating the Goddess in Every Woman* for the full scoop on granny goddesses.

iconogasm: cultural climax, marketing opportunity
The positioning: Older . . . maybe. Wiser . . . definitely.

Sports

Awesome. This is the era of the female athlete, but the daily sports page still doesn't get it. "I peruse the sports section looking for news about women. I have to tell you, it's usually a discouraging exercise," laments Mollie Hoben, copublisher of *The Minnesota Women's Press.* While journalists plead they're working on better coverage, most papers are caught in their jockstraps, unaware the XX chromosome train has finally left the station.

If the local gazettes are ten legs behind, the magazine industry is breaking the tape. Time Inc. is off and racing with *Sports Illustrated Women/Sport.* The only swimsuits here are issued by Speedo, who may expect to pay $25,000 for a full-page ad. Conde Nast, home to fashion plates *Mademoiselle, Glamour,* and *Vogue,* is now fielding *Conde Nast Sports for Women.* Both fem zines are priced to trot—$2.50 to $2.95—and will break new ground in sports reporting just like their heroine subjects.

Title IX reached its twenty-fifth year in 1997, with noticeable results. "Resolved: that no one shall on the basis of sex be excluded from participation in or denied the benefits of any education program or activity receiving Federal funding." In 1971 Little League had no girls on the roster; in 1997 more than

400,000 girls of summer swung a bat. Pre-Title IX, a puny $100,000 was spent on women's athletic scholarships; in 1997, $177 million was fielded. In 1996, 100,000 college women competed in various sports, seeded by high school sports programs in which one in every three girls takes part. More women and girls are realizing their athletic dreams, developing a positive sense of self as they double-backflip, spike, check, dunk, bike, climb, throw, kick, and pass just like the guys.

iconogasm: cultural climax, marketing opportunity
Support a women's or girls' team by putting your corporate name on their roster.

College and Pro Sports

On the college and pro circuits, women's basketball is holding court. The hinge points: national broadcast of the 1996 NCAA's Women's Collegiate Final Four and the 51–0 Olympic gold victory by the U.S. women's basketball team in 1996. Ever since, the public, media, and sponsors have found their hustle hard to resist. Schedules of the two newly founded women's pro leagues, the American Basketball League and the National Women's Basketball Association, make it possible to catch the fever year 'round. To the naysayers' chagrin, the second-tier city home courts are supporting their pro women with consistent, often high game turnout. Even better, where once the only hope for a professional future was with the European women's leagues, now there are 160 well-paying positions on the home-team bench. Best of all, the newly minted success of the female professional basketball leagues has set the stage for women's pro hockey, fastpitch softball, and soccer. Babe Didrickson Zaharias is grinning; she could have played them all so well.

iconogasm: cultural climax, marketing opportunity
The momentum is building. Women are on a full-court press, and the ball's in your court.

chapter 6: society

Society. This is a big concept to wrap your head around. Webster's claims society is a group with some things in common. For a country as diverse and freewheeling as the U.S.A., what would "some things" be? Awe and admiration for a young tiger in an old duffer's green sports jacket? A shared national day of anxiety, April 15? A collective cry of anguish for victims of a terrorist strike or Mother Nature PMS-ing? Could that common bond be as basic as a communal insanity for President's Day bargain hunting, running with the stock market bulls, the right candidate on the right side of the fence on Election Day, and a national love affair with salsa, salsa, and more salsa? Examining the uncommonest of common ground is what this chapter is all about. The most common "thing" of all: the threads—red, white, and blue.

sign #23:  value vertigo

Feel like this country is socially dizzy, disoriented, discombobulated? You're not alone. The media's issue of the day is that America is experiencing a nervous values breakdown, that we are in a state of moral crisis and have no commonly shared identity anymore. At Planet Iconoculture, we call this idea *value vertigo*, a society-wide sense of dislocation and rootlessness.

Nowhere is *value vertigo* more apparent than in the decline of public life in America and the associated rise of private, self-directed interests. Traditional American values based in the public arena—duty, responsibility, etc.—have eroded, reflected in lower turnout at PTA meetings and the voting booth. People are bowling more, but league play is in the gutter. As the public sphere shrinks, privatization creeps into all forms of previously civic institutions. Gated communities are the populist answer to crime, while planned communities like Disney's Utopian Village make suburbia look like ghettos. Garbage, mail, and security services are becoming increasingly privatized, with home and charter schools the refuge from the fast times at Ridgemont High.

Victims

Hand in glove with *value vertigo* is Victim America, the result of overboard demands for rights and entitlements for every special-interest group. Litigation mania continues despite Shakespeare's 400-year-old advice to kill all the lawyers, while psychotherapy tells us that contrary to Copernican theory, each of us *is* the center of the universe. Meanwhile, a new generation of me-firsts is being weaned by teachers who subscribe to the theory that self-esteem should be the cornerstone of the education experience.

Before expatriating yourself, however, note that public life is beginning to bubble up again in many communities. Look for more attempts to resurrect civic life like that made by the city council of San Luis Obispo, which (unsuccessfully) tried to mandate the building of front porches on all new homes. Better luck next time around.

iconogasm: cultural climax, marketing opportunity
Bolster consumers' cultural sea legs by building feelings of stability, balance, and connectedness into products and communications.

Institutions

Value vertigo is rearing its ugly head in our communal loss of faith in large institutions. If icons were toppled in the 1980s, in the '90s they have been ground to a fine powder. The national debt, federal government shutdowns, and regional bankruptcies like that of Orange County have confirmed for us that many of our elected officials have the fiscal sense of an eight-year-old. Militias are the extremist version of the broad dissatisfaction and mistrust of the government, and a tax revolt the size of the Boston Tea Party is brewing.

In other arenas, Corporate America has reengineered itself into believing that mission statements are more important that actual people, and Americans are increasingly forgoing slice 'n' dice Western medicine for do-it-yourself homeopathic cures. Professional sports heroes are being exposed as mere mortals, while working-class joes like the UPS man are elevated to hunkier status than super-peccy models. Only Hollywood seems immune to this wholesale discounting of those in positions of power.

iconogasm: cultural climax, marketing opportunity
Look to grassroots-level people and organizations when shopping around for marketing partners and spokesfigures.

Crime

It's in your face. The fastest-growing crime problem: juvenile offenders. The increases in juvenile arrests, murders, weapons violations, aggravated assault, and robbery have experts worried that this downward spiral is spiraling out of control. Is Public Enemy number one our children? Say it isn't so. Communities across the nation are getting tough on youth offenders, trying violent young criminals in adult court, imposing curfews and school uniforms, and fining parents for the misdeeds of their renegade offspring. More than half of the states are punishing parents for their little hooligans' crimes: up to $25,000 for defacing property and a night in the clinker for rampant school truancy. (From all-family cereal to all-family rotten-tomato throw in the same century?)

Read the case histories and you'll discover the harshest reality. The circle of self-destruction makes you shiver and puke—at three, suspected victim of child abuse; at fifteen, suspected of abusing his eight-year-old sis; at sixteen, standing trial for car theft. If that puts a lump in your throat, ponder this: By 2010 the under-eighteens could post a 31-percent population growth. Expecting teen violence to escalate as the welfare safety net is shredded, local outposts of the National Center for Neighborhood Enterprise are taking to the streets to save the children with community-inspired job programs, gang negotiations, and drug counseling.

iconogasm: cultural climax, marketing opportunity
Targeting teens and children with real-life community support is an investment in everyone's future.

Hunger

When was the last time you were really *really* hungry? For some 33.9 million people below the poverty level, there's no midnight raid on the fridge. Their cupboards are bare. Coming to the rescue is a simple yet very powerful new law on the books, the Bill Emerson Good Samaritan Food Donation Act (the late Representative Emerson and Representative Pat Danner cosponsored the bill). This legislation releases organizations, donation volunteers, and corporate givers from the tummy-ache liabilities that loomed from giving leftover food products to the needy. Passed in late-1996, the Act facilitates recycling an estimated 14 billion pounds of food otherwise going to the garbage each year. Leading the effort to feed America's hungry is an association of charities devoted to collecting and dishing out leftovers, Food Chain. They currently have 119 members but expect to grow as the loaves and fishes multiply.

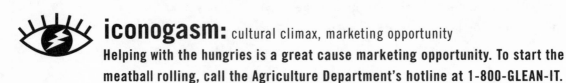

iconogasm: cultural climax, marketing opportunity

Helping with the hungries is a great cause marketing opportunity. To start the meatball rolling, call the Agriculture Department's hotline at 1-800-GLEAN-IT.

Neighborhood

What do you do when you've toiled all your life to own the digs of your dreams? Wall it in! Seems gated ghettos are not just for the Trumps anymore. From Scottsdale to Kansas City to Jackson Hole and uppity echelons in between, America's middle class is security-zoning the American Dream. Typical of these protected prosperity pockets is Dana Point, a neighborhood in California's Monterey Bay. Residents are hermetically sealed off from their Latino immigrant neighbors, except for special entry given to a Spanish-speaking support culture of gardeners, cooks, and baby-sitters. Roughly one-third of this 6.1-mile coastal city is safely behind bars.

Of course, violent crime is the mortar of fear and separatism that built these walls. We keep pinching ourselves, asking . . . you're talking Haiti, not the U.S.A., right? Welcome to the not-so-United Islands of Brown, Yellow, Black, and White.

iconogasm: cultural climax, marketing opportunity

The melting pot is stone cold. Keep an eye on products targeted to *us*, not *them*, and be ready for the backlash that will bring us back together.

Education

What's up in the old schoolhouse these days? Education has emerged as a principal site of some of the more passionate passion points of our times, including prayer, violence, immigration, affirmative action, and class privilege. The golden-oldie readin', 'ritin', and 'rithmetic vision of the schoolhouse has graduated into education as a *way of life* for inquiring, acquiring minds that want to know it as well as have it all.

Education is still the great equalizer, critical to bridging the got-it-all/got-nothing Grand Canyon. But does literacy have to be a luxury in the third millennium? There are 85,000 public schools nationwide, and as this book goes to press there is no national curriculum that tells what kids must learn in subjects such as math, science, literature, and history. No core standards to help determine who passes, who flunks, and yet American kids take more standardized tests, to show how stupid they are compared to any other nation.

The ever-provocative, "culturally literate" E. D. Hirsch (remember the brouhaha he unleashed in the late '80s with his 5,000 essential names, phrases, dates, and concepts that any bona fide smartypants should know?) makes a potent case for a national curriculum and content-based testing as the way to level the educational playing field. Continuity is key. In *The Schools We Need and Why We Don't Have Them,* he pleads that wanderlust is keeping our kids from making the grade—one-fifth of all Americans relocate each year, and one-sixth of all third-graders attend at least three different schools between the first and third grades.

All things being equal, are they ever equal? Gender roles and their relationship to learning are getting a lot of attention these days as the law bumps up against tradition and research. Study after study has shown that girls and women often do not have equal opportunity in the classroom when testosterone (read: boys) is added to the mix. Girls are frequently harassed, insulted, and intimidated by hormone-happy boys striving to make their presences very known. The results: All-girls schools and all-women colleges and classes are thriving, particularly in Canada, where all-female public schools are legal. Here in the States, the Supreme Court decided that public schools must be gender-friendly, forcing all-male bastions like the Virginia Military Institute and the Citadel to accept female candidates.

The debate over single-sex education continues, however, with many arguing that there should be havens for each gender to talk and learn among themselves. Supporters argue that all-women and all-men institutions provide a structure in which students can become leaders. Critics argue that such institutions nurture an intolerance for difference and fail to provide role models of the opposite persuasion. As the need to establish tight-knit *beehives* collides with the call for equal opportunity, expect the dynamics of gender to escalate as a passion point in education.

iconogasm: cultural climax, marketing opportunity

Go to the head of the class by instilling the value of learning in any setting every chance you get.

Manners

A very couth gentleman, Elbert Hubbard, quipped that etiquette is "the courtly manners of any two-legged predatory animal." Well, according to a *U.S. News and World Report* poll, 90 percent of American predators believe that incivility (crude, rude behavior) is a serious problem. The call for random acts of kindness instead of random shoves, sneers, and downright ugly insults is coming through strong (never loud or boisterous) and clear.

Nicey-nice training through books, courses, and friendly public signage abounds. In NYC, attitude-adjusting courtesy classes for the city's 8,900 bus-wheeling Ralph Kramdens are instructing them on the finer points of getting along with their riders. For a start, cut the sarcasm, swearing, and slapping. The *Star Tribune* in Minneapolis reports that new forums on doing unto others are being headed up by polite politicos William Bennett, Sam Nunn, and Patricia Schroeder. A most generous and graciously appreciated gift of $35 million seeded the Institute for Civil Society in 1996, which studies and advises on solutions to the crises of conscience and pervasive civic naughtiness.

The crux of this breakdown is being blamed on a cadre of cads—an overtherapied, shameless populace; rude role-model athletes who don't think once and never twice about spitting, punching, or delivering a swift kick to the groin; the down-dressing informality of even the president; selfish values; and a generally in-your-face, I'm-the-greatest, *hasta-la-vista* attitude at any age.

iconogasm: cultural climax, marketing opportunity

We better clean up our act, and that's going to take tons of training at virtually every level of society.

sign #24:  we the people

Brace yourselves. In the election-erection years ahead, grassroots politics will rule. Third-party yard signs will pop up faster than ticks on a coonhound, and the sins of the sanctimonious will finally catch up with the grand old parties. It will be *adios* to the impudent abuses of politico powers—campaign fundreaping, moral lapses, congressional privileges. Who will take care of national business? *We the people*, that's who.

If you doubt the grassroots momentum bringing politics back to reality and back to the people, take time to peruse smalltown newspapers. Community spunkiness is at an all-time high, with sparks a-flyin' over local zoning fights, school budgets, teen curfews, environmental skullduggery, urban wetlands, gambling, range cattle grazing, smoking bans, gang violence, salmon spawning . . . The immediacy of the impact on everyday lives coupled with citizen distrust, disgust, and disdain at the inability of state legislatures and Congress to act are a double shot of fertilizer on the sod of grassroots politics.

Initiatives

Go West, young politico. Go West! That's the land of the citizens' initiatives. In November '96 the real kicker wasn't the Clinton-Dole clash but rather the ninety propositions—more than double the forty-one contests of only ten years earlier—placed on ballots in twenty states. Oregon took high score with seventeen, sunny California posted twelve, and Colorado went to the mat with eight. Why the West? These states are hotbeds of political activism, gutsy idealism, and a perverse pride in flipping the eagle at the establishment. The trials that try women's and men's souls? Affirmative action, gender equality, medical-assisted suicide, medicinal marijuana, polluting, hunting rights, term limits, property taxes . . . Enough said; slam bam, get 'em on the ballot, and let's vote on 'em. All in favor, say "aye"! It can happen almost that fast now that private companies can be hired to collect petition signatures for initiative sponsors. (Seems business knows how to tap grassroots dollars as well.) Of course, the significance of the burgeoning number of initiatives is they're both a Richter scale taking a read on the public pulse and a mirror of future national debate.

iconogasm: cultural climax, marketing opportunity
Want to know what's really on America's mind? Take the initiative.

Voice

Grassroots politics continues to prove that the phrase "noble politician" isn't always an oxymoron. Go ahead. Toss your hat into the grassroots ring. From where we stand there are few planks or platforms to stumble over. The guiding principle, if there is one: You don't have to be a winner to be a winner. Making noble noise is worth it.

MAJIC—Mothers Against Jesse in Congress—is a case in point. With a mere $15,000 in donations, a card table, a fax, and a few cheerleaders, this group of North Carolina women who lost their sons to AIDS bonded together to make an earnest run at unseating Republican senator Jesse Helms. The *New York Times* reported that this grassroots gaggle had little illusion of ultimate success, yet these were mad moms with a mission. Helms's antigay bravado concerning AIDS victims "deserving what they get" offended them deeply. In the end, Majic didn't begin to have the arsenal to knock off the five-term senator, but they pledged it wouldn't be the last you hear from them. As founder Patsy Clarke pledged, "My eyes have been opened to much injustice, much bigotry, and much hatred. I no longer, with my very, very comfortable life, just hold my tongue and do my knitting and my needlepoint."

Tikkun, a bimonthly Jewish journal critiquing politics, culture, and society, has raised the banner big-time for the "Politics of Meaning." Positioned as a "vision that moves beyond the narrow, outdated or punitive solutions currently offered by liberals and conservatives," it's a run for higher ground, out of the floodplain of two-party mud. In a nutshell, Politics of Meaning is a fresh theoretical orientation and a strategy to change American society, and the POM politicos are aching for a "new bottom line" that emphasizes ethical, spiritual, and caring concerns. They are sick of downsizing corps and a Congress and White House at odds on how best to "screw the poor." *Tikkun* (a Hebrew word meaning to heal, repair, and transform) is the ringleader for a fertile group of alternative seedbeds—*Utne Reader*, The Unitarian Universalist Association, and the Reconstructionist movement in Judaism, to name a few. They rallied for the first time in Spring 1996 in Washington, D.C., at the National Summit on Ethics and Meaning, and now the dog-and-political-pony show is on the road to cities across the country. 2000 OR BUST! The goal is to blow the nation's politics-as-depressingly-usual head right off. No hidden agenda here.

iconogasm: cultural climax, marketing opportunity
The power is shifting back to the people. Companies need to recognize the people's bottom-line issues.

The Greens

If green is your favorite color, and the environment, individual and community rights, and democracy your leaning, party down with the Green Party. It's been around a long time in Europe and is a major player in many of the seventy-two countries it calls home. In the U.S. the Greenies have generally been ignored or labeled tree-hugging whale savers by the mainstream. But Ralph Nader's candidacy for prez in '96 made folks, especially the under-thirty-fives, genuflect in the Greens' general direction. (Younger voters see it not as a vote lost on an alternative party but as a voice registered for change.) To their credit, Nader, with his VP running mate, Native American activist Winnona LaDuke, set a budget of $5,000 for their symbolic run for Penn Avenue—a smart move that amplified the Mad Donkey and Elephant Spending Disease that plagued the process. Ralph's mythic national name recognition plus his plain, pungent talk (on Arkansas' fav son: "The bully coward in the bully pulpit") legitimized the Greens' often theatrical approach to cuckolding the big-corporation/big-government "duopoly."

iconogasm: cultural climax, marketing opportunity
A halo of less politicized advertising, fundraising, and hoopla could be the way to win the next elections.

Third Millennium

"When a majority of Generation Xers believe General Hospital *will outlive Medicare, you have a crisis."* —Pollsters Frank Luntz and Mark Siegel

Shouldering social responsibility for a whole generation is a heavy burden any way you slice it. Third Millennium, a national nonprofit advocacy and educational organization, aims to right the political and social wrongs by scrutinizing America's pitfalls through a lens of generational equity: "Our goal is to redirect the country's attention from the next election cycle to the next generational cycle—and in the process move a generation to action." They have gotten a lot of press from polls reporting the concerns of the coveted eighteen-to-thirty-four voter/market/consumer. One of the most quoted polling stats: By a 46-percent to 28-percent margin, more folks eighteen to thirty-four believe in UFOs than believe Social Security will exist by the time they retire.

Third Millennium members are zealots for controlling entitlement spending without bankrupting aging Xers. They also want the U.S. to grow up and act like a responsible adult, pay its debts, and live on, not over, its budget. They're waving flags for a retirement age upped to seventy, Medicare and Social Security benefits based on affluence and need, and personal investment of FICA for retirement accounts. Doesn't it make you wonder what doofus ever dubbed Gen X slackers?

iconogasm: cultural climax, marketing opportunity
Do what it takes to keep abreast of the vital, socially responsible age group called Generation X.

Natural Law Party

If in the mood to party hop, drop in on the Natural Law Party in our nation's New Age backwater, Fairfield, Iowa. The only third party to qualify for federal matching funds, its founder, presidential-hopeful, Harvard-trained quantum-physicist Dr. John Hagelin, professes there's only one way to recover from toxic government: "Bring the nation back into harmony with natural law, with the fundamental laws that govern and administer life." Besides a spiraling-out-of-control health-care crisis, genetically engineered food is IDed as the enemy of the people. To the rescue are Transcendental Meditation (used to boost intelligence), Ayurvedic preventative health care, a balanced budget by 1999, and a flat 10-percent tax leading NLP's 50-Point Action Plan to Revitalize America. Skeptical? Don't be. Pack up those charts and graphs, Mr. Perot. The Natural Law Party is all over that coveted crown of clean living and common sense.

iconogasm: cultural climax, marketing opportunity
Meditate on this: The separation of spirituality and state is in a fast fade.

sign #25:  boomeritis

Hate to harp on this, especially if you score a birth date between 1946 and 1964, but the bald-head truth is that *boomeritis* centers around the graying of America. As the 76 million pig-in-a-pythoners take on the last half to third of their lives, boomers are redefining the concepts of seniority and maturity. The generation that always wanted it all (and got most of it most of the time) is going through a collective spiritual journey in quest of the answers to the big questions of life. Marketers who can anticipate the needs of baby boomers will be the big winners during the first couple of decades of the next century.

Products

Material goodies have consistently been the leading soul satisfier of boomers. So why should we be surprised that the parents want to share their wealth of style with their offspring? Ma and Pa's favorite stylemeisters have moved fast to build brand loyalists from cradle up. Gap, Talbots, Guess, Polo, and Hilfiger are a few of the brands microsizing their wardrobes. Guess the attraction of lookalike moms and daughters, sons and fathers is too tempting to resist the splurge. The National Hockey League is even into the kidling act with Pucksters, a line of hockey threads for junior 'Bladers. And if you've been too busy driving the carpool to notice, that randy, swinging-singles icon of the 1980s, Club Med, has cleaned up its nude volleyball and now caters to families.

Some marketers are already capitalizing on the physical changes associated with aging. Are you (like us) finding house chores akin to competing in the Olympic decathlon? As our senses, strength, and flexibility fade like that T-shirt from the Wings Over America tour, housewares marketers are introducing new products to keep us cookin' and cleanin'. For that sorry thing you call your back, for example, pick up one of Quickie's Double Bubble snow shovels with a double grip (makes clearing the white stuff a lot easier). Overcooking your Tater Tots 'cause you can't read the genie-in-the-cupboard-sized dials on your Toast-R-Oven? Black & Decker has a model with easy-to-read dials that Whistler's mother couldn't miss from the living room. Hoover has a vacuum that tells you electronically where the dirt is, and Sunbeam has a scale with numbers you can read without having to squat down while buck naked (now that's a pretty sight). Rubbermaid has also jumped into the gray fray with its EZ Topper food containers, which have lids you can actually grasp, plus a seventy-inch Tub Scrubber. Now that's a tub scrubber!

iconogasm: cultural climax, marketing opportunity
Ponder how you can make your products more boomer-friendly as we become a nation of Mr. Magoos.

Autos

Ever wondered if that's really a hat driving the car in front of you? Imagine what it must be like for elderly drivers whose seats and pedals were designed for a younger, larger person. With the number of seniors growing, American car makers are listening to the needs of elderly drivers. Detroit is taking into account that many older people have poor eyesight, shorter attention spans, and arthritis. In response, they're making seats flatter and more adjustable, control knobs bigger, and displays larger and easier to read. The billboard-sized doors on the Ford Crown Victoria and Mercury Grand Marquis swing open extra wide, while the Cadillac Fleetwood chimes when a turn signal is left on. General Motors is even putting daytime running lights on some of its models to allow other drivers to see that pedaler-to-the-metal who learned to drive in a Tin Lizzy. Extra-wide rearview mirrors and adjustable pedals may soon be on the way, just in time for boomers entering their sixth decade.

iconogasm: cultural climax, marketing opportunity
Give serious thought to designing ergonomic, user-friendly versions of standard products for seniors.

Travel

Adventure travel is another pool in which boomers are dipping their wizening toes. The country's major adventure-tour companies say their average traveler is in his or her fifties and getting older. More and more mature travelers are forgoing cruises, bus tours, and RVs for adventure trips such as jungle treks and white-water rafting. Other tours for eldertrekkers include photography workshops in the Andes and anthropology conferences in Africa.

Today's greyhounds are more physically fit than any other generation of older people in history, a result of exercise, better food, and health care. Still, adventure tours for the sixty-plus crowd are typically a little less rugged, making more frequent stops and allowing those old bones to sleep on beds instead of the ground. After trying an adventure tour, seniors often get hooked, eager to take on new challenges and achieve goals. In addition to affirming self-worth in our youth-obsessed society, adventure travel teaches these older dogs with discretionary time and money some new tricks.

iconogasm: cultural climax, marketing opportunity
Tap into this group of consumers' lust for adventure and new experiences.

Disability

Ehh? What's that you say? *Boomeritis* should send a clear signal to marketers who have the ability to help folks avoid some of the disabilities associated with getting older. Experts in such things are beginning to observe a dramatic rise in the number of fortysomethings and fiftysomethings with heavy hearing loss. The Machine Age (and Led Zeppelin) has made our world a much louder place, and midlife boomers are paying the audible price. Betcha didn't know that at sixty decibels, a normal conversation is twice as loud as your thirty-decibel bowl of snappin', cracklin', and poppin' Rice Krispies. An estimated 28 million Americans have some hearing loss, one-third of which is due to long-term exposure to loud noise. (Generation X is determined not to repeat the subwoofer sins of the Disco Generation, with ear plugs the accessory of choice at hipper music clubs and concerts.)

iconogasm: cultural climax, marketing opportunity
Put a silencer on your products so that future septuagenarian and octogenarian boomers will be able to hear their great-grandchildren whisper secrets in their ears.

Creativity

As a group, baby boomers have always placed creativity at the top of their list of attractive attributes. That's good news considering some research showing that creativity doesn't somehow stop when one hits the mid-century mark. Lydia Bronte, author of *The Longevity Factor*, says, "Half of the people I interviewed started their period of peak creativity after age 50." On the other hand, if you follow the maxim that "creative thinking is the sex of our mental lives," that's a long time to wait for an orgasm.

Longevity in this country has redefined the concept of middle age as fifty to seventy-five, and that leaves a lot of years after raising the brood to boogie. In professions like dance that have traditionally dictated stage retirement in the early thirties, new venues for expression are emerging. Case in pointe shoes are fiftysomething ballet dancer Martine van Hamel, once a star with American Ballet Theater, and sixtysomething ballet dancer Gerard Lemaitre, who continue to prove age knows no leaps or boundaries by touring with Nederlands Dans Theater 3, a dance company for the over-forties.

Kicking up your heels at any birthday is the oldsters' credo at the Fabulous Palm Springs Follies. Here, the cast of vaudeville singers, hoofers, and jokesters, who have performed to more than 300,000 people since their 1992 debut, are all well-cured hams. The oldest in the cast is harmonica jiver Sister Magdalen Therese Peplin, ninetysomething years young.

But what if you've been an accountant all your working life? Creative contributions by mid-century entrepreneurs and volunteers of *all* professions are increasingly lauded in local and national news, so expect a continued value shift in America's vision of aging.

/TAP

TAP

TAP

iconogasm: cultural climax, marketing opportunity

Ask how this penchant for perpetual creativity can invigorate your product, company, or service.

Community

As America's hair turns gray, a mega shift is bearing down on how state and local governments spend money. Along with the aging populace, retirees are invading Sunbelt communities like sixtysomething Attila the Huns, shifting the ways in which budgets are allocated. Seniors, who are older than existing voter bases and on fixed incomes, typically have opinions on public spending that are much different from young families'. Seniors will often reject industrial development, wary of the noise and traffic, and block funding for educational programs and building new schools. Instead, these elder McGruffs vote for crime-prevention programs, new jails, and other "quality of life" improvements. Still, southern states are wooing seniors, seduced by retirees' "mailbox income" (pensions and Social Security). With many elementary and secondary schools feeling the hurt, some cities have had to let retirement communities, along with their huge tax bases, secede from their districts. Other towns are proactively trying to get seniors on their side by allowing them to audit high school classes, giving them tours of science and computer labs, and even throwing parties for them called "senior proms."

iconogasm: cultural climax, marketing opportunity

Watch out as maturing boomers who are used to having it their way take control of government spending at all levels.

Beauty   *Fountain   of Youth*

How 'bout putting the brakes on aging altogether? Hope is stampeding from every direction in a multitude of guises: bottle, book, tube, tonic, lotion, creme, bar, pill, diet, exercise, breathing, massage, meditation, surgery, suck-it-all-in lingerie. The fountain of youth is less a gurgle than a geyser as de-aging health and beauty products steam the market.

Even though extraordinary biomedical research to double and triple the average life span is being pursued by private corporations and think tanks at Harvard, MIT, the Picower Institute, and the International Longevity Center at Mount Sinai Medical Center, the vanity merchants are not content to sit back and wait for Mr. Science to crack the genetic wrinkle code. As the first crow's feet nest at the corners of boomers' baby blues, get ready for the exponential expansion of age-arresting gadgets, gallivants, and goos. The frenetic promise of perpetual puberty (or at the very least forty forever) seems to be the mother of invention of a growing amount of stop-the-clock gear: Renova prescription wrinkle reducer ("finally a tube of truth"); Green Magma, Arnie Palmer's Slurpee of choice ("it's given me more drive and energy than I had 20 years ago"); melatonin; DHEA; PrimeTime's three-pronged men's room punch (Formula 1 for vitality and acuity, Formula 2 for weight control, Formula 3 antioxidants for virility and prostate care); Facial-Flex ("you can actually reverse the telltale lines of aging and regain a radiant, youthful looking face with a 2-minute workout"); skin preservation systems; kombucha tea; Revitalize shampoo ("new hair is filling in where before I had close to no hair on top of my head"); and for the Donald Trump–sized checkbooks graying out there—Human Growth Hormone to firm up sagging muscles and slough off fat cells ($20,000 for a year's supply). Hope you have an IRA!

iconogasm: cultural climax, marketing opportunity
Count on boomers to accept the wisdom of aging but to fight its biology every inch of the way.

Future

If you surf no other trend, make sure you hitch a ride on those aching backs of aging boomers. As more boomers enter their mature years, the terms "old" and even "senior" will be replaced by more positive ones like "people of age" or even "wise ones." Boomers have never been known for taking the status quo in stride, so growing old gracefully is a laugh.

As the first wave of boomers hits sixty in the year 2006, the first few decades of the twenty-first century will see a number of paradigm shifts. The health, housing, and financial industries will shift into sixth gear to capitalize on the wants and needs of this huge, wealthy market. Look for alternative forms of domestic life like cohousing and intergenerational living to bloom in the years ahead. Expect a radical shift in what and who is considered sexy as all types of fountains of youth bubble up from Madison Avenue. "Foodaceuticals"—foods that promote health and prevent disease—will lead the consumables pack, while many more products and services will be made senior-friendly to finally end marketers' fifty-year obsession with youth. Sweet!

iconogasm: cultural climax, marketing opportunity

Boomeritis is an age-defying disease. Is the promise of vigor and long life hiding inside your product or service?

sign #26:  dollars and sense

Troubled waters are running under America's bridge as an economic shift reshapes the nation, dividing the country into two camps along dimensions of income, jobs, education, race, and even IQ. A host of factors will determine who's a have and who's a have-not in the new millennium, with knowledge of and access to information technology at the top of the heap. For the first time in this nation's history, the Founding Fathers' utopian vision of America as a level playing field, versus the Old World social hierarchy, is in serious jeopardy.

Class

The economic shakedown is creating the bugaboo no one in this country likes to talk about—class. Although most of us like to think of ourselves as within spitting distance of the middle class, the fact is we're increasingly falling into one of two sides of the great class divide. As America *themeparks* itself into an entertainment- and service-based society, well-paying blue-collar jobs are going up in smoke, squeezing the middle class like a trash compactor.

The income gap in the U.S. is fast becoming as wide as the Mississippi. The nation now has the biggest rich-poor gap since the Census Bureau began keeping track in 1947. Entry to the middle class now requires a college degree, a much different story than in the postwar era or in Europe, where most countries keep the lead dogs and the rest of the pack running together through high minimum wages and mandated corporate training.

Why make a case against social Darwinism? Beyond the ethical issues, new economic theory suggests that where inequalities are the greatest, *everyone* suffers. The theory is supported by research showing that haves and have-nots either prosper together or decline together in both cities and suburbs.

Something equivalent to the GI Bill would be necessary to level the playing field. But with a civil war declared on government spending, expect an economic Mason-Dixon line to further divide this country.

iconogasm: cultural climax, marketing opportunity
Help stem the great social divide by carrying a big middle-class stick.

Inheritance

Inheritance, historically a practice for only the elite, is part and parcel of the economic quake as millions of Cold War warriors stage their last battle. The voodoo economics of the 1980s were very good for most of those with a nest egg to invest, and baby boomers stand to be the benefactors of this now ostrich-sized egg. Baby boomers are going to be the recipients of the largest collective inheritance in world history, gleaning more than $10 trillion as their Depression-era, know-the-value-of-a-buck parents eventually die. This mother of all Lottos will represent by far the biggest transfer of wealth from one generation to another. Although a higher rate of inflation, the rising cost of end-of-life care, and the fact that seniors are living longer and retiring earlier will not put a Mercedes in every driveway, 115 million bequests with a mean value of some $90,000 *will* fill a few.

With the check in the mail, boomers and the financial-services industry have caught patrimony fever, obsessed with estate planning via trusts, mutual funds, insurance policies, and tax shelters. Bean counters have taken to calling themselves "inheritance counselors," showing fortysomethings and fiftysomethings with dying parents where to hide when the tax man comes a-knockin' at their doors. Don't put your head in the sand as this legacy is handed off to the generation who thought that $300,000 studio condominiums were a good idea.

iconogasm: cultural climax, marketing opportunity
Get your piece of the inheritance pie as boomers make room for dessert.

Anti-Inheritance Backlash

For those planning to hit the jackpot when it's time for Mom and Dad to enter the big bridge tournament in the sky, be informed that many of today's seniors are planning to check out without their luggage. An anti-inheritance movement is beginning to boil and bubble, marking a clear break with the traditional pursuit of passing on assets to the children. Coined "dying broke" by *Worth* magazine, the movement is based around the conscious decision to leave nothing to one's heirs, predicated on the belief that financial life should end at the same time as one's vital signs. Rather than building a nest egg to lay on relatives, those who are dying broke (DBs) proactively use up all their financial resources while still alive. DBs thus get the opportunity to see their estates put to full use, spending both on themselves and others. DBs use their savings for vacations and home improvement, while carefully insuring they will have enough money to live on should their genetics be better than believed.

Instead of building trust funds for grandchildren, DBs pay off their college loans; instead of leaving children stocks and bonds, DBs help them buy homes. Not only do DBs get to see the fruits of their hard work benefit others, but recipients get to make earlier use of the resources for investment purposes or simply for a higher quality of life. Giving away money while you're still alive also avoids the steep estate taxes government levies to get its piece of the pie. Dying broke represents a new form of legacy, a more holistic way to approach the concept of inheritance. As death continues to become a less taboo subject, look for other ways people ensure that life isn't a dress rehearsal.

iconogasm: cultural climax, marketing opportunity

Expect lots more of us to go to the Other Side with nothing more than our grins and the clothes on our backs.

Debt

Thought taking on large sums of debt went away with those born-to-shop 1980s? Living in the red is still business as usual for many, if not most, Americans, a bigenerational fiscal policy patterned after the federal government's. As our proclivity toward spending outweighs our saving habit, businesses will have to reposition their products and services toward a debt-oriented society. Strategies based in *debt marketing* will emerge, geared toward selling products and services in an economy where consumers' liabilities exceed their assets.

iconogasm: cultural climax, marketing opportunity
Put yourself in the black by figuring out how to help consumers get out of the red.

Boomer Debt

Baby boomers are still charging into debt, a legacy of their grooming as professional consumers. Kids of the 1950s and 1960s were the first children in history to be approached as a legitimate target market. In the 1970s, aspiring boomers learned to want it all, and in the prosperous 1980s, they got most of it. Now in these skinny-as-a-Pringles-with-Olean times, many baby boomers are finding it difficult to give up their spending ways. Most bankruptcy filers are in fact well-educated thirtysomethings and fortysomethings stuck in the material world.

Like all shopaholics, boomers with Armani on their backs get an emotional high from buying stuff, feeling satisfied and empowered by the purchase process itself. Carolyn Wesson, author of *Women Who Shop Too Much*, found that some women actually get sexually aroused by the sound of the credit card machine having its way with their Visa.

Help *is* on the way. In addition to counseling, another boomer icon, Prozac, appears to help ease the urge for conspicuous consumption. Baby boomers' willingness to live in a perpetual state of debt has major implications for the way they spend the back half or third of their lives. Bank on a radical shift in the lifestyles of "people of age" as boomers are forced to bring home the prosciutto well into their sixties and seventies.

iconogasm: cultural climax, marketing opportunity
As boomers go, go, go, create debt-management programs so they won't owe, owe, owe.

Gen X Debt

Generation Xers may have rejected some of the values of boomers, but they have wholeheartedly embraced their older siblings' propensity toward debt. It's back to home for many Xers strapped by megadebt. Forced to bunk in their childhood single beds with the original *Star Wars* sheets, 35 percent of men and 24 percent of women in their twenties are again shacking up with Mom and/or Dad. The American Expressing of college campuses (they stump more than 1,000 colleges each year) coupled with the cutbacks in government student loans are generating a credit-card meltdown for young adults. "All you have to be is a live body on campus, and you get credit," reports Gary Stroh, head of the Consumer Credit Counseling Service of Los Angeles County. In southern California, the average card-carrying twentysomething is bench-pressing a $2,159 balance due. Compounding the problem, college tuition is being run up on plastic instead

of on government grants. The kicker is that government-loan interest rates are half those of credit cards, and the Fed is definitely gentler

and kinder when it comes to payment extensions if you lose your job.

So why are junior debtors crippling themselves with credit? Being born into a borrowing culture has made MasterCarding soooo easy. Having a credit card in your jeans is a liberating rite of passage and an instant perk pacifier—until reality bites. Big debt is keeping young adults in the nest longer, affecting careers, marriage paths, and family dynamics. Although a fair share of twentysomethings embrace conservative values, stressed out about the possible demise of Social Security and saving adamantly, most of this age group is extremely vulnerable to credit crash. Their general lack of experience and comprehension of fiscal responsibility (and disability) could be grounds for redubbing them Generation B (for bankrupt).

iconogasm: cultural climax, marketing opportunity

Build brand loyalty by educating twentysomethings about money management. How about making Citibank Credit Card 101 a prerequisite for graduation?

Wealth

Here's the deal: Moody's gives it a triple-A rating; it's an assets-backed bond selling at a favorable interest rate (ten years at 7.9 percent), has a long history of predictable repeat sales from an impressive inventory as collateral, and has a pending contract worth $30 million to sweeten the revenue stream. Would you buy into this privately held bond issue? It does have the ink of stability written all over it. An offering from Lehman Brothers, you ask? Try the Thin White Duke, David Bowie. In the bond industry, track records count, and the Duke is not a hazard. It may not surprise Ziggy Stardust loyalists that Bowie would be the very first rocker to turn himself into a financial entity; he's always honored his creative instincts. This time around, that verve and instinct have put $55 million in his jeans.

Who will bond next with the bond market? We'd buy Dilbert; Tom Cruise; our fav literary litigator, John Grisham; or the ever-moxy Madonna. This gives stuffy old bonds sex appeal. Thanks to David Bowie, celebs of every ilk will soon be singing "Let's dance!"

iconogasm: cultural climax, marketing opportunity

Taken to the next level, a local celebrity, business, or regional product could be a bond issue.

sign #27:  bunkering

In simpler times the Cleavers likely lived next door, kids wheeled around the block on balloon-tired Schwinns, and on summer nights the neighborhood "gang" could be heard prowling the shadows in a game of hide 'n' seek. Today, with 75 percent fewer June Cleavers waiting for the afternoon school bus with a plate piled high with peanut-butter cookies, the time and inclination to be neighborly just ain't there. *The new family* (check out sign #32) has more personalities than an eight-headed Sybil, kids in every conceivable extracurricular activity, and all of the all-family stresses that go along with a jampacked lifestyle.

How to keep body and soul together? By retreating into the inner sanctum of our *bunkers*, our homes. We drive into the attached garage, buzz closed the door, flip on the security system, and lock out an increasingly hostile world. We are the kings and queens of our technosmart fiefdoms. *Bunkering* makes life livable. Could it also turn us into a society of groundhogs, dashing out and back in, scared of our own shadows?

Home

Home is still where the heart is. Home on the Range is still off I-94 Exit 7 in North Dakota, and home for the holidays is still where most of us want to be. Whether home is a twelve-foot-wide Pathfinder trailer complete with a cozy couch where potatoes nuzzle tube-r-side, a Victorian rowhouse, Brooklyn brownstone, rambling ranch, colonial, log cabin, hogan, casita, loft, lanai, condo, tent, penthouse, yurt, townhome, zero lot line, duplex, bungalow, or cottage— wherever you sleep tight fending off the bedbug bites—it's home sweet home.

Technology makes it possible for us to hibernate like big old brown *bunkering* bears. Dial Dominos or a galloping gourmet to deliver rations, lounge in the lux of a 500-channel home theater, or chat via cell phone while bubbling in the master bedroom spa. It's here, Mr. Jefferson. Your vision of a self-sustaining household is being realized through techno gadgetry. These *bunkers* of ours are getting more mind-boggling every day.

iconogasm: cultural climax, marketing opportunity
Appeal to Americans' homing instincts as we batten down the hatches.

Decor

Junking up your own space has always been an obsession for people with extra income. But now the plastic-toting public seems enraptured with possession obsession. On the home front it's a furnishings fervor, a frenzy for buxom buttonback throw pillows, hours spent angsting over the right shade of white to lather the living room, and devoting every waking weekend hour to trawling for peonies in the backyard. At Iconoculture we affectionately call this wildfire passion for home and garden *Marthamania*. Thanks to Ms. Stewart, her crafty revival of homey chic is the trend that ate America. She's everywhere—prolific publishing, wassail-and-iced-gingerbread TV specials, mail-order catalogs, and absolutely the yummiest step-by-smiley-step inside poop (oh, gosh, we mean scoop) on how to make a buttercream cake.

All this attention to domesticity is a mass-market awakening. Martha Stewart and PBS's *This Old House* and all their prideful, putty, putsying clones can be credited with the rejuvenation of the American Dream. Being a "homebody" has a newly hand-rubbed luster.

iconogasm: cultural climax, marketing opportunity
Even the most mundane domestic chore is fair game for product development in these home-crazed days.

Second Home

Feathering a nest? This is serious fun. Just as two human fingerprints are never the same, the rule of thumb in decorating follows suit. *Bunkering* nurtures the need to create the absolutely perfect place to hang your Cubs cap. Once nothing more than the primal urge to mark our territory, today boundaries are etched in stone, stucco, rough-sawn cedar shakes, even hay bales. For those families in the clover, the pride of owning your very own patch of crabgrass has been usurped by the need to second-mortgage the hometown home in order to build a vacation home "up North," "out West," "on the course," "at the beach," or "on the lake." Supposedly it's the antidote for the stresses of modern life, buying into the upper-middle-class reasoning that the family that second-homes together plays and stays together.

Second nests are also a reward for years preoccupied with raising kids, footing mammoth bills for college, and decades spent in consuming careers. The American Dream[2] thrives at virtually every resort area from Taos to Scottsdale to the Cape to Santa Fe. (Santa Fe, by the way, is fighting back with restrictive zoning to stem the tide of outsiders land-rushing the arroyos.) This trend will only accelerate in the third millennium, as baby boomers inherit more than two-thirds of the nation's wealth.

iconogasm: cultural climax, marketing opportunity
To capture the housing dollar, cater to rampant home-away-from-home dream scenarios.

Fantasy

What's amazing is how frivolous serious folks get when it comes to creating the right sense of place for their home away from home. Endless hours go into conjuring a totally integrated environment. More often than not, the second home is like a stage play paying homage to the author's romantic daydream or inspired flirtatious fantasies.

Wind Whistle is the love child of architect James Stageberg and writer Susan Allen Toth. This sherbet-shingled whimsy perches high on a bluff overlooking the Mississippi's Lake Pepin, a PeeWee's tree house perfect for spotting bald eagles. The couple's passion for English gardens seems to be their muse as, outside and in, Wind Whistle is a double-dip dish of rainbow—blue and pink sofas; yellow, pink, and apple-green walls, posters, dishes, countertops, and cupboards. Even the Oriental carpets and roomy bathtub frolic in pastel.

Other homebodies have got the boot-scootin' boogie! The ever-renewing infatuation with all things Old West has ignited the log home market, range wrangler fashions, textiles, and buckaroo *bunker* furnishings. The Marlboro Man may have been pistol-whipped by antismoking advocates, but his cowboy ethos is very much alive and galloping in timber homes from lake-country Wisconsin to toney enclaves out West—especially virile in Colorado, Montana, and Wyoming.

It's the Ponderosa revisited as decorators load up the buckboard with heavy-sawn timber beds, elk-antler chandeliers, leathers, Pendleton blankets, Native American sculptures, baskets, and pottery. Visit Telluride or Aspen, Jackson Hole or Big Sky, and find Stetson-styled homes and brokers-turned-buckaroos ambling down Main Street. The glint off their $300 custom silver belt buckles could make a blind burro cry. All this Western stuff, down to the boots-with-spurs salt and pepper shakers and the double-cab Chevy 4x4 in the driveway, buy the homeowner permission to forget "my other life" and live in a fantasy state.

iconogasm: cultural climax, marketing opportunity
Fuel the fantasy. From clothes to couches to autos to eats, the $$ are in the details.

Catalogs

You don't even have to leave the leatherette BarcaLounger in your home entertainment center to order out for more neat stuff. Home shopping networks are habit forming, encouraging a shop 'til you drop (or until the remote blows up) lifestyle. QVC reaches 61 million American homes, feeding our fetishes. Animalmotif lamps ("in your choice of tiger, zebra, or leopard design"), solid brass toilet brush holders, the hand-tufted Guggenheim rug collection, Edwardian-inspired carved easels that hold "ORIGINAL ART at EXCEPTIONAL VALUES," and log cabin kits are for anyone who will call toll free for UPS doorstep delivery.

If you're searching for a business to jump into, the merchandise-by-mail biz may be the E-ticket to ride. The trend-tracking Direct Marketing Association figures 132 million Americans (that's 66 percent of the adult population) buy by mail. Got a hot idea for a new direct-mail souk? The future, and a slice of the more than $70 billion a year spending pie, is yours.

iconogasm: cultural climax, marketing opportunity
Dorothy Parker's words worth pondering: "The two most beautiful words in the English language are 'check enclosed.'"

Eating In

A new industry may soon be giving Lean Cuisine a run for their stroganoff. People with a passion for cooking are turning their hobby into thriving businesses with the help of the United States Personal Chef Association. A $500 membership sets you up with a bite-by-bite program for creating and marketing a culinary service that shops, chops, simmers, and sautées in the comfort of the client's kitchen, then packs his freezer with a month's supply of dinners. Monthly dues of $49 cover new recipes plus a hotline to field business questions.

USPCA founders Sue and Dave MacKay successfully cooked up the first Personal Chef as an antidote to the southern California lifestyle. Currently forty-six states are represented, plus three Canadian chefs and one in the Caribbean. This new cottage industry opportunity sidesteps the licensing red tape of catering by preparing all foods under the status of a personal domestic employee. By 1999, 3,000 new PC entrepreneurs are predicted to be broilin'.

What's really interesting is how this Aunt Bee concept has caught on outside the U.S. In Brazil, white collar workers are as stressed out and hungry as the American workforce. In Rio they buy monthly "subscriptions" for home-cooked, prefrozen diners—fifty-four entrées for under $200. (In the U.S. the price is about $130 for a week's meals plus groceries.) Watch for PCing to fill the *bunkers* of America with the fresh smell of banana bread, taking home cooking to new heights of convenience and taste.

iconogasm: cultural climax, marketing opportunity
Any service that diligently de-stresses home life has a huge future.

Home Schooling

Being smart is a national obsession, and it's got us looking for learning in all the right places. At home? If it was good enough for Ben Franklin, Flo Nightingale, Thomas Edison, Booker T. Washington, Agatha Christie, and Andrew Carnegie, home schooling is good enough for more than 1 million American children. Parents fearing a public school system devoid of morals, accountability, creativity, safety, multiculturalism, critical thinking, and (most important) fun are teaching their little prodigy at the kitchen table.

Home schooling is not just for conservative Christians anymore. Growing out of this homeward-bound trend is a support network of satellite schools which, for a tuition of $160 to $280 a year, provide books and week-by-week lesson plans for home teachers. Urban home schoolers bond together and form co-ops to enrich learning with group activities. With consistently high scores on standardized achievement tests landing home-schooled students on top college campuses and on scholarship lists, this once-wacko alternative is proving that yes, Toto, there's just no place like home.

iconogasm: cultural climax, marketing opportunity
Don't play hooky on the home-school trend. Here's a huge market for educational products.

Identity

No, your neighbor hasn't seceded from the Union. And no, that bunny flag he's flying is not a symbol of nationhood dedicated to the ideals of small, furry creatures. Decorative flags of bunnies, snowflakes, leprechauns, and other cute-alia are gradually sweeping their way west, a home decorating trend started in Richmond, Virginia, twenty-five years ago. Cheery as Katie Couric at 7:00 A.M., decorative flags allow people to extend friendly greetings to neighbors without actually having to talk to them. The average flag waver owns nine different designs, rotating them every week or two to keep the neighbors looking up. Among the hundreds of designs, flags depicting the pineapple, a traditional sign of greeting and hospitality, are the most popular.

Don't be fooled by the artsy-craftsy appearance of these penguins, shamrocks, and daffodils, however. Flag mania is big business, flapping its way into mail-order catalogs and retail stores ranging from Macy's to Wal-Mart. More than just an inexpensive way to decorate the house, flags are a symbol of our desire to reengage in communities, individual pieces of cloth within the larger fabric of society.

iconogasm: cultural climax, marketing opportunity
Raise the flag for individuality. No matter how folksy, we want to be honored.

chapter 7: nature

Are those fig leaves we see people wearing around town? Well, mayb[e]
not, but Americans are returning to the garden every other way they ca[n.]
We are experiencing an unprecedented interest in the natural world [as]
well as a deep fascination for the supernatural world. The more we kno[w]
about Earth and what lies beyond, it seems, the more we want to kno[w.]
Take a bite out of the twenty-first century by tempting Adams and Ev[es]
with the luscious fruits and secret mysteries of the universe.

sign #28:  gaia

Never fool or underestimate the power of Mother Nature. In a blink we jettisoned the Industrial Revolution and are now full-speed ahead through the Information Evolution. Reeling from the sheer speed of change, people are grasping for balance. To soothe the aches and pains of technological whiplash, many are beginning to root their lives and livelihoods in the eons-old philosophy of *gaia*—exalting Earth as a living, breathing, feeling organism, with humans as caretaker. Learning from the nation's indigenous peoples, Johnny-Appleseed-come-latelys are honoring and nurturing a symbiotic kinship with the wind, water, land, and creatures of the planet. In *Roget's Thesaurus* circa 2012, "environmentalism" and "equilibrium" will be synonyms, confirmed by Earth-centered politics, economics, and cultural endeavors. The nation, already giving a strong voice to its Native American roots, will internalize its forefathers' *gaian* reverence and responsibility for the health and longevity of the planet.

Native American Culture

Gaia's rebirth has been midwifed by our fascination with Native American culture. Take a trip to Santa Fe for full immersion in the capitalistic manifestation of all things *gaia*. Everything Native American is for sale—hand-whittled Kachina dolls that woo the sky and Earth spirits into blessing the garden with bountiful crops; Acoma pueblo clay pottery; hand-tooled turquoise; and smudge sticks, those sweetgrass and fresh mountain sage incense cigars (just light one up and fan the fragrant smoke to cleanse the air of trickster spirits). Most enchanting are the palm-sized stone animal totems created by the Zuni tribe of New Mexico. Believed to hold mystical meditation powers, these gems are said to arbitrate between human forces and the higher powers of the natural worlds. For example, Long Tail (the Zuni mighty mountain lion) fortifies your courage, clarifies personal and career vision, and demands high standards and commitment. For anywhere between $15 and $1,200, depending upon the reputation of the sculptor and the stone, you can bring the Long Tail spirit to bear and show that bummer boss who's really boss.

The opening of the National Museum of the American Indian on the Washington Mall in 2001 will officially anoint our indigenous culture as a national treasure. Within its million-plus baskets, rugs, pottery, musical instruments, and tools, the NMAI will express the wisdom embedded in Native American artifacts, that beyond their everyday uses, "every object has a breath." In fact, there is no word in most Native American languages for the Western terms "art," "religion," or "culture," implying that art and religion are not *parts* of culture but *are* culture itself.

How is Native American culture going to impact mainstream American life? Will the vision quest, a personal trek into the wilds to capture your soul, usurp Super Bowl Sunday? Probably not, but a *gaian* pregame ritual might very well hype those burly warriors as they purify their minds and muscles at a Lakota Sioux *inipi* or sweat lodge. The ancient spiritual-cleansing ceremony is moving off the reservation into more local neighborhoods. Take a peek over your neighbor's fence and you may see folks gathering around fire rings to experience a legacy of teachings that explores the natural, mystical relationship between the Earth and all who live upon it. The roasting ritual promises to sear away the participants' insecurities and fears, illuminating a vision of strength and purpose. Other markers of Indian identity also have been appropriated by mainstream America. Even Time-Life has given away dreamcatchers, crafted works of natural materials designed to ward off bad dreams and catch good ones, as a promotional premium.

iconogasm: cultural climax, marketing opportunity
Respectfully borrow *gaian* philosophy that views Earth and its inhabitants as interrelated.

Neoagrarianism

Gaia is welcoming back the family farm, a staple of American identity and experience. Look for this awakened reverence for a bountiful, healthy Earth to rototill an enthusiastic backyard agrarian movement. Families tired of spandex-skinned, cardboard-tasteless tomatoes and yearning for the crunch of a lemon cuke are hoeing and weeding the urban landscape. Fresh, organic foodscapes in both backyards and community gardens are looked to as the source for chemical-free fruits and veggies, the seeds of a broader sustainable agriculture movement.

Permaculture, the slam-syllabling of "permanent" and "agriculture," is also going wild. Permaculture is a process/lifestyle designed to reclaim the soil by taking all the knowledge of traditional farming and overlaying it with today's technowizardry. The net result is a form of organic gardening that creates and nurtures artificial but sustainable living systems that look, act, and feel just like original biosystems. Got that?

At the more than 1,000 experimental gardens worldwide, landscapes are planned and planted based on the number of functions a plant performs. Establishing an interwoven community of plants, or "guilds," as they're called, is the key. A working guild may include an invisible structure of sweet potatoes, garlic bulbs, and daikon enriching the soil down under as veggies flourish above. An indigenous fruit orchard stands guard nearby with its protective roots and afternoon umbrella of shade. Birds, bees, and bacteria share their talents, while a man-made wetland filters waste through the roots of bulrushes, cattails, and reeds.

Permaculture is also a cost-effective toxic wastebasket, with cattails cleansing the oily selenium fields at Chevron's Point Richmond, California, refinery. In the Ukraine, a Rutgers University biochemist is testing the Indian mustard plant on Chernobyl's scorched soil, and the Environmental Protection Agency is tilling parrotfeather and stonewort in the hope that it will decompose TNT in Georgia. Scientific applications that support the *gaia* idea prove that "progress" and environmentalism are not mutually exclusive.

Iconotip *du jour:* Keep your eyes, ears, and tastebuds tuned to Kenny Ausebel and his Seeds of Change certified-organic seed company. This environmental engineer is leading the charge of backyard gardeners, chefs, vintners, and scientists to reclaim the plants of the planet. You only have to put an ear to the ground to hear a cry of clear and present danger: Ninety-seven percent of the cultivated plants our grandpappys feasted on in 1900 have been lost, replaced by an army of engineered food droids. The enemy, according to Ausebel, is modern agriculture's obsession with the hybrid. Hybrid varieties are perpetrated by multinational, petrochemical-based farmers for uniform breeding, uniform harvests, and uniform profits. Problem is, hybrids almost always produce uniform, less-than-yummy produce. From an eco-crusader perspective, all this inbred, incestuous sameness leaves a crop more vulnerable to disease, setting the stage for history to repeat an Irish-potato-style famine of humongous proportions.

iconogasm: cultural climax, marketing opportunity
Tie an umbilical cord to the Earth-as-mother movement to reclaim the future.

Travel

As a metaphor for the journey of life itself, travel can be *gaian* in spirit. As *roadtripping* (sign #15) showed, we're interested in not only where we're going but also how we get there. A common thread running through many travel trends is the quest to visit places as a participant, to blend into a local habitat, to immerse ourselves in a different culture. More and more we need to bring home (besides the pictures and trinkets) a new way of seeing the world. The gradual extinction of the Ugly American is being fueled by our interest in different cultures and a growing sensitivity to the environment, with consumers more likely than ever to choose the high road when deciding where and how to travel.

This *gaia*-a-gogo is playing out through eco, or green, travel, one of the fastest-growing segments of the pack-your-kit-bag industry. As *The Denver Post* eco-scooped, green travel can take social responsibility to heights that litter-sensitive Boy Scouts only dream about. At the heart of green travel are goals of educating visitors about local culture and ecosystems, hiring locals, and putting a portion of profits back into communities visited. Greenies also move in small groups: on water, for example, they'll use a kayak rather than a motorboat to avoid giving that manatee an Evinrude-sized headache; on land, they'll stay on the marked trail so as not to disrupt the cryptogram, the desert's fragile ecosystem. Stephen Foehr is the green meenie of green travel, his *Eco-Journeys: The World Guide to Ecologically Aware Travel and Adventure* the natural source on the subject. Foehr speaks of the connections that can be made between the traveler's own home and a new environment, that the experience of traveling green becomes part of each traveler's "psychological backyard." After returning from such a trip, the green traveler is much more likely to practice an ecologically aware lifestyle, providing long-term benefits to the environment and community back home.

iconogasm: cultural climax, marketing opportunity
Look for Americans' innate wanderlust to be recast as the desire to be a part of—rather than a visitor to—new places.

Volunteering

Do the eco-right thing. Put away that yellow polka-dot bikini. After all, how can you lie on the silken sands of Waikiki slurping rum coocoos when Planet Earth is in peril?! To the rescue . . . you! Preserving eco-sensitive sanctuaries is a mission for every human, according to global watchdog Earthwatch. Since its inception in 1972, more than 40,000 Dr. Livingstone wannabes ages sixteen to eighty have signed up with Earthwatch to save the world at some 161 global sites. That's $26 million in citizen-supported projects like eco-expeditions to count Zimbabwe's black rhino, chart the mating behaviors of Alaskan caribou, dig for dino bones and ancient Iberian artifacts, and survey glaciers in the French Alps.

Reaping the intrinsic rewards of scientific grunt work doesn't come cheap. On one eco-trek, for example, travelers paid $1,595 plus airfare to go to Peru's virgin rain forest in order to share a mattress under a thatched roof with howler monkeys, a toucan or two, and the team leader from the Smithsonian Institution. *Gaians* were there to preserve katydid biodiversity, finding insects resting on foliage, fogging them, and then attracting them with ultraviolet lights. All at night, mind you.

iconogasm: cultural climax, marketing opportunity

Expect "Go Big Green!" to be the war whoop of the future as more *gaian* armies march in support of Mother Earth.

sign #29: tarzan

We're going to beat our chests and scream it out loud: There's a growing physical and emotional craving for what remains of the primitive side of nature. *Tarzan* is what we call this raw, sensual trip to a time unspoiled by the spin doctoring of civilization. Within *tarzan*, Earth's habitats and inhabitants are perceived as visceral places and creatures, the fruits of nature considered authentic and honest.

Modern day Tarzans and Janes are reclaiming the savage soul, trying to get back to the jungle that resides somewhere within. Whether your own private Africa is an urban jungle or the Amazon wilds, *tarzan* prescribes that life is one long safari. Sports utility vehicles and combat boots are *tarzanesque* survival gear. Hemp sweaters and knapsacks tell the world you're pro-fiber. World music—the fav among pop music's elite—is *tarzan* for the ears. *Tarzan*'s mission, should you decide to accept it: Go face-to-face with the unknown and explore virgin territories with a commitment to keep the Earth fit and strong. Fruits of the Spirit, The Body Shop, Clean Water Coalition, Sierra Club, Greenpeace, and thousands of anonymous *tarzans* are swinging from the trees, living life large while guarding the balance of nature.

Food

Luckily, *tarzan* is edible. You can taste it in the trend toward fresh, direct-from-nature do-not-pass-go foods. The mainstreaming of organic foods, whole-food grocery stores, and co-ops is a neon sign of the times that we want the real thing. Foods from God's own pantry even come in the mail, a mad postal shopping spree for guaranteed untainted produce, fruits, and meats. Bite into a Harry and David Anjou. Heaven should taste so sweet. Jamison Farm Lamb, the

Potato of the Month Club, and Alfresco Brand Organics conjure a pastoral vision, a purity of place where nature is the antidote for civilization.

Tarzan is also embodied in the trend toward grain-based foods and authentic, traditional cuisine. If you have not yet, pick up a copy of *Saveur* magazine to get a sense of how food and place can be one and the same. You'll never look at eggplant in the same way again. Cheeses and wines are state-of-the-art *tarzan*, micromarketed by region and even climate. Beverages are blowing *tarzan* through the jungle roof with the juices of exotic fruits like guava, papaya, mango, Zudachi orange, and wild elderflower. Load that ginseng-laced juice with some electrolytes, vitamins, and nutrients, and you've got an action-enhancing body quencher before you can say Jack LaLanne. Vinegars, chutneys, and sauces are mixing flora in ways that nature never intended.

Restaurateurs have latched on to *tarzan* in an equally big way by offering *al fresco* dining, adding wood-burning stoves to their open kitchens, and roasting and grilling everything that doesn't move. Chefs are even leaving their big white hats at home to venture into the forest in search of wild foods. Why bring home the bacon when you can bring home morels, enokis, fiddleheads, and stinging nettles?

Is that *tarzan* we see wooing *chi* under that big tree? Yep, spirituality is doing the wild thing through ancient elixirs like kombucha, that liquid made from a mushroom bigger than your head. It's fermented fungi with a twist, an oozing cocktail that will leave your inner being shaken, not stirred.

 iconogasm: cultural climax, marketing opportunity
Return your products and services to the Garden of Eden through purity and sensuality.

The Great Outdoors

Nothing like going right to the source. You can unearth *tarzan* in the great outdoors by climbing a rock face, trekking the Boundary Waters, kayaking the Yellowstone. These are the juiciest, tastiest, most satisfying passion points in life, nature boys and girls will tell you. Whether hiking, flyfishing, or mountain biking, outdoor adventure is the off-the-beaten path to find the *tarzan* lurking in all of us. *Tarzan* is not a place; it's a state of mind. Women are running with the wolves, while Iron Johns beat their manly drums. Extreme sports are another cultural milieu for wild ones. Mountain runners and ice bikers press the boundaries of human endurance, their bodies becoming extensions of the environment. With muscles of molten rock and rivers of sweat, extremists are walking, talking symbols of our need to be a part of the essence of nature.

iconogasm: cultural climax, marketing opportunity

Take leadership in the outdoor movement by equating your brands with the wonders that are nature.

Health and Beauty Aids

Fragrances are kidnappers. Jungle scents awaken danger and excitement. A splash of the sand and sea transfixes us. Memories are intrinsically linked to that wet-dog-and-pine-laced hike you took when you were just a tike. If we can't get to the mountains, health and beauty aid marketers are there to bring the mountains, rain forest, desert, or ocean to us. Origins, Shiseido, and Biolage are blending art and science into a new generation of botanically based products, bringing *tarzan* to the masses. These brands draw upon our primal need to be in touch with the Earth (and smell good, too).

How can other HBA marketers turn green stuff into greenbacks? Consider "crosstraining cosmetics" for that athletic guy or gal passionate about skin and hair products that are sport authentic. "Extreme fragrances" can offer maximum performance and cutting-edge efficacy. *Tarzanesque* scents can turn sweat into muscle moisturizers and guard exposed skin against the sun's rays. Oil and emollients, modeled on natural protectants found in the animal kingdom, provide shelter from the jungle monsoon. Feminine and masculine merge into a sinewy, strong, beautiful single-sex fragrance. Cool-down de-stressers bring the body back to earth after a face-off with the rougher, tougher side of Mother Nature. Badly battered regions—feet, knees, shoulders, neck, wrists, fingers—get their own unique stress-foliating formulations. Other fragrance habitats calling to be explored: North Africa's High Atlas Mountains, home to Bedouin brides and amethyst crystals; Tasmanian waterfalls; the Tundra at midnight; the rushing torrents of the Pacific Northwest.

iconogasm: cultural climax, marketing opportunity
Head off to the wild and into the mystic to romanticize brands.

Gardening

Time out. Take a deep breath. What is that fecund, mossy aroma? It's the smell of money wafting from the bountiful annual harvest of the gardening industry. It's a backyard, sideyard, rose-arbored revolution, as your-garden-or-miners raise beds and find happiness right there in their own backyards. The herb and garden craze is an outgrowth of the voluntary simplicity movement, mainstreaming environmentalism, and the pure delight in making something other than a mutual fund grow. However the seeds were sown, the crop is definitely a bumper.

From Portland, Maine, to Portland, Oregon, there's a whiff of fish emulsion in the air. A pox on those chemical weed killers and fertilizers! Organic is definitely the way to go. What's springing up? Connoisseurs are putting in weird, exotic plants sourced from the four corners of the globe. One-up your nosy neighbor by putting in some wild hellebore from Croatia, ferns from China, Siberian oaks, or some South African fuchsia. Antique roses such as the Madame Hardy, sourced from nineteenth century Victorian and French gardens, haven't been this popular since, well, the nineteenth century. Like heirloom vegetable seeds, antique flowers retain a singular, identifiable quality unavailable in modern, overhybridized agriculture. Suburban *tarzans* are building ponds or "water gardens" in their backyards, another instance of what-once-was-new-is-new-again rearing its wet head. The truly dedicated are practicing xeriscaping—low-maintenance, water-wise gardening—while the truly obsessed are using irrigation and waterwheels on their hobby farms out in the country.

iconogasm: cultural climax, marketing opportunity
Steep yourself in consumers' desire to bring *tarzan* home.

Birding

If you haven't heard, the jet-set crowd is out; the egg-laying crowd is in. The industry circling around our fine feathered friends is getting as big as a vulture on a bad day at Black Rock. Birdhouse envy is rampant as designer digs from log cabin to urban moderne to cozy colonial swing from neighborhood branches. Sexy suet holders, bathtubs, nesting starter kits (organic strings and moss), chirping audio CDs, and Audubon Society–endorsed binoculars are selling like hot cockatoos. Bird gourmets should be sure to check out the four different custom-blended seed cuisines available at All Seasons Wild Bird Store.

Up for a vacation migration to an exotic locale? *Bird Watcher's Digest* is filled to the brim with ads touting tours to breeding habitats all over the world (Costa Rica, Turkey, South Africa, New Zealand, Belize, and Trinidad are hot, hot, hot). The customers for all this bird-tripping are the over-forty-five crowd, who also flock into stores like Wild Bird and The Nature Store to outfit their yards or condo terraces. Birding gives empty nesters whole new families, an opportunity to rediscover the little tweets in life.

iconogasm: cultural climax, marketing opportunity
Look for other ways consumers can discover *tarzan* in their own backyards.

sign #30:  outer limits

Rod Serling took us there in 1959, and the nation has never come back from *The Twilight Zone*. We love being so scared we wet our pants, and we are fanatics for unexplainable phenomena—strange deaths, nothing-is-a-coincidence coincidences, alien invaders, astrological charting, out-of-body sidetrips, and hoary otherworldly visions that inhabit the night. As our spaceship speeds along its trajectory to 2000, expect the millennium heebie-jeebies only to intensify. Stay tuned to the *outer limits*. There's frightening and enlightening fun (and bug-eyed grays) ahead.

UFO

These saucers aren't under your teacup. Beam yourself to Seguin, Texas, international (and in all probability intergalactic) headquarters for the Mutual Unidentified Flying Object Network. Of course UFO sightings aren't new; MUFON has been cataloging them for twenty-five years. What *is* of late-breaking interest is the swelling public interest in extraterrestrial encounters and abductions and their links to comets, crop circles, and livestock mutilations (even aliens gotta eat). Network membership is at an all-time high, with 5,000+ believers signed on and turning their eyes skyward. Walt Andrew, our man on the scene in Seguin, attributes the growing fervor to the public's "sophistication" ("This is the greatest mystery of the Space Age. People don't trust government UFO coverup investigations") as well as the voracious videocamming of flying saucers.

Fate Magazine, Fortean Times (the journal of strange phenomena), and *True Reports of the Strange & Unknown* (a *Reader's Digest* of the weird) hover around newsstands monthly, while 700,000 read *Weekly World News*, which feeds an insatiable national hunger for factoids and altered-state photos. Add in hit shows like *The X-Files* and *Millennium* (its debut drew the highest Nielsen rating of any show in Fox history) plus countless reptile-eyed, the-truth-revealed alien exposés, and our best guess is there really is a market for a steely antenna in our collective navel.

iconogasm: cultural climax, marketing opportunity
Look, up in the sky! It's a bird! It's a plane! It's money in your pocket!

Paranormal

Here's the tip-off: When the government announces "There is no cause for alarm," suspicion races into overdrive and conspiracy theories sprout faster than shiitake mushrooms. One hyperventilating c-theory of late has "moles" from inside the Pentagon revealing new generations of mind-control technologies known as LTL (less than lethal) weapons. *Fortean Times*, that woo-woo compendium of worldwide weird phenomena, has reported in depth on the LTL high-power microwaves that supposedly beam voices into the enemy's brain to confuse synapses, halt action, or erase memories and then fill the vacuum with an altered personality. Watch for this to come out of the CIA's sci-fi closet as an electromagnetic zapper used for crowd control. Paranoidically speaking, this could conceivably put the kibosh on antigovernment demonstrations.

Another mind-boggling mind grope comes from the Farsight Institute in Atlanta. This is the headquarters of scientific remote viewing, a mental telepathy technique (trance?) that allows trained individuals to view what's happening in distant places, planets, or future time. Reportedly the Defense department has their own corp of agents who infiltrate Saddam's bunker by remote viewing. The farseers at Farsight claim to have ongoing interaction with friendly extraterrestrials and have recently offered the U.S. government access to their "new science" in exchange for a partnership in building a campus to expand their mind bending. Can't you see Newt voting to fund Farsight? Are we pushing your *outer limits* yet? Hope so.

iconogasm: cultural climax, marketing opportunity

Here's fertile territory worth exploring for theming a new ad campaign, for basic research into the paranormal realm, or just for fun.

Stars

"Everything born or done at this moment in time has the qualities of this point in time." —Sydney Omarr, astrologer deluxe

Do you check your horoscope every morning to see if the stars will be with you or against you? If so, you're one of the 20 percent of Americans who believes in astrology or one of the many more who reads horoscopes "just for fun." With more than 90 percent of this country's 1,556 daily newspapers carrying an astrology column, and more than 100,000 practicing astrologers in the U.S., America has gone positively star crazy.

The concept behind astrology is that planetary movements and the coordinates of celestial bodies work in synchronicity, shaping the events here on our little orb. Although the scientific revolution put a 200-year hex on looking to the heavens for inspiration, astrology is part of a new global resurgence of alternative belief systems offering answers to tough questions. Parallel interests in ghost sightings, divine apparitions, angels (*George* found 78 percent of Americans believers), faith healing, near-death experiences, UFO encounters, and voodoo are in large part a backlash against *technomorphing* (see sign #39), the effects of warp-speed technological change. Our crystal ball tells us that with the turning of the millennium, belief in astrology and its extraterrestrial cousins will have more people tracing constellations than in the days of Copernicus.

iconogasm: cultural climax, marketing opportunity
Create a big bang through celestial products and services.

Spirituality

As we plunge headlong toward the end of the second millennium, religious sightings are multiplying like bagel shops. The Windy City has been a virtual mecca of miracles, with the divine-inclined seeing signs of the King (no, not Elvis) in the branches and bark patterns of trees. Mary-shaped bloodstains have been

spotted in a downtown shoe-repair shop, while a three-foot plaster statue of Jesus in a St. Charles gift shop has been noted to possess a heartbeat.

The Host of hosts apparently roadtrips once in a while; his image has been detected in—no kidding—a Pizza Hut billboard in Wichita. What's accounting for this flurry of deep-dish divinity? Those in the know, such as Sandra Zindars-Swartz, author of *Encountering Mary*,

say it's a reflection of anxiety as we approach the big 2000. Other Mary mavens say miracle mania reflects a search for the sacred in everyday life, an effort to put religion back into the hands of worshipers as traditional institutions are busted for committing their own mortal sins. Expect the visions to escalate as the countdown to ecstasy continues.

iconogasm: cultural climax, marketing opportunity
Harness the power and the glory of the supernatural and paranormal in products, services, and communications.

Travel

One of the freakiest travel *outer limits* we've spied lately is written as a smudge of blood—vampire tours. This is true. Cross our hearts with a silver cross and pray the bedroom window is double locked. New Orleans bound? Pack the garlic. No hipster or Anne Rice fan could resist the palefaced, bloodshot glances of the nocturnal bar crowd at LaFitte's Blacksmith Shop. An Iconofriend swears he danced with a vampire but doesn't have the neck punctures to prove it. Certain Rice writings and the bloodcurdling film *Interview with the Vampire* piqued curiosity, but of late it's become the fashion for practicing vampires to come out of the coffin. Real vampires in real interviews talk of drinking their best friends' blood—definitely a *biomorphing* trend, you say—as a sign of brotherhood and love.

Where do newly fed 'n' wed vampires honeymoon? Where else? Off to Castle Dracula. The eight-day tour, complete with masked ball, is the brainchild of the Transylvania Society of Dracula and Romania's Romantic Travel. Prince Vlad the Impaler's digs, a staged witch trial, and medieval cemetery visits all are part of the adventure.

iconogasm: cultural climax, marketing opportunity
Trip to the outer limits and connect to consumers' phobias, fetishes, and fantasies.

chapter 8: relationships

"Americans of all ages, all stations of life, and all types of disposition, a
forever forming associations . . . of a thousand different types—religiou
moral, serious, futile, very general and very limited, immensely large ar
very minute. . . . Nothing, in my view, deserves more attention than th
intellectual and moral associations in America." —Alexis de Tocquevill
Democracy in America, 1830s

Unless you're living a Unabomberian lifestyle, much of your life revolv
around relationships with other people. Because we are a multicultur
nation, Americans rank high on the social meter, eager to form affiliatio
to get a sense of group identity. As our national culture continues to con
apart at the seams, we're keeping our community quilt together throug
various types of close-knit relationships. Tap into our enduring need to t
a part of something bigger than the individual.

sign #31:  beehiving

Ahhh, these times they are a-changin', and at the heart of these changes is the redefinition of the most important touchstone of community. New, smaller communities are forming as our larger ones break down, a result of the wholesale fragmentation of America. We call these new communities *beehives*, tight-knit affinity groups or coalitions bound together by common social or political interests. Where you look and with whom you share physical, emotional, educational, and spiritual hallelujahs and high-fives will not necessarily be the traditional venues of home, neighborhood, work, and Main Street. New *beehives* of shared interests and values are buzzing on the horizon, reshaping relationships inside and outside of the honeycomb.

Brandhiving

In our consumer society, communities are bound to form around shared interest in a brand. Saturn, of course, has proactively defined its consumers as a *beehive* through promotions such as inviting all its owners to a picnic in Tennessee. Philip Morris is a master *beehive* marketer, linking its consumers through its Marlboro Gear catalog and train promotion. Brand *beehives* are also created by consumers themselves, independent from any efforts by Corporate America. Booberry, the General Mills cereal, has had quite a hive on the World Wide Web, where enthusiasts discuss, well, Booberry stuff.

Perhaps no other brand *beehive* is as compelling as Harley-Davidson. The purveyor of hogs deluxe is doing wheelies over its Harley-Davidson Owners

Group, a worldwide *beehive* of more than 200,000 chopperholics in 750 local chapters. These folks share little except a common passion for the wild wind in their ponytails and all stuff Harley. The community is composed of otherwise strangers who saddle up for a free membership the first year and pay thirty-five dollars per year after that. The booty: two magazines plus eligibility for cool bikerama goodies including insurance, travel services, emergency roadside help, and even tuition reimbursement for safety courses. Members' shared value of the free spirit within transcends the standard social divisions of gender, class, and racial lines, illustrating how *beehive* marketing can be an alternative means of reaching consumers.

iconogasm: cultural climax, marketing opportunity
Build a brand *beehive* by defining your product or service as a communal gathering place.

Gays and Lesbians

They're out, and they're proud. Gays and lesbians both are key *beehives*, diverse yet tight-knit communities with their own social codes. Pink triangles and

rainbow stripes are the *hives'* logos, telling the world that you're in gay-friendly country. As a marginalized group, gays and lesbians integrate social activism in ways most heteros do not. Some lesbians have been known, for example, to stamp their money, "These are lesbian dollars," a sign of their loyalty to one another and to marketers who acknowledge their existence.

A growing number of marketers are actively wooing the gay and lesbian *beehives*, some donating a portion of revenues to gay-related causes. Both the Pride Network, a long-distance telephone service, and Pride Fashion direct a percentage of sales to AIDS research. Marketing to gays is a niche strategy Corporate America is gradually embracing as it recognizes the brand loyalty and spending power of this target audience.

Consider TZABACO (za-bak-koh), a catalog committed to "serving expressly, but not exclusively, gay men and lesbians, and to portraying our lives and values in a positive way." TZABACO is positioned as a hip mix of all the good stuff in J. Crew, Williams Sonoma, and Sundance wishbooks with a tinge of J. Peterman dialogue tossed in. The premier issue of the catalog personalized the products via Mike and Alex, on the road to their cabin in the Sonoma Hills of California. All the accoutrements of "a less complicated life"—bunkhouse, longjohns, mukluk slippers, plaid cozy shirts, hunter-green Adirondack-wannabe Southport chair—are ready and willing to help you scale back your checkbook. Hey, simplicity ain't cheap. Obviously these dudes and their yellow lab, Bob, are blessed with enviable good taste. You don't have to be gay or lesbian to buy TZABACO gear, but you do need to recognize the tremendous buying power of this market. Yankelovich Partners estimates $17 billion is spent each year on travel alone. Peruse the TZABACO catalog for clues on how to connect with this huge audience.

iconogasm: cultural climax, marketing opportunity
Target *beehives* whose members believe in strong group affiliations.

Beehive Bunkers

Don't look for all graying boomers to be rocking on their own front porches in 2020. Some waves of this aging tidal swell will be undercapitalized in their retirement, pressed to afford even the rocking chair. Extended or amended career paths will probably retire any plans for retiring. Their well documented do-it-all, see-it-all, be-it-all, have-it-all past will lead to a variety of collective-living situations in the future. Twisting baby boomer Hillary Clinton's borrowed philosophy, it will take a village to retire a boomer. Communities of long houses, reminiscent of the Seminole tribal tradition of several families living together, are already on the rise. Nurturing healthy, productive, interdependent, proud

residents is their mission, providing a much-needed community to people who too often end up living alone.

One successful model of a bunkering *beehive* is Sunset Hall. This L.A. Spanish-style hacienda is home to a coven of socially and politically aware activists in their seventies, eighties, and nineties. Some residents first met when unionizing the garment industry more than sixty years ago. These folks find comfort and kinship while debating NAFTA, attending in-house contemporary issues and pop culture classes, field-tripping to the Getty Museum, or licking envelopes and manning phone banks for their favorite causes. Activism is the fountain of youth in this real-life cocoon. Sunset's seniors, like their boomer kids and grandkids, laugh in the face of acting your age. Look for boomer versions of Sunset Halls to be the busy-bee longevity lounges of the future.

iconogasm: cultural climax, marketing opportunity
Target *beehive* bunkers to find consumers where they live.

AARP

Mirror, mirror on the wall, what's the biggest *beehive* of them all? Why, it's AARP, the American Association of Retired Persons. If you've just celebrated your first half-century birthday and feel too pooped to party, let your instant membership in AARP do the talking. Hands down, AARP holds the potential to be a monster lobbying force through the first half of the twenty-first century. In preparation for the boomer surge, AARP has been garnering political and economic power over the last decade. You'd think the mega *beehive* had been chug-a-lugging Energizer Ensure with the redesign of their now boomer-friendly geezer zine, *Modern Maturity*. AARP is bestowing (for a fee, of course) its valuable seal of approval on lots of products and services, including mutual funds, annuities, mobile homes, health and life insurance programs, a prescription pharmacy service, and both Visa and MasterCard. Its ambitious vision is a harbinger of the *beehive* to be: "AARP excels as a dynamic presence in every community, shaping and enriching the experience of aging for each member and for society." Watch for AARP to flex its bulging elder muscles and put new wrinkles on Medicare, Social Security, and other policies facing seniors.

iconogasm: cultural climax, marketing opportunity
Don't miss the buzz in the mother of all *beehives*. The AARP seal of approval is becoming as powerful in the '90s as the Good Housekeeping Seal was in the '50s.

Technohives

Every hour around the clock, tens of thousands are wiping their fingertips for the first time on cyber welcome mats. There are roughly 24 million people on the Internet or subscribing to online services, plus another 17 million who access the World Wide Web. Online *beehives* are constantly evolving into new Net neighborhoods filled with community chatter, Main Street shopping, and political gossip. Once you're snagged in the Web, it's hard to leave home without it.

As any technobeehiver can tell you, there are thousands of online support hives bringing together people with health, employment, parenting, or relationship concerns. AOL's Better Health and Medical Network, CompuServe's Disabilities Forum, Microsoft's Breast Cancer Awareness Forum, and Prodigy's Grief and Death Bulletin Board are particularly hot hives in cyberspace. Special-interest groups such as Ecolink have also set up camp on the Internet, connecting crusaders sharing a common cause.

Another swarming technobeehive is Motley Fool, the biggest little stockhouse in cyberspace. Motley's message boards, honey hives vibrating with the financial buzz, share hot tips, competitive analyses, hype on corporations' new products, and rumors and ravings about favorite acquisitions. More than 350,000 guest hits are recorded each month, a testament to the freewheeling-individual, online-investor community exchanging information previously held tight to the vest by industry insiders. Now everyone with a modem can play the bullish game—if they can bear the consequences.

iconogasm: cultural climax, marketing opportunity
View websites and homepages as places for bees to hive.

191

sign #32:  the new family

What is a family these days? As our social and economic plates fracture like the San Andreas Fault, we are in the midst of a whole-hog redefinition of what constitutes a family. The traditional nuclear family is already well on its way to becoming an anachronism, a Cleaverian or Bradyesque wisp of another time and place. All forms of families are gradually earning legitimacy, including trigenerational, multiracial, and multiunit families. The classic markers of the family unit—race, age, parents' sexual and gender orientations—have become much more fluid, and there has been a significant blurring of parental and children's roles. Although more diverse and not necessarily related by blood, families remain strong, cohesive networks of people, the *beehive* of all *beehives*.

Nontraditional

It seems Americans will do just about anything to maintain some semblance of collective family life. With little or no time during the day to share, many moms and dads feel that bedtime is the right time to bond with the little ones. The practice, termed the "family bed movement," is getting a solid endorsement from a growing number of experts. The result is a gradual chipping away of one of our culture's big bambu taboos.

Those who subscribe to familial posturpedia believe it more natural than segregated sleep quarters, providing kids with a greater sense of security in these scary-as-a-nightmare-in-the-dark times. With children's bedtimes getting later, and parents' bedrooms not the private chambers they once were, communal dreamcatching makes more sense than some might admit. Be prepared for other no-nos proscribed by Dr. Spock (the pediatrician, not the Vulcan), such as family nudity, to eventually become more socially acceptable.

Another traditionally private practice, giving birth, is going public, as increasing numbers of family members and friends join Mom in the delivery room. Two-thirds of all hospitals in the United States have opened up "birthing rooms" to accommodate larger groups of people, but most of the laborin' and neighborin' is happening at home or at birthing centers. There are now 145 such centers in the nation, where about half of the 20,000 annual deliveries are attended by various family and friends. Husbands, children, parents, and best buddies comfort and coach the mother, often in a partylike atmosphere. Some rub the mother's back or help her breathe, while others are content simply to watch or to munch on hors d'oeuvres. Recent immigrants from countries where midwives or doulas deliver babies account for a large percentage of public births, although a significant number of native baby boomers are choosing to go public as well. The heightened interest in multicultural rituals and traditions is fueling the trend, as is the greater interest in turning medical events into holistic, positive experiences.

iconogasm: cultural climax, marketing opportunity
Help turn family experiences into celebrations of togetherness.

Traditional

Although the traditional family may be on the cultural ropes, don't expect it to go down without a fight. Block parties, town meetings, and community service all are flourishing as boomers reaffirm their parents' postwar family values. Can you say "soccer mom"?

Even more indicative of the tenacity of traditional values is the return of "Mrs." as a title. A generation after feminists fought to claim their own identities, in part by not assuming their husbands' surnames, many twentysomething brides are now eagerly becoming "Mrs." when they get hitched.

What's the reason for this backlash of Faludiesque proportions? "The baby bust generation [born between 1965 and 1976] tends to be a little more traditional, waiting longer to get married, and when they do, looking for more traditional marriages," says James Madden, associate publisher of *American Demographics*. "Mrs." hearkens back to a time when couples stayed together (for better or worse) and to a mythic age of stability defined by prescribed gender roles. The return of "Mrs." parallels other prefeminism trends, including more stay-at-home moms, lower divorce rates, and the growing number of men reclaiming their "rightful" places in the families. Are dowries around the millennial corner?

iconogasm: cultural climax, marketing opportunity
Follow the golden rule by recognizing the safety and comfort traditional values offer.

The Great Outdoors

Need to justify a week off from work? Think of an outdoor excursion—camping, hiking, fishing, biking, shooting the rapids—as an incubator for family values. A recent Roper Starch poll reported that 63 percent of Americans credit their passion for outdoor recreation to the fun times they had while growing up. About half those claim that the seeds of an active, environmentally friendly relationship to the Earth took root before the age of eight. So it follows that more young parents are sharing with their young ones their passion for Deep Woods Off, tall knotty pines, and the aroma of bacon sizzling over an open fire.

Family camping is the wholesome trip *du jour*. Books and magazines are devoting barrels of ink to tips on tents, nature hikes for tikes, and building the perfect campfire (*Rodale's Guide to Family Camping* actually details eleven fire-savvy methods:

trapper, tripod, hunter, dingle crane, flat-rock, keyhole, Dakota . . . you get the idea). Fashion is downsizing as little camping bods deserve and are getting as much attention as big folks. Outfitting the kids in the right gear is serious work for parents and serious business for retailers. "When my 6-year-old daughter said she wanted to scale Mount Rainier," one mom recounts, "I got her Vasque Kid's Klimbers ($50). . . . The quality heel counters would keep her from rolling an ankle, and the reinforced toe cap would protect her toes from rocks."

The wonderment and promise of this trend are immense. Teaching children to see, understand, and appreciate the great outdoors gives them skills that positively affect personal confidence and competence in navigating the human and physical environments. If your focus is family, this is your country to explore.

iconogasm: cultural climax, marketing opportunity
Stake your claim in the great outdoors to cross the great divide in family values.

The Workplace

Balance. This is the biggest perk managers can offer their employees in the workplace of the future. *Business Week* reports that 73 percent of large corporations in the United States have adopted flextime in their employee handbooks, if not in daily practice. Some companies, including Hewlett-Packard, Motorola, Eddie Bauer, and Xerox, are carving their competitive edge with programs and policies geared to balancing the work-life relationship. The family-friendly workplace is curbing worker burnout with innovative offerings ranging from onsite twenty-four-hour daycare for children, private grade schools and summer camps, and eldercare for the moms and dads of aging boomer employees. Eddie Bauer headquarters even offers express meals for those stressed-out worker bees who need an answer to the age-old question "What's for dinner?"

iconogasm: cultural climax, marketing opportunity
Find ways to target consumers through the workplace instead of the marketplace.

sign #33:  kid quake

What is that danged racket coming from the kids' room? It's getting louder and louder, shaking the windows and rattling the rafters of the nation. *Kid quake* describes the seismic effects children are having on society. Kids are reshaping our family and social dynamics in a much different but equally significant way from what baby boomers did when they rocked America's house in the 1950s and 1960s.

Kids are often, for all practical purposes, the queens and kings of the family hive, acting as gatekeepers for what goes in and on in households. With one in every four kids living in a single-parent home, children have assumed responsibilities that adults from previous generations never dreamed about. The generational astigmatism is compounded by the fact that children today are growing up in a world very different from the one in which their parents were raised. Still, kids are more active, more anxious, and more like their parents than ever before. As today's children become the first teenagers of the new millennium, an idea about as eerie as an Ed Wood movie, look to kid culture as an indicator of our collective future. Hold on to your backward baseball hat as the *kid quake* continues to rumble into the next century.

Social Responsibility

So who's taking up the slack for Ma and Pa Kettle in the new millennium? Big business, for starters. Social responsibility is the inroad for companies such as Nike, who uses it to assume their place at the head of the table. Realizing its power to do good where good is needed most, Nike initiated P.L.A.Y.—Participants in the Lives of America's Youth—with a $10 million advertising/promotion campaign to support its program of kid-driven community activism. The program even has a Kids' Bill of Rights, created by the founding foot fathers to guarantee that younger citizens "will have the natural and absolute right to feel safe in our own backyards, community playgrounds or neighborhood parks—extended drug-free, violence-free zones." Here it is, word for righteous word:

A Kids' Bill of Rights

All kids deserve and demand an escape from the daily pressures facing us in our society— somewhere to go, something to do, someone to be. A kids' movement is awakening. Kids are taking the initiative and responsibility for positive, energetic actions charged with fun and free motion. These are our inalienable rights: Active life, sport, and the pursuit of fun.

1. Right to participate
2. Right to have fun
3. Freedom of choice
4. Right to easy access and clean facilities
5. Right to safety
6. Right to parental involvement
7. Right to quality programs
8. Right to equal access for boys and girls
9. Right to have in-the-know coaches
10. Right to have a voice

iconogasm: cultural climax, marketing opportunity

To leap over your competitors, take the protection and promotion of kids' rights to Jordanesque heights.

Food

Noticed more kids reaching for endive and radicchio rather than links and patties?

There are signs that a vegetarianism movement the size of an elephant squash is sprouting up in our children's gardens. Boomer parents are finding that their kids are becoming vegetarians more frequently and at earlier ages, often surprised at the little pumpkins' independent decisions to decarnivorize. Kids attending a city summer camp in Berkeley, California, are legally entitled to be offered a vegetarian alternative and can choose from a wide variety of tofu-inspired dishes.

Children themselves don't care a pig-in-a-blanket about the health issues associated with eating meat, just the morality of it all. Kids make the literal connection between real-live animals and meat that adults often ignore, seeing that ground chuck as a chunk o' Elsie rather than a plastic-wrapped commodity. (Watch out for the day when kids realize where leather comes from.) The reasons for the increase in veggiekids are unclear, although the environmental movement and boomers' own aversion to fat are certainly factors. Always looking for the semiotic needle in the haystack, we think that Barneymania contributed to the rise in pedovegetarianism. Kids may believe that Grandma's mystery-meat surprise hotdish-casserole-thing-in-a-bowl may once have been a purple dinosaur, Arthur the Aardvark, or another scaly friend. Don't the words to the song go, "I love you, don't eat me . . ."?

iconogasm: cultural climax, marketing opportunity
Read kids' leaning toward flora versus fauna as the roots of a meatless culture.

Education

Another icon of good ol' Western hierarchy appears to be tumbling. More and more schools are opting out of naming class valedictorians or are redefining the award. Private schools in particular, like St. Anselm's Abbey School in Washington, D.C., are looking for excellence both inside and outside the classroom, viewing the whole valedictorian concept of my-GPA-is-bigger-than-your-GPA as too competitive and too narrowly focused. Grades are seen as just one part of the overall learning mix, with service to school and community equally important factors in the academic experience. With selection of a valedictorian often too close to call, administrators, teachers, and even other students are instead choosing a "Student of the Year." The judging process for this is sort of like a beauty contest without the swimsuit competition, designed to reward the student with the best overall talent and skills. Not pinning the big V label is also having some longer-term benefits, like relieving some of the pressure eighteen-year-old overachievers naturally feel when pitted against other smartypants in elite colleges.

iconogasm: cultural climax, marketing opportunity
Expect other traditional symbols of children's rank to morph into more well-rounded, team-oriented forms of recognition.

Technology

We have seen the future of education, and it is cyberspace. The more progressive schools in the country are starting to put their money where their modems are, placing computers in as many kids' hands as possible. The Buddy System Project in Indiana, for example, puts computers, modems, and printers in 6,000 fifth- and sixth-graders' homes and is considered to be a model program for education in the twenty-first century. In addition to encouraging critical thinking through multimedia options, computers allow students to work at their own paces and free up teachers for one-on-one instruction. Students and teachers find that downloading information from databases makes textbooks seem like stone tablets, out of date before the ink's dry.

It's not surprising that cyberkids are more motivated and get better grades than those without access to computers, which opens up major issues about equitably slicing the technological pie. As the year 2000 rings in, only 3 to 5 percent of the nation's classrooms will be cruising the Internet, with affluent suburban schools much more likely to be online. State funding for the Buddy System is supplemented by the Lilly Endowment and the Ameritech Foundation, a mixing of public and private money which signals a parallel trend in the future of education. With technology becoming cheaper and schools gradually reallocating textbook budgets toward computers,

expect to see many more kids toting laptops along with their lunch boxes as we graduate to the new millennium.

iconogasm: cultural climax, marketing opportunity
When planning marketing initiatives, remember that kids are natives to information technology, while adults are immigrants.

Sexuality

One trend contributing to the *kid quake* is the coming out of gay teens and preteens. According to the American Psychological Association and the National Association of School Psychologists, it is only a natural evolution of the sexual revolution for children to question and explore their partner preferences in early adolescence. When the choice for Annie is not the boy next door, a whole set of harassments, insecurities, and suicidal tendencies may begin. Queer youth—gay, lesbian, and bi—are finding a comforting embrace from trained psychologists, the National Gay and Lesbian Task Force, and groups on the Net. *Wired* magazine reports about the "safe space" Usenet moderated newsgroup (soc.support), throwing a lifeline for socially isolated, confused, and despondent kids. Another supporter is *Y.O.U.T.H.* (Young Outspoken Ubiquitous Thinking Homos) magazine (probably not on the reading list at Omaha Jr. High).

iconogasm: cultural climax, marketing opportunity
Recognize and respect the different lifestyles of the most diverse generation in history.

sign #34:  toto too

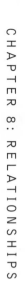

Noticed that dogs are everywhere you look these days? In addition to dog-friendly restaurants and offices, you can buy a full line of doggie clothing to make that quadruped look like the cat's meow. At the Dogpatch in Los Angeles, your dog can spend the day painting or making ceramics. How did these cute but kinda dumb mammals jump like a scared Chihuahua up the evolutionary scale? As man's best friend, dogs represent trust, loyalty, and dependability, precious commodities in this icon-toppled world. Dogs are no longer seen as a lower species but as a pet companion, endowed with therapeutic, life-affirming qualities. America's obsession with canines is spreading to other animals, with wild birds and hedgehogs becoming the pets *du jour*. We see animals and animalia—products and services dedicated to things that chirp, purr, hiss, or bark—becoming an even more central part of life in the twenty-first century as people look to their furry friends for companionship, comfort, and camaraderie.

Welcome Mat

As in 1920s society culture, dogs have become popular accoutrements. It's no longer enough just to own a dog; now you have to wear it. Dog-friendly companies are on the rise, as are other public places willing to let your diminutive life partner share a spot at the table. Portable minidogs, as we all know, are *de rigueur* for the rich and famous. Madonna snuggles with a Chihuahua named Chiquita, while Oprah cuddles with a cocker spaniel named Solomon. Liz Taylor even wrote her Maltese, Sugar, into her will, proof that love for a pet lasts longer than that for a few husbands. Other popular yappy breeds are bichon frises, shih tzus, pugs, Malteses, Yorkshire terriers, and that old standby, toy poodles.

There *are* ways to bond with one's animal companion other than by using it as a living, breathing shawl. Popular in Scandinavia for years, skijoring—cross-country skiing while hooked up to a dog leash and letting the dog do all the work—is gaining ground in the States. Training your dog for a career in entertainment is another way to let that pup be all he can be. The heightened demands for dogs in television, movies, and advertising have produced a cottage industry dedicated to getting one's pet into show biz. Doggie talent scouts advise that droolin' ingenue where to live, how to act, and how to prepare for the big audition. It's the end of the world as we know it.

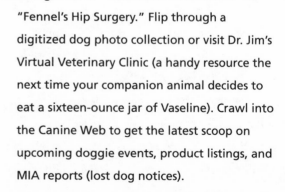

iconogasm: cultural climax, marketing opportunity
Develop new ways for pet owners to bond with their creatures of comfort.

Community

For 54 million Americans, the *beehive* of choice is . . . the doghouse. The United States leads the world in dog ownership, with about 42 percent of homes Bowser abodes. New pups and their owners are even going to "socialization" parties, grrrrrr get-togethers to swap bones, trade housebreaking stories, and share the love of canine camaraderie.

The technological version of pooch parties is the cyberscene at the Canine Web. This site for interactive puppy schmoozing is a global fire hydrant to get the latest poop on anything furry and four-legged. Read personal accounts of the trials and tribulations of life as a dog, such as "Dave's Flat Coat Is Born" or

"Fennel's Hip Surgery." Flip through a digitized dog photo collection or visit Dr. Jim's Virtual Veterinary Clinic (a handy resource the next time your companion animal decides to eat a sixteen-ounce jar of Vaseline). Crawl into the Canine Web to get the latest scoop on upcoming doggie events, product listings, and MIA reports (lost dog notices).

iconogasm: cultural climax, marketing opportunity
Create opportunities for dogs and their owners to travel in packs.

Products

What to get that Rover who has everything? How about an electric dog-food dispenser, a gizmo that unloads food into a bowl at twelve-hour intervals? This makes it easier for a dog owner to leave town without checking doggie into a kennel. So their dogs don't skip town, many owners have small microchips with identification numbers implanted under their dogs' skin. Recommended by humane societies, animal shelters, and veterinarians, the technology is superior to collars, tags, and tattoos should Lassie get lost or stolen.

Something more personal? When it's time to turn in, dogs are turning up their wet noses at blankets and jumping into their own down-filled beds. Addison Berkey and Diana King have even introduced four-poster beds for that royal canine. If Zorro is the artistic type, pick up *Unleashed: Poems by Writers' Dogs*, scribblings inspired by famous writers' four-legged companions, or *Dog Jingles*, canine-inspired Christmas music. Pet stores are selling Halloween costumes for dogs, so they can properly accompany people on trick-or-treat runs. Maybe this explains the burgeoning field of dog psychotherapy.

Because a pup is, like us, what he eats, many dog owners want the same kind of all-natural, nutritious foods for their companion animals that they eat themselves. Expect to see more products like Barley Dog, a powdered barley grass health supplement. Made with brown rice, garlic, and barley grass, Barley Dog features antioxidant vitamins C and E, beta carotene, live enzymes, amino acids, purifying chlorophyll, proteins, and essential trace minerals. Kal Kan has introduced "prenatal" dog food for that pregnant pooch eating for two (or ten). We'll also be lapping up more dog beverages like Thirsty Dog from the Original Pet Drink Company. Thirsty Dog is a lightly carbonated, mineral-enriched bottled water flavored especially for canine palates. Slices of lemon or lime, however, are not included. If all the romance is gone from your relationship with your partner in fur, make a pilgrimage to the Park Bench Cafe in Huntington, California. The Park Bench caters to dogs with its Canine Cuisine menu, offering items like

Hound Dog Heaven (a hamburger) and Hot Diggity Dog (a hot dog). You don't have to leave home to get good eaties for Petey, however. For $79.95 a year, the Bone of the Month Club sends that lucky dog an organic, holiday-themed treat on six special occasions. Roll over, Milk Bone.

The Wet Nose Award, however, goes to the Three Dog Bakery, a Kansas City–based retailer serving dogs' culinary needs since 1990. The Three Dog Bakery is taking a bite out of the Great Dane–sized dog-food business, marking its territory in upscale, all-natural snacks. Alarmed at the scary ingredients listed on the labels of ordinary dog foods, founders Mark Beckoff and Dan Dye saw an opportunity to market good and good-for-Scooter canine comestibles. They offer more than fifty types of poochie pastries, including Snicker Poodles, Scotty Biscottis, St. Bernard Bars, and Collie Flowers. Business at the Three Dog Bakery has been booming, inspiring Beckoff and Dye to open up more stores in other Midwestern cities. The Three Dog Bakery also sells its bowser baked goods to thousands of mail-order customers, including Oprah. New York City has its own poochie pastry shop, the Bow-Wow Bakery, which makes a salt-free and sugar-free puppy pizza that would make even Wolfgang Puck sit up and beg for more.

iconogasm: cultural climax, marketing opportunity
Hound your competition by offering added-value products for animal companions.

Services

Toto is too smart, of course, to be bought off with a good meal. For each new canine product there is an equally luxurious service to please the comaster of the house. Dog day-care centers, for example, are there for owners who work all day and feel guilty about leaving a family member home alone. Dogs get exercise, companionship, and sometimes training and grooming. And what did you learn today, Fido? Pet-friendly kennels *sans* cages are also popping up, kinder and gentler options for that dog on holiday. Check out, or rather, check in, at Pets Are Inn, a boarding facility for dogs and cats in Alexandria, Virginia, which places pets with families while owners are away. Dog-friendly hotels are also on the up and up, not only allowing guests to bring their dogs with them but offering various yummy services for man's best friend. The Ritz-Carlton in Chicago, for example, offers puppy pillows and personalized dog biscuits. Having a professional photographer take a doggie portrait with or without owner is another must for the canine-crazed. Call David Sutton in Chicago, the king of dog photography, for the gift that keeps on giving. When you do take the beast out for a spin, you'd best keep him on a short leash. Bite claims are ripping a $1 billion hole in owners' pockets every year, making insurance that covers dog bites a hot property.

iconogasm: cultural climax, marketing opportunity
Offer custom critter services as we continue to go mad over finny, furry, and scaly pets.

Spirituality

"And I will remember my covenant, which is between me and you and every living creature of all flesh." —Genesis 9:15

Even religion is adapting to Americans' interest in animalia. If you're a parent and have owned a pet, you've probably been hit with the tough one: "Will Fluffie go to heaven when he dies, Mommy?" Greater minds than yours or ours, including Aristotle, Aquinas, More, and Descartes, have pondered the animal-soul enigma, but more and more, religious leaders and scholars are being asked if Scout will be waiting in heaven. Congregation members are also asking their ministers, priests, and rabbis to bless their dogs, cats, birds, and reptiles, and some churches and synagogues have responded with special Pet Blessing services. In case you were wondering, Judeo-Christian religion experts believe that animals have soulful qualities but are not on an equal footing or pawing with humans when it comes to the afterlife. Conversely, most Native

American and Aboriginal cultures do believe that humans and animals will tango together in the big dance to come. Don't even ask what Hindus and Buddhists believe unless you've got a couple of lifetimes to kill.

iconogasm: cultural climax, marketing opportunity

Bless your animal products and services to find your way into consumers' hearts and souls.

Health and Beauty

America's obsession with health and beauty has spread to keep dogs fetching. Check out Sun Spot All-Natural Sun Protection, which not only keeps Rover from turning into a Raisinette but also repels outdoor pollutants and insects. As drug therapy for humans advances, more effective pharmaceuticals and analgesics for dogs continue to appear. How about some Purina Gelcaps for that splitting pooch-ache? Perfume for dogs is also wafting from below. Dog perfume is a $10 million market, with more than forty companies now marketing canine fragrances. Is that Gee Your Fur Smells Terrific we detect?

Dogs have "safe sex" ringing in their pointy ears too, you know. Dog breeders are gradually moving away from wham-bam-thank-you-Sam reproduction toward artificial insemination. Breeders screen parents-to-be for diseases and then find ideal matches anywhere in the world via computer. Genetic engineering to make the perfect dog is next. With research indicating that dogs have complex psyches, there are growing numbers of dog psychologists around the country. Doggie shrink Dr. Nick Dodman has narrowed canine personality disorders to three basic types: aggressive, compulsive, and fearful/anxious. Can you say "Pooch Prozac"?

Dogs are also being widely used for human therapy. In fact, there are approximately 2,000 animal-assist programs around the country, many of which use dogs to help humans heal physically and emotionally. Unconditional Love, in Chicago, for example, provides dogs to children and adults with special needs, while Canine Assistants in Alpharetta, Georgia, trains dogs to help disabled people. Dogs can be trained to dial 911 but have not to date been able to have pizzas delivered to the neighbors just for some yucks.

Holistic health care for dogs is healthier than ever, even deserving its own magazine, *Wolf Clan*. For those who don't want to subject their companion animals to the weird science of Western health care, there are people like Joel Hyman of Santa Monica. Mr. Hyman is a master herbalist with a potpourri of holistic potions to treat that lucky dog, cat, bird, reptile, or horse. His animal remedies are completely pure, derived solely from herbs like wormseed, wormwood, and peppermint. Bowser rolling around in the dirt again? Scrub-bubble that grubby puppy with Joel's herbal body cleanser (twenty-five dollars), a four-stage, 2½-week process that will whisk away those nasty parasites hitching a free doggy ride. Kitty's coat all a-tangle? Try Joel's liquid hair conditioner (ten dollars for sixteen ounces) made from nettle to get that fur bouncin' and behavin' naturally. Taking your macaw home for the holidays? Put him on ice with Joel's special sedative (twenty-two dollars for thirty capsules) made from licorice, jojoba, and fu ling (no fooling).

iconogasm: cultural climax, marketing opportunity
Adapt people trends to the dog-eat-dog world of pet products and services.

chapter 9: fear

The more we know about the world, it seems, the more we have to fe
This irony—that knowledge leads not to greater security but to great
insecurity—is making us more wary about what we both can and ca
see. If it's not gun-totin' mamas and papas, it's invisible toxins and gern
just waiting to whack you with bacterial bullets. As a vital surviv
instinct, fear is driving us to arm ourselves with metaphoric Uzis to dri
the evil forces back to their evil empires. Expect the number of things w
fear to grow, and with it the defense mechanisms designed to keep t
wolves at bay.

sign #35: shields up!

Shields up, Worf! That's the *fin de siecle* mantra as we try to protect ourselves and our families from all the lurking dangers. *Shields up!* is driven by our primal urge to defend our nests, as well as the fact that guarding loved ones is a powerful source of identity and purpose in life. By raising our shields, we believe we really are safe and in control, when in fact an acorn (or worse) can fall on our heads at any time.

Heightened concerns about making it through the day without getting a bump on the head are fueling a new breed of safety and security measures. History has taught us that technology and fear are a dangerous combination, an ominous proposition as we find new ways to liquidate witches who want our shoes. Count on more shields to go up in the twenty-first century as the haves continue to pull away from the have-nots.

Security

Although the number of violent offenses in some cities is actually falling, crime remains our biggest fear and worst nightmare. Those not fleeing to the hills or to planned communities like Disney's Utopian Village are building moats around what they hold dear. Gated communities are springing up in every suburb to try to keep the bad guys out, while the Clubbing of America has made antitheft devices ubiquitous symbols of our urban landscapes. More home-control software is being installed into new houses not only to monitor all things with an electric plug but also to keep the Romulans from invading. Cell phones are used as a safety measure as much as to wheel and deal. Orwell's Big Brother is becoming a reality as cameras record our every move and turn us into a surveillance culture. Through closed-circuit video, parents are even keeping electronic eyes on baby-sitters, once considered icons of trust and dependability.

Self-defense is again hugely popular, inspired perhaps by Jackie Chan's superhuman abilities. Classes in kick boxing and boxing are packed with those of us who want to know how to take on those ninjas who are after our wallets or running shoes. Gun registration is up, particularly for women, as are classes in how to shoot and, if necessary, kill. The most telling sign of the times regarding security is that John Wayne Bobbitt, immortalized for being in the wrong place at the wrong time, has marketed overnight penis shields to help other men avoid a similar fate.

iconogasm: cultural climax, marketing opportunity

Consumers are looking for something to hang on to. Throw a life raft into the turbulent sea of our times.

Technology

The fight against parents' worst nightmare, child abduction, has a new weapon. DNA kits are popping up on shelves across the country, ammo against the worst-case scenario when you need to find or identify a missing child or convict a kidnapper. According to the U.S. Justice Department and F.B.I., every year there are more than 100,000 attempts to abduct children by nonfamily members, with almost 5,000 of them successful.

Long used by law enforcement to make positive IDs, DNA is easily and painlessly gathered from a child's mouth. As genetic material, DNA is a far superior means of identification than fingerprints or footprints (which smudge), photographs (which fade), or blood (which degrades). The kits include a cotton swab, plastic gloves, a test-tube vial, and labels. Child Trace, created by former Miami Beach homicide detective Joe Matthews, sells at Wal-Mart and hospitals for less than ten dollars. A percentage of sales goes to the National Center for Missing and Exploited Children. Product information about Child Trace was made available at some General Cinema theaters when *Ransom*, a movie about child abduction, was showing. Guardian DNA stores the sample for you and throws in a video on child safety to boot. The product sells for up to seventy-five dollars, although some pediatricians sell it for fifty dollars, with a consultation included in the price.

Genetic-based shields are not limited to kids, of course. Adults buy the kits to sample a relative with Alzheimer's or sample themselves in case they have to be identified after a disaster like TWA Flight 800.

iconogasm: cultural climax, marketing opportunity

Expect other genetic-based safety shields to clone as the secrets of human identity are uncovered.

Clothing

Ozone depletion. Polo shirts. Global warming. Floppy hats. Acid rain. Hooded pullovers. See the connection? Ozone-blocking sportswear offers a new way to protect skin from Old Sol, a sign of the times as other manufacturers seize the epidermal day by getting a jump in the soon-to-explode area of fashionceuticals (healthy clothing). Retailers may want to forget workday casual, in fact, and instead think bullet-proof casual! Seventh Avenue is dreaming the impossible dream, recycling the kind of clothing worn by the knights of the Round Table. Urban Body Armor of Jersey City sells a complete line of customized, bullet-proof clothing, capitalizing on consumers' fears of being caught in the direct line of fire. UBA's coats, jackets, vests, and pants are made out of Kevlar, the same antiballistic stuff worn by the police and the military, hidden beneath a layer of brown or black leather. Clothing has always been used to shield our tender skin from hostile environments, so it makes perfect sense that armor has returned in these violent times, a half-millennium or so after it went out of fashion. Interest in bullet-proof clothing is surging in urban America as pistol-packin' party poopers make their presence unquestionably known at concerts, movies, and social gatherings. The demand for high-tech armor is so great, in fact, that UBA can afford to choose its knights in shining Kevlar carefully, asking each potential dragon slayer why he or she needs an amazing dreamcoat. Professional protection doesn't come cheap, either, with a UBA vest starting at a cool $450. Big-time marketers might investigate this trend toward protective clothing by trading off some style for safety. How 'bout a Medieval Gap or some Sir Lancelot Levis?

iconogasm: cultural climax, marketing opportunity
Seventh Avenuers should explore ways to doctor their *schmatas* to create fashionceuticals with a mission.

Scams

Old granddad's habit of hiding money is beginning to look a lot less wacky. Scams galore await those who aren't careful about protecting their assets from all the technovultures out there. P. T. Barnum's ghost walks about, with a telefund sucker born every minute. If your phone rings during dinnertime and it's not MCI or AT&T trying to get you or get you back, chances are it's a telefunder. Telefunding is the solicitation of money for charity over the phone, usually by for-profit, professional fundraisers. Although 99 percent of all charitable organizations are on the up and up, according to *New Choices* magazine and the National Charities Information Bureau, that 1 percent of phony baloney charity translates to $1.3 billion every year. With that kind of money at stake, fraudulent telefunders aren't operating out of back rooms. Instead, telescammers use marketing-research databases and high-tech switching equipment capable of dialing thousands of numbers an hour. The systems are smart enough to pass the call on to a salesperson only if a human voice, versus a recorded message, is recognized. Telethieves have your charity rap sheet (giving history) in front of them and are trained to squeeze water from a rock.

Despite recent crackdowns, telefunding is booming because of the growth in the number of charities as a whole. Particularly vulnerable are those on the dreaded "sucker list," people who've been taken at least once and are thus considered easy pickin's. Proving telefraud is difficult because there is little evidence and because few people file charges after being stung. Classic scams include associating oneself with the police ("badge" fraud) or with a religious organization ("collar" fraud). Experts recommend that to avoid being a scammee, you should request written information about the charity, not send cash or use a credit card, and not accept prizes (sorry, Ed). Look for a major backlash against

anyone soliciting money over the phone as Americans try to regain a sense of privacy and security in their own homes.

"We need to reconfirm your access code." "We want to make sure we have your correct credit card number." "We need your Social Security number for registration purposes." Beware, cyberfreaks, there are scammers lurking. You may think you are safe in your digital nest, but the Justice Department's Computer Crime Unit warns that where there's a Web, there's a black widow spider. Because the medium is so new and huge, there are no definitive figures on how many bank accounts have been emptied or credit cards maxed because of information falling into the wrong hands. John Barker, director of the National Fraud Information Center in Washington, guesstimates that more than $100 million a year is heisted online. The tried-and-true scams—quack health cures, phony credit repair, get-rich-quick opportunities—flourish on the Internet. A whopping 95 percent of participants in pyramids (where you buy into chain-letter instant bonanzas for an investment of $250 to your life savings) lose money. Fraudulent betting pools and online casinos are working out of hideouts in Bombay, Hong Kong, and the former U.S.S.R. Like telethieves, catching and prosecuting Net bandits is almost impossible because they just pack up and move to other sites under new names. Caveat Net surfer!

iconogasm: cultural climax, marketing opportunity

Help consumers protect themselves by arming them with anti-scam strategies and techniques.

Future

With the guidance of emerging technologies Mike Davis envisioned in *Spin* magazine, we're about to embark on a new era in shielding ourselves from harm. In Davis' vision, today's security systems will look like toy handcuffs compared to what lies ahead in crime prevention. Biometric recognition systems will become the stuff of everyday life, with retinal scanners, hand and voice keys, finger mappers, and thermal face imagery used to distinguish the good guys from the bad guys. Home security will borrow from military surveillance technology, with electronic guardian angels (the AAA of security) on alert should anything go bump in the night. Micropowered impulse radar systems and infrared lenses for night vision will detect that prowler in the bushes before you can say "home alone." Brace yourself for scanscaping, the twenty-four-hour surveillance of public places, something already common in the U.K.

The workplace is another frontier for hypersecurity in the future. A wake-up call for the workplace is about to sound as thousands of 'round-the-clock businesses call for the installation of alertness-detection devices that electronically monitor sleepyheads in truck cabs, cockpits, nuclear plants, and all-night eateries. Shut-eye alert systems will monitor baby blues with heavy lids so that when the *zzzzzzs* start, so will the cool-air systems, brighter lights, and louder Muzak. Only the bright-eyed and bushy-tailed will survive the future workplace, a twenty-first century Darwin might muse. This is life imitating smart, confirming Drexel University futurist Arthur Shostak's prediction that "the only jobs that will be good jobs in the 21st century will be ones that smart machines cannot perform."

iconogasm: cultural climax, marketing opportunity

Poke Big Brother in his unblinking eye and reclaim the individual's right to privacy.

sign #36:  detox

A pox on toxins, say the *vox populi*. We're seeing a broad interest in eliminating toxins and poisons wherever possible, to *detox* our bodies from unnatural substances. *Detox* is being spurred by a rising sensitivity to real or imagined chemicals and pollutants. After ingesting bad stuff for decades, we are starting to feel sick from the cumulative effect. Like the first environmentalism movement of the 1970s, *detox* subscribes to the belief that naturalness is inherently healthier for us and the planet. Watch out as boomers, the first generation raised on artificial ingredients and colors, reject the wonders of science and get back to the garden.

Health and Beauty

Suspicious of that product made with ingredients spelled with twenty letters, four of them "x"? We are. Americans are increasingly choosing natural health and beauty products over those cooked up with a pipette and Bunsen burner in a lab that closely resembles your junior high science class. Homeopathic health-care products made of herbs and roots are spreading like kudzu. Botanical health and beauty aids like Aveda's Shampure and Purefume are the path toward herban renewal, a *gaian* recipe linking user to Earth. Even if they *are* made in a lab, we just don't want to know about it. Exfoliants and hydrators are other *detox* HBAs, taking the bad stuff out and putting the good stuff into skin. Spas and salons have emerged as professional *detox* centers, shrines for restoration and purification. Even agents once considered health protectors like PABA have been put on the toxicity list, replaced in sun lotions by more skin-friendly ingredients. We're also smelling a major antiperfume movement, as purists with their noses stuck in the air claim their space is being invaded by no-good Charlies.

Consumers are opting for natural cleaning products made with yummy sounding ingredients like fresh citrus and green apple. Is that drain cleaner or a spritzer? Clothing made of organic cotton or hemp is taking off as we think twice about exposing our tender skins to fabrics grown with pesticides, and reusable menstrual pads such as Glad Rags offer the same kind of all-natural alternative. Suspicious eyes are being cast on drycleaning as well, as chemical solvents cause bad karma for stuffed shirts. Those mercury dental fillings also have teeth chattering, perhaps a source of disease or (worse) radio signals from distant stations or planets. Woo-woo!

Toxins may in fact be at the root of an alarming biological phenomenon occurring in humans. According to two different studies, the amount of semen an average man ejaculates has decreased significantly over the last generation or two. In a recent Danish study (the people, not the pastries), scientists found that the quantity of sperm in a typical man's release in 1990 was only half of that in 1940. A recent French study confirmed the Danish findings and also found that today's sperm are like ninety-eight-pound weaklings compared to those of just twenty years ago. Holy zygotes, Robin! What's the cause of this precipitous decline in the number and health of our li'l swimmers? No one really knows, but chemical pollutants might be behind the gobbling up of our go-getter guppies. With nothing less than the fate of the human species at stake here, we think it's time the National Institutes of Health issued a seminal study!

iconogasm: cultural climax, marketing opportunity
Detox your brands to be viewed as the solution rather than the problem.

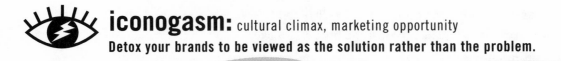

Water

Like the Earth, the human body is mostly water. H_2O is thus viewed as both a prime source of toxins and a means to *detox*. Water joes will tell you hydrotherapy is the way to purge those poisons shacking up in the internal ecosystem. Colonics are all the rage among the beautiful people, making their insides as fresh-scrubbed as their outsides. With toxins, gas, and feed matter removed through a colonic, the irrigatee supposedly gains greater energy and is less susceptible to acne and headaches. A visit to an enematorium will have you wondering if the last 2,000 years were just a rumor.

Ingesting purified water through the more standard route is considered by many to be the way to literally drown one's sorrows. The ocean-sized bottled-water market (2.8 billion gallons and $3.4 billion per year) is a telling commentary on how Americans feel about what is oozing out of their faucets. Toxic water has captured the attention of legislators, who have pushed drinking-water law reforms through Congress. Revisions to the Safe Drinking Water Act of 1974 were recently passed, reducing the amount of pathogens and pesticides allowed to be present. The next step is for notices of contaminants and their effects to be provided to water customers. Science geeks with pocket protectors have also gotten water religion, with the 1996 Discover Award given to National Laboratories's UV Water Purifier. Huzzah!

iconogasm: cultural climax, marketing opportunity
Remember Great-grandma's homily that cleanliness is next to godliness.

Air

Fear concerning airborne toxins appears to be in the wind these days. We've noticed a startling rise in the number of people wearing breathing masks in cities, disturbing anecdotal evidence that something may be atmospherically amok. The greater incidence of asthma, particularly among African-Americans and children, is real cause for alarm. "Sick building syndrome" has emerged as a real health threat, with the recycled air on airplanes of particular concern. Invisible indoor pollutants have claimed squatters' rights in our homes and offices, even after valiant efforts to seal ourselves off from

outdoor pollution. New carpeting, we now know, is grounds for major headaches and breathing ailments, as are some cleaning products and paints. Dust and fabrics treated with formaldehyde keep us sneezin' and wheezin', while that innocent-looking photocopier is a living, breathing toxic fume waiting to happen. My atmosphere-controlled place or yours?

iconogasm: cultural climax, marketing opportunity
Feature *detox* capabilities as a broad-based, compelling position across product categories.

Home

That money pit you call your home may also be about as safe as camping out in Chernobyl. Visit your local Home Depot or Menard's to find a plethora of kits designed to *detox* the air and water from houses, or consider the variety of professional services available to exorcise more serious toxic demons. Radon tests tell you if Mother Nature wants you to look elsewhere for digs, while carbon monoxide tests reveal if something wicked this way comes. High-tech air purifiers are gaining as much acceptance as well-entrenched water purifiers, now used not only for drinking but for bathing and laundry as well.

If your house was built, say, before the Beatles were on Ed Sullivan, asbestos insulation may be yet another cause of home toxicity. Asbestosbusters, however, are just a phone call away, one of a growing number of services specializing in what could be considered *fear marketing*. Be ready to fork out $10,000 or more to de-asbestos your house, however, or $7,500 and up to strip the lead-based paint off. Peace of mind don't come cheap, ya know.

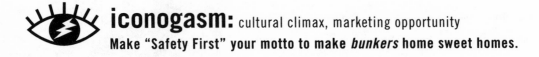

iconogasm: cultural climax, marketing opportunity
Make "Safety First" your motto to make *bunkers* home sweet homes.

Food

A larger percentage of the grocery aisle is being *detoxed* as shoppers look for 100-percent-natural foods. Higher risk groups—children, pregnant women,

HIV+s, and seniors—are justifiably careful about what they put into their bodies. Naturally raised meats are growing in popularity as consumers worry that that bovine may be hormone happy. Similarly, fish caught from unpolluted waters is increasingly the order of the day since that flounder might have had a close encounter of the sewage kind. Government officials in Great Lakes states, in fact, suggest fisherfolk troll elsewhere if trout is on the menu.

Organic foods have become popular, no longer limited to those who attended Woodstock. Organic alternatives in the produce and dairy sections are proliferating as more shoppers feel the extra cost is warranted. Kosher foods have gone mainstream, seen as cleaner and thus healthier than nonkosher foods. You don't have to be Jewish to like toxin-free rye bread!

iconogasm: cultural climax, marketing opportunity
Preempt concerns about food safety through *detox* positionings.

Technology

Technology is catching up to consumers' interests in living as toxin-free as possible. Why clean the pool with chlorine when a solar-powered water purifier does just as well? While you're at it, forget those nasty laundry detergents. Antibacterial laundry disks reduce water's molecular clusters and ionize oxygen to wipe dirt and microbes clean.

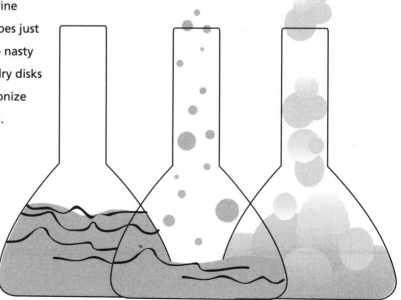

Life Sciences, Inc., a St. Petersburg biotechnology firm, is marketing the EnviroScreen, a higher-than-high-tech water analyzer. The EnviroScreen detects and measures more than 100 organic and inorganic compounds that may very well be floating in the nation's water supply. Metals and salts like fluoride, chlorine, silver, and iodine are increasingly present in reservoirs and streams, slowly turning our bodies into modern-day Tin Men. The EnviroScreen is designed for use by food processors and other manufacturers who pour water straight from the tap into their products. At $35,000 to $50,000 a pop, the EnviroScreen is not quite ready for home use yet, but the device represents an important breakthrough in keeping bacterial ninjas out of food and health and beauty aids.

In another strain of *detoxicating* rhythms, "supercriticals" are back by critical acclaim. Supercriticals are the queens of clean, all-natural super-cleansing technologies that have been around in some form or another for a century. Tougher standards for air and water quality, plus a public consumed with *detox*, however, have made the process more popular than ever.

General Foods is one company to use the technology, nixing its old decaffeinator methylene chloride (a possible carcinogen) in favor of a supercritical scrub-a-dub-dub bean clean for Sanka. The result is more taste with fewer health risks. NutraSweet's Eggcellent takes the low-calorie cake for using a supercritical process to strip dehydrated eggs of 74 percent of their fat and 90 percent of their cholesterol, literally whipping "lite" products from mayonnaise to waffles into a frenzy. The food industry is just one of many to use supercriticals, with drug czars and oil barons also using the process. Anyway you shake 'n' bake it, it's great health news for consumers interested in squeaky-clean products.

iconogasm: cultural climax, marketing opportunity
Look for "superclean" technologies to help us win our superdirty war.

sign #37:  germonella

The growing awareness of and concern about invisible culture is not limited to toxins and pollutants. There's a whole other world out there that we can't see, and it's populated with bacteria, viruses, and germs while we can't say that these parasites are living life large, they are living in and on our own bodies. While some micro-organisms wear white hats and are even vital for our survival, others are hostile and make us sick just because they can. Many of your itsy-bitsy lifeforms are wilier than coyotes, outsmarting Ph.D.s with their resiliency and persistently bad manners. We are just beginning to realize the threat the Lilliputian universe poses, with an underlying fear that *germonella* will evolve into the twenty-first century version of the Black Death.

Society

Not missing a beat, of course, the media is all over *germonella* like white on rice. News of a necrotizing fasciitis (flesh-eating virus) is sure to sell magazines and newspapers, because readers will think their leg might be the next course on the microscopic menu. Ebola is alarming for its gruesomeness as well as for the speed and ease with which it can travel. Mad Cow Disease has, as far as can be proven, harmed no one (except the unlucky cows and the British beef industry) but caused widespread panic among carnivori the world over. Popular culture has seized the *germonella* day, catering to our fascination

X

with an apocalypse of teeny-weeny proportions. Books and movies such as *The Hot Zone*, *Outbreak*, and *The Coming Plague* reflect our fear that small ones may be the Big One. With the Cold War over, nuclear weapons are out, and germ warfare is in as the ultimate killing machine in movies like *The Rock*. The belief that the Iraqis may have used germ warfare in the Gulf War makes the threat of *germonella* that much more real and ominous.

Unfortunately, *germonella* is not limited to a few scattered cases of bad-tempered viruses or the stuff of novelists' and screenwriters' imaginations. Incidences of food poisonings caused by salmonella and Legionnaire's disease caused by airborne viruses are on the rise. The mysterious Hanta virus resulted in some deaths, and even tuberculosis and cholera are showing signs of a comeback of Travolta proportion. After E. coli was found in some hamburgers, we all were a bit surprised to learn that meat and chicken are only visually inspected and that there's a medium-rare chance of that Special Yummy Burger being an undercooked, ticking timebomb. AIDS, of course, has raised everyone's attention to the clear and present danger of viruses. The incredible number and variety of "lower" forms of life that are constantly among us—molds, mildews, yeasts, and such—make life miserable for the allergy-inclined. If you knew what was going on in your pillows and sheets, you'd never get another good night's sleep. That innocent looking air conditioner? That box o' trouble is a breeding ground for microscopic winged monkeys. Perhaps scariest of all is the ability of the small world to mutate and laugh scornfully in the general direction of antibiotics. *¡Ay, caramba!*

iconogasm: cultural climax, marketing opportunity
Consider how your company can assume a more important role in a world obsessed with germs.

Products

Fortunately, some marketers are helping us get microcritters before they get us. 3M's O-Cel-O sponge is a wonder in cellulose, loaded up with virus-fighting elements. One wipe and your kitchen counter is free from the teeming multitudes remaining from that chicken-Kiev-to-be. Brillo cleaning pads are available with a "microbe shield," and Keri's antibacterial lotion kills germs while it softens! First Brands offers two cat litters, Scoop Away and Johnny Cat, with germ fighters to keep kitty's quarters minty fresh. It's no longer enough for a water purifier to purify water. The Fontana Germicidal-UV model uses a bacteria/virus-killing UV lamp to eliminate microorganisms like cryptosporidium cysts and other unpronounceable minutiae. Playskool recently launched a line of playthings made with Microban, an organic substance that makes infectious bacteria such as salmonella, E. coli, and strep run home crying. Microban is also used in carpets, toothbrushes, mattress covers, socks, cutting boards, Teva sandals, and other products used in hospitals and dental offices.

iconogasm: cultural climax, marketing opportunity
Position appropriate products around their abilities to kill germs on contact.

Hospitals

If the hospital is your only lifeline, research warns us to get in and out as quickly as possible. More than 2 million sickies enter U.S. hospitals each year only to get sick with some other sickness that they weren't sick with in the first place. Huh? At least one in twenty patients goes in to have an appendix yanked and gets pneumonia. Similarly, if the heart bypass doesn't get you, the hepatitis will. Wee ones and geezers are most susceptible to hospital-acquired infections. Uncle Sam reports 80,000 folks each year check in only to check out *permanently* from bugs they picked up while getting well.

Hospitals have always been full-fledged germ incubators because of patients' sicknesses, but infectious-disease experts are now pointing their latexed fingers at infected equipment—breathing tubes, IV needles, catheters— and nurses and docs with dirty digits! Lowell Levin, a professor of public health at the Yale School of Medicine, tells it like it really is: "Doctors and nurses... [are] like bumblebees, going from one flower to another, pollinating." Ouch. The sting comes with lost life and (for all you capitalists) an added $4.5 billion to the U.S. health-care bill.

Pneumonia, the big killer (30,000 people die yearly), adds about a week to a patient's stay and $5,700 to the bottom line. Most critical is the lack of sterile care, causing, according to epidemiologist Dr. Walter Heirhotzer, "a probable modern plague" at your local hot zone hospital. Ironically, medical technology is light years ahead of where it was in the 1970s, but patients are getting sicker. Expect a full-steam-clean-ahead push for hospitals, rest homes, and clinics to be accountable for their microscopic actions.

iconogasm: cultural climax, marketing opportunity

Develop prescription-serious germ fighters to put the health back in health care.

Future

The source for all things cyber, *Wired* magazine presents a scenario for the future that should send chills through our social spine. Imagine the next generation as the plague years, with the "Mao Flu" claiming the lives of 4.1 billion people (75 percent of the world's population of 5.5 billion). The hypothetical viral mutation kills one's immune system with amazing quickness and 99.8 percent efficiency, like "HIV on speed." Every exhaled breath takes on the power of nerve gas, giving rise to "sterile communities" costing millions of dollars to enter. Less well-off urbanites flee to the countryside, reducing the chances of coming face-to-face with someone already infected. Health passports called "Hygiene Cards" are required to travel, making air travel a nightmare of paperwork, medical releases, and quarantines.

In place of nations, "Hygienic Alliances" have formed, and old people are nowhere to be found. The textile industry has flourished by marketing virus-fighting clothing, as has McDonalds by introducing the immensely popular McCure Meal. *Wired*'s scenario is a lightning rod to cool down the hot zone before it becomes a reality.

iconogasm: cultural climax, marketing opportunity

Be the first one on your block to breed antiviral health and beauty, household, and wearable products.

chapter 10: technology

Every day the ghost in the machine becomes a little more real. A[s]
machines get bigger, better, and smarter, they're becoming inextricab[ly]
linked to our own course of evolution. More dimensions of everyday li[fe]
are being encoded into zeros and ones, leaving fewer aspects of work o[r]
play free of information technology. The once nonnegotiable line[s]
between reality and the imagination are even up for grabs as virtual li[fe]
rocks the physical laws of nature. Get ready for a trip of Wonderlan[d]
proportions as we crawl farther into the technological rabbit hole.

sign #38:  torquing

Despite rumors to the contrary, America's love affair with size and power is still sizzling. Would a country that invented the Cadillac, the 22-ounce steak, and Sam's Club have anything else? Technology is leading to a new generation of bigger and better products, reaffirming our lust for heft and, occasionally, excess. We call this type of technology *torquing*, the desire for high power and performance without compromising style or comfort. *Torquing* suggests, in fact, that power *is* style, and style is power, leading to products that allow you to fully engage in life. Driving the *torquing* trend is a passionate pursuit for bragging rights and one-upsmanship, to have the biggest or best you-name-it on the block. *Torquing* represents a backlash against aspects of 1990s asceticism and the *unplugged* trend, which say (silly us) that less is somehow more. As we plunge over the white cliffs of the next century, more technology will still be more as technology fulfills its manifest destiny.

Sports

Knees a little wobbly looking down that icy 45-degree descent? Skiiers and golfers with a case of the yips are finding newfound confidence in oversized equipment. Big Kahuna skis and Big Bertha golf clubs offer vivid proof that size definitely matters when it comes to athletic performance, particularly for older enthusiasts. Titanium has displaced graphite as the *torqued* material *du jour,* the Titanium Bubble the hot golf club on the PGA tour. Professional baseball players are slugging it out with the Carolina Club, a wood bat made from a naturally *torqued* variety of ash. Even young whippersnappers are living life large with four- and five-foot skateboards, able to leap tall railings in a single bound. In-line skates are *torquing* up with "cyber bindings" and the revolutionary concept of brakes.

iconogasm: cultural climax, marketing opportunity
Think big when designing and developing new products.

Fashion

Next time you're standing hip deep in the Willamette River trying to reel in a few lunkers, you may wish you ordered those Neoprene waders you saw advertised in *Field & Stream*. Lightweight, insulated materials like Neoprene, Kevlar, and Polartec are *torqued* fabrics, designed to keep wearers snug as a bug in a Gore-Tex rug. More than that, however, clothing made from these types of materials tells others on the slopes, in the streams, and down the streets that the wearer is serious about his or her sport. Even ski and diving goggles have been *torqued*, now available in prescription lenses so you don't mistake a tree for a slalom post or a shark for a dolphin.

Nike, of course, is in a constant state of *torque* evolution, progressively raising the technological level of its shoes. The company has masterfully juggled a dual "top-down" and "bottom-up" strategy by positioning its *torqued* shoes as the preferred brand of both professional athletes and inner-city basketball players. The brave new world of body-enhancing apparel is *torquing* cotton in ways Eli Whitney never dreamed, turning ordinary underwear into butt-shaping wonders and breast-enhancing miracles. As the first line of defense against the elements, clothing will continue to express style as performance and performance as style through *torqued* design, materials, and construction.

iconogasm: cultural climax, marketing opportunity
***Torque*-up that frock to allow consumers to wear power on their sleeves.**

Shields

Consumers' perceived need for shields against a hostile environment is the perfect justification for *torqued* products. The increasing popularity of bullet-proof clothing suggests we haven't come too far from our medieval, dragon-slaying ancestors, a sad commentary on our gun-happy society.

A more subtle form of cultural armor is the hiking boot, a protective device guarding tender feet against hostile ground forces. That *torqued* bootie designed to get up and down the Himalayas is ideally suited, we think to ourselves, for the urban jungle that is the American city. All around us are symbols of our underlying fear that we are exposed to great physical and emotional harm. We carry Swiss Army knives and wear Swiss Army watches as inconspicuous weapons in our war against an unknown, unseen enemy. We command four-wheel-drive vehicles loaded with every safety feature imaginable as psychological insurance against potential tragedy. The ultimate symbol of *torquing* today is the Hummer, a street-legal tank offering unsurpassed confidence when driving those few blocks to the convenience store. Why not, when we feel we really are in a war zone?

iconogasm: cultural climax, marketing opportunity
Position *torqued*-up products in safety terms.

Communications

How do you make an old dog do new tricks? You *torque* it up. Machines a half- or full-century old have been made new with improvements to their performance, the addition of new features, or redefinitions of their purposes. The telephone, a vestige of nineteenth century technology, has been *torqued* into the twenty-first century through features like caller ID, call waiting, and call forwarding. Through cellular technology, the telephone is morphing into a personal monitoring device, with car phones already used by many just for security purposes. The radio, using essentially the same technology as the original models of the 1920s, has been *torqued* into a $350 Bose clock radio. The television has remained a state-of-the-art machine through constant innovation. The home theater hooked up to a satellite dish is nothing more than a *torqued*-up version of the black-and-white, vacuum-tubed, rabbit-eared set of 1946. The laptop computer is an example of classic *torquing*, pure power packaged in a sleek, ergonomic box. Expect new twists on the *ménage à trois* as the television, telephone, and computer get collectively *torqued*.

iconogasm: cultural climax, marketing opportunity
Resurrect mature products from their technological graves through *torquing*.

Smart and Smarter

After centuries of dreaming about it, we're on the cusp of developing machines that can actually think. "Smart," or "thinking," machines are the ultimate evolution of technology, an extreme form of *torquing* that combines the human quality of intuition and the machine's analytical skills. The car, for example, is about to be *torqued* through a variety of smart-car safety devices. Drunk-driver detectors will deny over-the-limits ignition if they smell alcohol, cabin-filtration systems will wash that smog right out of our (cars') hair, and night-vision windows will let us see through the dark.

We may be hearing "Look, Ma, no hands!" from open car windows if the National Automated Highway System Consortium has its way. The NAHSC is in the midst of developing an intelligent highway, able to control the speeds and directions of cars. Envision cars zipping along bumper-to-bumper, steered, braked, and powered by computers. This literal information superhighway would be built along only the busiest routes of a large city that has major automobile congestion. Sure sounds Jetsonian, but a prototype is already in the works. Chrysler has used a driverless roadway at its Chelsea, Michigan, proving ground to test new models, which are installed with emergency braking systems should the cars decide to jump ship. With light-rail a distant dream for budget-crunched cities and Americans' love of the automobile a fixture of our national culture, smart cars and highways may turn out to be the best compromise between private and mass transit.

iconogasm: cultural climax, marketing opportunity

Get smart and *torque*-up products with brains instead of brawn.

Foods and Beverages

Feeling a little piqued? *Torque* yourself up with some high-powered foods, beverages, and nutritional supplements. Americans are gobbling up engineered edibles for extra energy in our take-no-prisoners world, at least those who believe voluntary simplicity is some sort of alien plot. Supplements like Up Your Gas (no kidding), Ultra Energy Plus, and Energia are designed for people who want to live life across the red line. Even big names are endorsing *torqued* nutritive supplements, with Scottie Pippin dribbling for Ginsana and Arnold Palmer sticking his putter out for Green Foods. DHEA and melatonin are the latest "foodaceuticals," a mixed marriage between food and pharmaceuticals. As New Age sleep aids and fountains of youth, these wonder nondrugs promise not only a good night's rest but more nights *to* rest.

Balance bars and Powerbars are ready to pump you up, along with other supercharged and naturally prepared foods making the rounds. For maximum *torque*, let a Vita worm slide down your throat. These slippery invertebrates plucked from the African jungle are chock full of nutritive value, kind of like nature's One-A-Day vitamin. Wash it down with any number of high-octane beverages like Ultra Fuel, Kick, Powerade, or Water Joe. *Torqued* beverages targeted to Generations X and Y include Skeleteens, Fukola,

FOOD BAR

loO lbs   loO lbs

Brothers of Invention, and Orbitz. These funky, fruity drinks come in scary colors and taste just like they look. Seniors eating less are drinking liquid *torque* with brands like Boost, Ensure, and Resource to get their daily allowances of vitamins and minerals. Even the fast-food industry has *torqued*-up their menus through pure size, offering burgers bigger than your head and 64-ounce drinks. We can hear it now: "Six all-beef patties on a sesame-seed bun . . ."

iconogasm: cultural climax, marketing opportunity
Cook up high-powered foods and beverages for consumers looking for a jolt or boost.

Personal Care

Torquing is being used to help us look and feel better. A walk through a Sharper Image store or Brookstone catalog is a stroll through *torquing* personal-care heaven, with every product imaginable available to scrub, scrape, or scratch your body. Scrub mitts and loofas are *torqued*-up washcloths, heavy-duty showeralia that say you don't take your largest organ for granted. Cosmetics too are being *torqued* to prescription-serious levels as aging boomers fight wrinkle mania with ceramides, liposomes, and nanospheres.

How far can *torquing* go in personal care? Retailers might offer a computer diagnosis to reveal an individual's complete skin chemistry, including its elasticity and thickness, pore size, burn predisposition, and allergies. Why not a room air analyzer to make sure the aromatherapy one chooses *feng shui*s with the rest of the room? Such technotherapies can be agents for positive health and/or beauty change, the next logical level in personal care.

iconogasm: cultural climax, marketing opportunity
Torque-up personal-care products to keep the Me generation looking and feeling good.

sign #39:  technomorphing

History has starkly illustrated the direct link between our tools and machines and the society we construct. Just as the Bronze Age, the Renaissance, the Industrial Revolution, and the Space Age launched people into radically different trajectories, today's Cyber Age promises to alter the very building blocks of society—our beliefs, values, and actions. *Technomorphing* describes the evolutionary effects that warp-speed technology is having on our lives. The love-hate relationship we have with technology is only going to intensify as we go farther and farther into deep cyberspace. The winners of the Information Revolution will be those able to translate technology into human terms, to *technomorph* cyberbells and cyberwhistles into truly relevant, applicable, and meaningful terms.

Communications

Online culture is, more than anything else, about satisfying our fundamental needs for dialogue, discourse, and debate. The old Chatterbox Cafe down on Main Street may have closed its doors, but new cafés are opening up every day down on Modem Avenue. Websites, homepages, chat groups, and virtual jam sessions are our new tables and booths, where we're snarfing down heaping platters of all things dot.com. As online technology elopes with electronica like the television, telephone, and video camera, one can dial up the Internet through the Sony Trinitron, call someone over the Net, and see who you're talking to via CU-SeeMe videoconferencing. Online culture is singularly remarkable for its ability to bring together people who otherwise would never meet.

The very concept of language is in flux as writing gets a faceful of *technomorphing*. As e-mail eclipses paper correspondence across Corporate America to save cost and time, E-speak is the latest branch to bloom on the English tree. A new form of hieroglyphics called emoticons, or "smileys," is offering America's millions of e-mailers shorthand when speed is of the essence and voice tone or facial expression is impossible. Just tilt your head to the left to read :-(as "I'm sad" or :-))) as "I'm overweight." All caps mean ANGER or SHOUTING, and **asterisks** imply emphasis. E-mail symbolism and its chatty, often rambling writing style are changing the very nature of how we communicate at the office and, in turn, making corporate culture less formal. Old-school correspondence cops are naturally having fits, griping about the need for a beginning, middle, and end, or at least a point. E-mail also raises privacy and ethical issues that Big Brother technology always brings, especially for workers who wonder how often their bosses monitor their "work flow" by rubbernecking via e-mail.

Read any good screens lately? With more and more literature available online and on CD-ROM, there's a revolution going on in publishing not seen since Gutenberg cranked up his press. The more creative cyberscribes are invading the Internet with a whole newsy generation of electronic zines. Zines are self-published micromagazines, often with an irreverent or iconoclastic message or tone. Check out *Factsheet Five* to get a sense of the swirling maelstrom of zine culture. Abandoning the printed magazine medium for the digitized masthead only makes dollars and sense, given the high costs of printing and postage (more than one paper zine publisher has been seen fleeing Kinko's at 3:00 A.M., five-fingered copies in tow). The 50,000+ electronic zines are often birthed by college graduates making their creative best out of dead-end careers. They contraband a megabyte of their bosses' servers and digitize their latest musings on politics, pets, sex, libertarianism, or rock 'n' roll. These zines and their online fan clubs are authentic cyberhives in our *technomorphing* garden.

Digerati know how to talk the cyber talk and walk the cyber walk. In *Digerati: Encounters With the Cyber Elite*, intellectual hunter/trapper John Brockman interviews the field generals of the communications revolution— Microsoft's Bill Gates, Netscape's Jim Clark, Steve Case of America Online, Broderbund Software cofounder Doug Carlston, *Wired* publisher Jane Metcalfe, and a whole heady herd more. Brockman lets each of the techno top brass spew and then lets his or her colleagues critique. It's sorta like Gertrude Stein meets Max Headroom—a browser is a browser is a browser. Future visions bandied about include cyber communities, content development, online civil rights, digital commerce, and computer psychotherapy.

iconogasm: cultural climax, marketing opportunity
Read the writing on the cyber wall and gain fluency in the communications medium of the next millennium.

Entertainment

Look up *technomorphing* in the dictionary, and you might see a picture of Microsoft headquarters. Those wacky wizards at Microsoft Research are funneling more than $2 billion a year into state-of-the-art computer research and development. Unlike the Bell Labs of old (now Lucent Technologies), the push is to *technomorph* technology into real-life products. What Microsofties are working on amps the mind—talking Windows, voice fonts (recorded vocal patterns of, say, Bart Simpson, Madonna, or Maya Angelou), artificial intelligence, and 3-D graphics hardware, to name just a few.

With a technological intellect and vision bigger than Jabba the Hutt's butt, George Lucas is a *technomorphing* force. Lucas was and remains the leader of digital effects in film. His empire includes Lucasfilm (home of Industrial Light & Magic visual effects), Skywalker Sound, a videogaming company, and licensing divisions. Today, practically all movies have digitally recorded sound, while five years back only 10 percent used it. If Lucas has his way, much moviemaking in the future will be a computer craft, with scenes kneaded together from a library of digitized images. How will all this impact the arts of acting and cinematography? We honestly don't know, but we do know that $3 billion+ worth of trash 'n' trinkets has been sold since the 1977 debut of *Star Wars*. The release of Lucas's *Tyrant's Test* prequel will be of epic *technomorphing* proportions.

iconogasm: cultural climax, marketing opportunity

Learn from the *technomorphing* masters that technology is only as good as its applications, which can be eye-popping.

Travel

Can't afford to spring for a chocolate croissant 'n' latte at a sidewalk café on the Champs Elysee? Take a virtual vacation via Bonjour Paris, America Online's French tickler (keyword: Bonjour) for the baguette-challenged. The City of Lights site offers up a chance to practice your *langue français*, cybercruise the nightlife, feast on digital crèpes, visit eateries, and hear a collection of testimonials on the nuances of Parisian life.

Likewise, if you don't have the time or money to visit Jerusalem's Western Wall, your savior has arrived. Virtual Jerusalem, an Israeli company, has established a site on the World Wide Web where one can send a prayer over the Internet. After you e-mail your prayer to the site, Virtual Jerusalem will

print it out and stuff it in one of the wall's cracks. Best of all, this won't cost you a shekel. *Mazel tov!* These are but two specks in cyberspace's Cyclops-sized eye. To help you navigate this wanderer's wonderland, sites such as the Travelers Resource Center offer electronic roadmaps to a variety of travel-related information sources. Created by O'Reilly & Associates, publishers of techie magazines, TRC is a bundle of bulletin boards for the itinerant Internetter. Visit TRC's Traveler's Marketplace for a listing of travel publications for sale, or The Hitchhiker's Guide to New Zealand for everything you wanted to know about kiwi. So you don't get caught in the middle of a banana or papaya republic coup, dial up TRC's World Travel Watch for the latest on political upheavals and assassination attempts. The juiciest part of TRC is the digital guides to fifty or so countries compiled by natives who know the local scene and scenery best. Learn how to ask "Where's the bathroom?" in Latvian, or where to get a cup of decaf in Greenland. The TRC is formatted with full audio, video, color maps, and graphics for the hardware-endowed. Cyberspace or bust!

iconogasm: cultural climax, marketing opportunity
Tamper with the physical laws of space by *technomorphing* travel.

Work

As the world jumps from the Industrial Age to the Information Age in what is, from a historical sense, a cultural nanosecond, the very concept of work is morphing at Warp 13 speed. The Information Revolution is coursing through the veins of corpus corporatus, having as significant an effect on the American workplace as did Ford's assembly line. The principal currency of the new workplace—what one knows and what one does with that knowledge—is effectively splitting the nation's workforce into two social classes. A professional class ("information brokers") holds the skeleton key to the executive bathroom, while a service class is increasingly relegated to the broom closet. As the ability to manipulate data emerges as the new definition of skilled labor, blue-collar workers, who represented the heart of the postwar middle class, are fast becoming an endangered species. With polarization of the workplace accelerating into the next millennium, the parachutes most likely to open will be those somehow connected to managing information.

Technology and the workplace have, of course, always been kissin' cousins, but never before have they been as intimately attached and as symbiotically related. Although technology is largely responsible for breaking America's labor pool into two halves, the Information Revolution is also having a socialistic effect on the workplace by giving small-business Davids better chances at kicking the shins of corporate Goliaths. Universal access to cheaper, better hardware and software has made computer technology the great equalizer, leveling the competitive playing field in many industries. As speed and agility in the marketplace displace sheer clout as the more effective business strategies, more and more *technomorphing* mice are making their competitive elephants dance. In fact, faster, more accurate information (the key to guerrilla marketing tactics) has made "playing it safe" the riskiest way to run a business. Technology is also flattening the traditional hierarchical structure of most organizations as CEOs down to mail clerks all become masters of their digital domains.

iconogasm: cultural climax, marketing opportunity
Make sure you're on the right side of the guillotine as the Information Revolution spills out into the streets and technology gives power to the people.

Telecommuting

Are you reading this at home, less than dressed up with nowhere to go? Link Resources estimates that more than one-third of all workers are clicking the heels of their ruby-red house slippers and working at least part of the time out of their homes. That's about twice as many homeboys and homegirls as there were in 1988, just when Corporate America's Hindenburg-sized balloon started to leak. Downsizing and technology are driving the homeward-bound train, fueled by our emergence as a freelance nation working from virtual offices.

Although just about all you need to be in business is a phone jack and a power-surge protector, the $800 million home-office furniture market is hotter than a pistol as it tries to keep up with consumer demand. Business equipment and furniture manufacturers are blurring the lines between where the home ends and the office begins, while interior designers are faced with the unenviable task of matching that Dali print with the laser printer. With PC manufacturers making computers more home-friendly in color and design, can a joint venture between Apple and GE be far behind? An ice maker in the belly of a Mac may be just the thing for all those beverage-loving hackers out there.

iconogasm: cultural climax, marketing opportunity
Develop products and services for homies' life-as-work and work-as-life lifestyle.

Grackers

If you think cyberspace is currently inhabited only by twentysomething geeks, think again. The ranks whom we call "grackers" (gray hackers) continue to grow, with more and more of those ages sixty-five or older using PCs at home. Computer clubs at retirement communities are becoming more popular than eating dinner at 4:00 to save a buck and a half.

Thousands of grackers at Sun City West, an Arizona retirement community, belong to its computer club and attend classes such as "How to Buy a Computer." Compaq and other PC marketers have targeted grackers, aware that this is the first generation of retirees who used computers at work. With their PCs, seniors keep track of personal finances, write wills, trace family genealogies, create greeting cards, publish newsletters, and download photos of their grandkids. Get grackin'!

iconogasm: cultural climax, marketing opportunity
Start waxing your board now to surf the next, much bigger wave of grackers.

Technobacklash

Thought life in our digitized, hypertextualized age was made up purely of zeroes and ones? Hardly. There's a whiplash backlash against cyberculture, a longing to embrace visceral sensuality wherever we can. Simple pleasures like cigars, martinis, espresso, and bread have become so popular in part because they balance out the often harsh, impersonal nature of technology. As safe, affordable, hedonistic indulgences, the nice vices of our times complement the logic and rationalism associated with machines. Poetry readings, gardening, and mountain climbing are examples of our "native intelligence" making its voice heard in the Information Age. Marketers who creatively package products which help keep the left and right sides of our brains in balance will capitalize on the technobacklash.

Marthamania reigns because it brings aesthetics to the how-to table. Spas and salons are shrines of wellness because they let us celebrate the wonders of the human body before we head back to our computer screens. Aromatherapy taps into our desire for olfactory stimuli in an age when the sense of smell is no longer critical for survival. As we head into the genesis of the third millennium, there will be a Garden of Eden–sized need for pleasures appealing to body, heart, and soul.

iconogasm: cultural climax, marketing opportunity
Work both sides of the *technomorphing* fence as people try to balance the push of technology with the pull of nature.

sign #40: virtuality

Virtuality represents the emergence of alternative and interactive realities through technology. The very concept of reality, in fact, is changing as cyber technology blurs the lines of what is real and what is imagined. *Virtuality* allows people the opportunity to experience different environments without physically moving, breaking down the constraints of time and space. Although *virtuality* is primarily used for entertainment purposes, our best and brightest are finding ways to apply alternative realities for constructive and therapeutic purposes. In the new millennium, *virtuality* will become as accepted as other once-revolutionary technologies such as the automobile, the television, and the electric fork. Well, okay, not the electric fork.

Virtual Travel

As we turn the century, we are segueing from an era of postmodernism to one of *virtuality*, where reality and imagination are blurred. *Virtuality* is the real-life stuff of Hollywood fantasy, a postreality world in which experiences occur only in the brain. If you're all dressed up and have nowhere to go, fret not. Just pull on your cybergloves, adjust those virtual-reality megashades, and melt away the constraints of time and space. Thanks to *virtuality*, you'll be squeezing every juicy experiential drop out of life, and all from the cozy comfort of your digitized chaise longue.

Why *go* to Mars when you can *think* you are on Mars? All sorts of virtual-travel experiences will be possible through a combination of technology and sensory stimuli. Soon we will be able to take virtual vacations as the sights, sounds, and smells of a particular place are made real. Go to Hawaii for your coffee break, picking your own Kona beans on the way. Flatlining, the state of near-death, will become a popular destination, with round-trip tickets the overwhelming choice.

The first generation of virtual travel is already hatching through "discovery vacations" at the Disney Institute in Orlando. Guests are encouraged to live out their fantasies (G-rated, please) through more than eighty hands-on interactive programs. Animate a cartoon! Create a topiary! Talk flicks with Siskel and Ebert! Or ask architect/furniture designer Frank Gehry how to carve a kitchen chair out of that pile of corrugated cardboard you've been meaning to recycle since the late-'70s. Courses run about $275 a day, about what you'd spend on snacks for the kids anyway. The potential of such online junkets borders on infinity.

iconogasm: cultural climax, marketing opportunity
Reality bites! Exploit consumers' desire to dwell in the imagined through virtual experiences.

Virtual Therapy

Once you've donned the glasses and gloves, it may be difficult for you to return to our temporal plane, where gravity is not negotiable. But when the real world is scarier than make-believe, technowizardry can come to the rescue. At the Kaiser-Permanente Medical Group in San Rafael, California, agoraphobics spell relief V-I-R-T-U-A-L R-E-A-L-I-T-Y.

Medical researchers are experimenting with curing a couchful of angst disorders by using the magic glasses. Scaredy cats terrified of walking the plank (or crossing the Golden Gate Bridge) wear VR headsets that lead them through a series of height-defying gymnastics aimed at conquering the freakout phobia. Thanks to this head-blazing therapy, patients are sweating less and taking the high road more often.

iconogasm: cultural climax, marketing opportunity
View *virtuality* as a New World way to solve Old World problems.

Mysting

As entertainment continues to become America's principal *raison d'etre*, get ready for Hollywood and Silicon Valley to dish up new ways to have out-of-body experiences all in your mind. *Mysting*—full immersion in virtual realities—will be the hippest form of recreation in the next few decades. Who needs Ticketmaster when mysting takes you right up onstage jammin' with Hank Williams, Jr., or fast-breaking with the Orlando Magic, or wheeling the Indy pace car? Climb the Himalayas to visit with the Dalai Lama, or address the masses at Vatican Square. In *virtuality*, what does the Pope have that you don't have (besides a really big hat)? Break bread with James Beard, or break into Fort Knox. Go fly a kite with Benjamin Franklin, or offer Monet a few pointers on those haystacks of his. The Cleavers' den is morphing into the family's optic-nerve center with trips, tournaments, and tantalizing adventures within a flick of an eyelid.

iconogasm: cultural climax, marketing opportunity
Play mystie for consumers interested in alternative universes.

The Virtual Future

Marketers are just beginning to fully appreciate the possibilities of *virtuality*. Car dealers are experimenting with virtual test drives, where consumers can take a new car for a spin without leaving the showroom. As technology allows us to alter perception, however, *virtuality* will be applied in an infinite number of ways toward the senses. Imagine Microsoft Looks, software designed to offer alternative-appearance scenarios. Offering consumers the opportunity to experience life in more interactive and entertaining ways is an especially prime opportunity to reach Generation Xers and Whyers. Create a virtual fantasy for someone who wants to feel like Gordon Gekko walking into a board room in *Wall Street* or like a leggy supermodel walking down a runway. Virtualizing your customer's cyberimage alongside someone of their choice (Warren Beatty, say?) is another sure way to move products off the shelves at warp speed.

In the future, *virtuality* will change the way we make decisions. Business and personal problem solving will be aided by virtual scenario planning—cyber what-ifs complete with outcome forecasts. Scenario planning for complex projects like architecture or interior design is already taking advantage of VR technology. Angsting over that early morning decision about whether to wear the acrylics or the woolies? Don't bite your fingernails; boot up Sockware.

iconogasm: cultural climax, marketing opportunity

Ask not what *virtuality* can do for you but what *virtuality* can do for consumers.

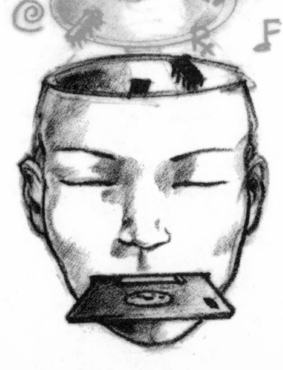

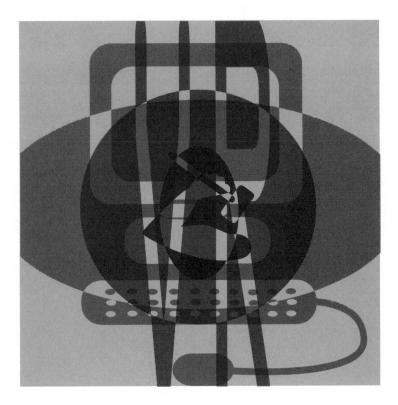

glossary

Altered States   The desire to experience alternative psychological states and turn fantasies into realities

Artisan   The return to hand-crafted, one-of-a-kind objects and activities that express personal style

Back to the Future   The use of history as an active resource; the recycling of the past, best expressed by "memory marketing"

Beehiving   The formation of tight-knit affinity groups bound together by some common interest

Biomorphing   The ability, desire, and technology to reshape our bodies in subtle or extreme ways

Boomeritis   Boomers' continued search for self-gratification within a context of responsibility and accountability

Bunkering   The trend that redefines the American home as a sanctuary from a hostile world

Carpe Diem   The quest for fun, passion, adventure, and guilt-free "experiences of the Now," counter to Christian theology of delayed gratification and sacrifice

Chi   Based in the Eastern concept of strength and harmony from within; maintains that power and control are a function of faith and trust in one's own abilities

Cultural Infidelity   Proactive interest in experiencing multiple cultures and new cultural hybrids grounded in popular and consumer culture

Detox   Broad interest in eliminating toxins and poisons wherever possible

Dollars and Sense   The trend crossbred of early-1990s frugality and 1980s luxury, which holds that scrimping and splurging are not mutually exclusive; signals a greater concern about long-term financial security as gaping holes emerge in traditional safety nets

Fingerprinting   Search for and articulation of one's unique identity; in consumption-based society, fingerprint is expressed through a person's "consumer portfolio" and collection of the individual's unique mix of *beehives*

Gaia   The symbiotic relationship between humans and the Earth, and the belief that the planet is a living, breathing, feeling organism

Germonella   The growing awareness of and concern about "invisible culture"—bacteria, viruses, and germs

Gray Matter   The unquenchable thirst for knowledge and learning as part of the self-actualization process

Healthwatch   Characterized by concerns about access to health care, broad embracing of alternative medicine as East meets West, and the continual search for miracle cures and therapies; fueled by boomers' desire to slow or stop the aging process

Joie de Vivre   Quest for pure, enduring joys of life rooted in sensuality, aesthetics, and earthly delights; driven by boomers maturing and Generation X *carpe diem*

Kid Quake   The seismic effects children are having on society

Merit Badges   The shift in values to collect experiences versus things; the recasting of social status from what one has to what one does

The New Family   The increasing fluidity of what constitutes a family, and the blurring of parents' and children's roles

The Other Side   The exploration of alternative attitudes toward death; driven by baby boomers confronting their parents' and their own mortality

Outer Limits   The growing fascination with unexplainable phenomena

Roadtripping   The trend toward meaningful, purposeful, experiential travel

Shields Up!   Protecting oneself and one's family from all forms of risks via a new breed of safety and security measures

Smart and Smarter   The development of smart or "thinking" products as the ultimate evolution of science and technology; reflects the mantra that information equals power

Soul Searching   The compelling hunt for genuineness, deep satisfaction, and meaning in life through relationships with self, other, and higher consciousness

Stealthing   Consumers' desire to fly underneath society's radar in order to beat the system

Synesthesia   Unprecedented interest in understanding and appreciating the senses; desire to maximize and blend sensory environments tied to a holistic paradigm of united mind/body

Tarzan   The physical and emotional craving for a time unspoiled by the spin-doctoring of civilization

Technomorphing   The effects of warp-speed technological change on our lives, and translation of such change into human terms

Themeparking   The encroachment of entertainment into all aspects of everyday life

Torquing   A new paradigm of technology in which performance is style and style is performance

Toto Too   The elevation of pets to animal companions as part of our quest for companionship and camaraderie

Unplugged   The movement to streamline life in an overly complex world; marked by a stripping away of pretense, hype, and marketingese in popular and consumer culture

Value Vertigo   The society-wide values breakdown experienced by Americans as a sense of dislocation and rootlessness

Vice Versing   The accommodation of "nice vice" and acceptance that hedonism in moderation is natural and even healthy

Virtuality   The technological blurring of reality and imagination; also breaks down constraints of time and space

We the People   The grassroots trend moving the focus of political power from national to community arena

Wisewoman   The focus on and value of older women's views of life and society, fueled by the movement of influential female boomers into their 50+ years

Zentrepreneurism   Fusion of personal vision and professional mission, typically with activism as instrumental part

resources: people, places, things

CHAPTER 1

Elderhostel
75 Federal Street
Boston, MA 02110
617-426-8056
617-426-8351 fax
www.elderhostel.org

Successories, Inc.
919 Springer Drive
Lombard, IL 60148
800-535-2773
800-932-9673 fax
www.successories.com

Ehama Institute
31440 Loma Pritea Way
Los Gatos, CA 95030
408-847-6448
408-454-9129
ehama1@aol.com
www.ehama.org

Excelsior-Henderson Motorcycle Manufacturing Company
607 West Travelers Trail
Burnsville, MN 55337
612-894-9229
612-894-9705 fax

Polaris Industries, Inc.
1225 Highway 169 North
Minneapolis, MN 55441
612-542-0500
612-542-0599 fax
www.polarisindustries.com

Jewish Home and Hospital Long-Term Health Care Program
120 West 106th Street
New York, NY 10025-3712
212-870-5075
212-870-5958 fax

House of Blues
8430 Sunset Boulevard
West Hollywood, CA 90069
213-848-5100
213-650-0237 fax

B.B. King Blues Clubs
143 Beale Street
Memphis, TN 38103
901-767-1310

The Derby
4500 Los Feliz Boulevard
Los Angeles, CA 90027-2006
213-663-8979

CHAPTER 2

ESPN X Games Headquarters
1845 Quivira Way
San Diego, CA 92109
619-523-7800

Regenix
8631 West Third Street, Suite 420E
Los Angeles, CA 90048
800-908-8885
310-358-8892 fax

**Dolly Parton Wigs
Beauty Trends**
P.O. Box 9323, Dept. 63021
Hialeah, FL 33014-9323
305-826-8283

Beverly Hills Institute for Facial & Body Sculpting
9001 Wilshire Boulevard
Suite 202
Beverly Hills, CA 90211
800-SCULPT-1

**The Sharper Image
Corporate Headquarters**
650 Davis Street
San Francisco, CA 94111
415-445-6000
www.sharperimage.com

Gauntlet International
2377 Market Street
San Francisco, CA 94114
415-431-3133
415-431-3170 fax
www.gauntlet.com

Smell and Taste Research Foundation
845 North Michigan Avenue
Suite 9090 West
Chicago, IL 60611
312-938-1047
312-649-0458 fax

Breadsmith
3510 North Oakland Avenue
Shorewood, WI 53211
414-962-1965
414-962-5888 fax
bread@franchise1.com

Paul Herb
Massage Therapist
3500 Grand Avenue South
Minneapolis, MN 55408
612-822-9333
612-822-1833 fax

Oxford Health Plans
800 Connecticut Avenue
Norwalk, CT 06856
800-889-7658
www.oxhp.com

Mayo Clinic
200 Southwest First Street
Rochester, MN 55905
507-284-2511
507-284-0161 fax
www.mayo.edu

Pathways
3115 Hennepin Avenue South
Minneapolis, MN 55408
612-822-9061
612-824-3841 fax
pathways@mtn.org

American Geriatrics Society
770 Lexington Avenue, Suite 300
New York, NY 10021
212-308-1414
212-832-8646 fax
info.amger@americangeriatrics.org
www.americangeriatrics.org

National Institutes of Health
9000 Rockville Pike
Bethesda, MD 20892
301-496-1766
www.nih.gov

University of Pennsylvania
Center for Bioethics
3401 Market, Suite 320
Philadelphia, PA 19104-3308
215-898-7136

CHAPTER 3

Upledger Institute
11211 Prosperity Farms Road
Suite D325
Palm Beach Gardens, FL 33410
800-233-5880
561-622-4771 fax

Marsha Sinetar
c/o Dell Publishing Group
1540 Broadway
New York, NY 10036-4094
212-354-6500
212-492-9698 fax

Norman Shealy, M.D.
c/o Stillpoint Publishing
P.O. Box 640
Walpole, NH 03608
603-756-9281
603-756-9282 fax

Promise Keepers
P.O. Box 103001
Denver, CO 80250-3001
800-888-7595
www.promisekeepers.org

Mendele
Yiddish Chat Group
listser@yalevm.ycc.yale.edu

Kabbalah Learning Centre
7088 Beracasa Way
Boca Raton, FL 33433
561-347-7095
561-361-3132 fax
www.icanect.net/kabbalah

The Living Vine
3001 West Irving Boulevard
Irving, TX 75061
972-986-1026

Old Friends Information Service
1 Camino Sobrante, #21
Orinda, CA 94563
800-841-7938
ofis@aol.com
www.oldfriendsinc.com

AARP
601 E Street NW
Washington, DC 20049
800-424-3410
202-434-6483 fax
www.aarp.org

AARP Widowed Persons Service
601 E Street NW
Washington, DC 20049
202-434-2260

Compassionate Friends
P.O. Box 3696
Oak Brook, IL 60522-3696
630-990-0010
630-990-0246 fax
TCF_National@prodigy.com
www.jjt.com/~tcf_national

Grief Recovery Institute Helpline
800-445-4808

National Self-Help Clearinghouse
25 West 43rd Street, Suite 620
New York, NY 10036
212-354-8525
212-642-1956 fax
www.selfhelpweb.org

Kelco Funeral Supply
2700 Freeway Boulevard
Minneapolis, MN 55430
612-560-4300

The Chalice of Repose Project
St. Patrick Hospital
554 West Broadway, Suite 436
Missoula, MT 59809
406-329-2810
406-329-5614 fax
www.saintpatrick.org

Missoula Urban
Demonstration Project
629 Phillips Street
Missoula, MT 59802
406-721-7513

CHAPTER 4

Jacob Leinenkugel
Brewing Company
1 Jefferson Avenue
Chippewa Falls, WI 54729
715-723-5558
715-723-0857 fax
www.leinie.com

Get Juiced
4515 North 16th Street, Suite 110
Phoenix, AZ 85016
602-241-1160

Surf City Squeeze
Corporate Headquarters
4521 Campus Drive, Suite 510
Irvine, CA 92612
714-856-0220
714-854-7596 fax
surfcity1@aol.com

American Birding Association
P.O. Box 6599
Colorado Springs, CO 80934-2470
719-578-9703
719-578-1480 fax
www.aba.org

Land Rover Driving School
1-800-362-4747

Terminator III Racing Team, Inc.
519 Westport Boulevard
Huron, OH 44839-1458
419-433-2003

The Marsh
1500 Minnetonka Boulevard
Minnetonka, MN 55435
612-935-2202
612-935-9685 fax

The Center for Shamanic
Arts & Training
Lynn Andrews Productions
P.O. Box 751086
Petaluma, CA 94975-1086
707-765-0733

Chapel of Love
Mall of America
240 North Garden
Bloomington, MN 55424
612-854-4656
612-854-4642 fax

Cracker Barrel Old Country
Store, Inc.
305 Hartmann Drive
Lebanon, TN 37088-0787
615-444-5533
615-443-9399 fax

Cowgirl Hall of Fame
Restaurant
519 Hudson Street
New York, NY 10014
212-633-1133
212-633-1892 fax

**National Cowgirl Hall of Fame
& Western Heritage Center**
111 West 4th Street, Suite 300
Fort Worth, TX 76102
800-476-FAME
817-336-2470 fax

Mall of America
1550 East 79th Street, Suite 450
Bloomington, MN 55425
612-883-8800

The Motley Fool
www.fool.com

CHAPTER 5

**National Association to Advance Fat
Acceptance (NAAFA)**
P.O. Box 188620
Sacramento, CA 95818
800-442-1214
916-558-6881 fax
naafa@world.stol.com

National Genealogical Society
4527 17th Street N
Arlington, VA 22207-2399
703-525-0050
703-525-0052 fax
www.genealogy.org/~ngs

Louisiana Heritage Center
P.O. Box 94125
Baton Rouge, LA 70804-9125
504-922-1208

**Family History Library
Church of Jesus Christ of
Latter Day Saints**
35 NW Temple Street
Salt Lake City, UT 84150
801-240-2331
801-240-5551 fax

Musical Feast of Harlem
467 Central Park West, #6D
New York, NY 10025
212-222-6059
gospeltour@aol.com

Harlem Spirituals, Inc.
690 8th Avenue
New York, NY 10039
212-757-0425
hstours@pipeline.com

Burley Design Cooperative
4020 Stewart Road
Eugene, OR 97402-5408
541-687-1644
541-687-0436 fax
burleybike@aol.com
www.burley.com

Pueblo to People
2105 Silber Road, Suite 101
Houston, TX 77055
713-956-1172
713-956-8443 fax
info@pueblo-to-people.com

**Greyhound Lines
Corporate Headquarters**
P.O. Box 660362
Dallas, TX 75266
214-849-8218

National Runaway Switchboard
800-621-4000

Monastery Hill Bindery
1751 West Belmont Avenue
Chicago, IL 60657-3019
773-525-4126
773-472-4820 fax
monhill@interaccess.com

Nunes Farms
P.O. Box 311
Newman, CA 95360
800-255-1641
209-862-1038 fax

Penzey's, Ltd. Spice House
P.O. Box 933
Muskego, WI 53150
414-679-7207
414-679-7878 fax

Postmark America
Mall of America
254 North Garden
Bloomington, MN 55425
612-854-1849
612-854-2032 fax

CHAPTER 6

**National Center for Neighborhood
Enterprise**
1424 16th Street NW
Washington, DC 20036
202-518-6500

Food Chain
912 Baltimore, Suite 300
Kansas City, MO 64105
800-845-3008
816-842-5145 fax

**MAJIC (Mothers Against
Jesse in Congress)**
c/o Patsy Clarke
7814 Coach House Lane
Raleigh, NC 27615
919-848-3471
    or:
c/o Eloise Vaughn
3312 Felton Place
Raleigh, NC 27606
919-772-6609

Association of Green Parties
131 Gracey Road
Conton, CT 06019
860-693-8344

Third Millenium
817 Broadway, 6th Floor
New York, NY 10003
212-979-2001
thirdmil@reach.com
www.thirdmil.org

The Natural Law Party
51 West Washington Avenue
Fairfield, IA 52556-3327
515-472-2040
515-472-2011 fax
info@natural-law.org
www.natural-law.org

**Consumer Credit Counseling
Service Headquarters**
P.O. Box 22045
Los Angeles, CA 90022-0045
909-808-4222
213-890-9590 fax
www.cccsia.org

Direct Marketing Association
111 19th Street NE
Washington, DC 20002-6701
202-955-5030

**United States Personal Chef
Association**
3615 NM 528, Suite 107
Albuquerque, NM 87114
800-995-2138
508-899-4097 fax

CHAPTER 7

National Museum of the American Indian
470 L'Enfant Plaza SW, #7103
Washington, DC 20560
202-357-3164

Rodale Institute Bookstore
611 Siegfriedale Road
Kutztown, PA 19530
800-832-6285
610-683-8548 fax

Seeds of Change
P.O. Box 15700
Santa Fe, NM 87506-5700
888-SOC-SEED
888-FAX-4SOC fax

Mutual Unidentified Flying Objects Network
103 Oldtown Road
Seguin, TX 78155
210-372-9216
210-372-9439 fax

CHAPTER 8

TZABACO
1150 Industrial Avenue, Suite A
Petaluma, CA 94952
800-770-2758

Sunset Hall
2830 Francis
Los Angeles, CA 90005
213-387-5277
213-387-5208 fax

National Gay and Lesbian Task Force (NGLTF)
2320 17th Street NW
Washington, DC 20009-2702
202-332-6483
202-332-0207 fax
202-332-6219 tty
ngltf@ngltf.org
www.ngltf.org

Canine Web
http://snapple.cs.washington.edu/canine

Three Dog Bakery
1706 Holmes
Kansas City, MO 64108
816-474-3647
816-474-2171 fax

Sutton Studios
P.O. Box 1558
Evanston, IL 60204
847-328-0346

Joel Hyman
Herbalist
1453A 14th Street, #205
Santa Monica, CA 90404
310-393-0056

CHAPTER 9

Child Trace
14865 West 105th Street
Lenexa, KS 66285-4100
800-235-2574
913-888-1066 fax

In Vitro International Guardian DNA
16632 Millikan Avenue
Irvine, CA 92714
800-355-0078
714-851-0563 fax

Bogs, Ltd.
539 Norwich Avenue
Taftville, CT 06380
860-892-4560
860-892-4562 fax

National Charities Information Bureau
19 Union Square West, 6th floor
New York, NY 10003
212-929-6300
212-463-7083 fax
www.give.org

CHAPTER 10

Brookstone Company
17 Riverside Street
Nashua, NH 03062-9908

Virtual Jerusalem
www.virtual.co.il

Traveler's Tales
101 Morris Street
Sebastopol, CA 95472
www.ora.com/ttales

The Disney Institute
1960 North Magnolia
Lake Buena Vista, FL 32830
800-4WONDER

Kaiser Permanente Medical Group
100 South Los Robles, Suite 550
Pasadena, CA 91101
818-564-3000

BOOKS

Aging. New York: Chelsea House Publishers, 1996.

All Roads Are Good: Native Voices on Life and Culture. Washington, DC: Smithsonian Institution Press, 1994.

The Children of America. The 11th Commandment: Wisdom from Our Children. Woodstock, VT: Jewish Lights Publishing, 1996.

Roger E. Allen. *Winnie-the-Pooh on Management: In Which a Very Important Bear and His Friends Are Introduced to a Very Important Subject.* New York: Dutton, 1994.

Lynn V. Andrews. *Dark Sister: A Sorcerer's Love Story.* New York: HarperCollins, 1995.

Rachel Ashwell and Glynis Costin. *Shabby Chic.* New York: ReganBooks/HarperStyle, 1996.

James A. Autry. *Confessions of an Accidental Businessman: It Takes a Lifetime to Find Wisdom.* San Francisco: Berret-Koehler Publishers, 1996.

James A. Autry. *Life and Work: A Manager's Search for Meaning.* New York: William Morrow, 1994.

James A. Belasco and Ralph C. Stayer. *Flight of the Buffalo: Soaring to Excellence, Learning to Let Employees Lead.* New York: Warner Books, 1993.

William J. Bennett, ed. *The Book of Virtues: A Treasury of Great Moral Stories.* New York: Simon & Schuster, 1994.

Sarah Ban Breathnach. *Simple Abundance: A Daybook of Comfort and Joy.* New York: Warner Books, 1995.

John Brockman. *Digerati: Encounters With the Cyber Elite.* San Francisco: HardWired, 1996.

Lydia Bronte. *The Longevity Factor: The New Reality of Long Careers and How It Can Lead to Richer Lives.* New York: HarperCollins, 1993.

Mel Brooks. *The Wit and Wisdom of the 2000-Year-Old Man in the Year 2000.* New York: HarperCollins, 1997.

Zsuzsanna E. Budapest. *The Goddess in the Office: A Personal Energy Guide for the Spiritual Warrior at Work.* San Francisco: HarperSanFrancisco, 1993.

Michael J. Caduto and Joseph Bruchac. *Keepers of Life: Discovering Plants Through Native American Stories and Earth Activities for Children.* Golden, CO: Fulcrum, 1994.

Joseph Campbell, with Bill Moyers. *The Power of Myth.* New York: Doubleday, 1988.

Jack Canfield and Mark Victor Hansen. *Chicken Soup for the Soul: 101 Stories to Open the Heart & Rekindle the Spirit.* Deerfield Beach, FL: Health Communications, Inc., 1993.

Chief Archie Fire Lame Deer and Helene Sarkis. *The Lakota Sweat Lodge Cards: Spiritual Teachings of the Sioux.* Rochester, VT: Destiny Books, 1994.

Shinta Cho. *The Gas We Pass: The Story of Farts.* Brooklyn, NY: Kane/Miller Book Publishers, 1994.

Deepak Chopra, M.D. *Creating Affluence: Wealth Consciousness in the Field of All Possibilities.* San Rafael, CA: New World Library, 1993.

Deepak Chopra, M.D. *The Seven Spiritual Laws of Success: A Practical Guide to the Fulfillment of Your Dreams.* San Rafael, CA: Amber-Allen Publishing, 1994.

Luann Colombo. *Beakman's Gear Up Your Gray Matter: 50 Questions and Answers from the Hit Show "Beakman's World."* Kansas City, MO: Andrews & McMeel, 1994.

Norman Crampton. *The 100 Best Small Towns in America.* New York: Macmillan Reference, 1995.

Stephanie Culp. *Streamlining Your Life: A 5-Point Plan for Uncomplicated Living.* Cincinnati: Writer's Digest Books, 1991.

Joy Dickinson. *Haunted City: An Unauthorized Guide to the Magical, Magnificent New Orleans of Anne Rice.* Secaucus, NJ: Carol Publishing Group, 1995.

Hope Dlogozima, James Scott, and David Sharp. *Six Months Off: How to Plan, Negotiate, and Take the Break You Need Without Burning Bridges or Going Broke.* New York: Henry Holt, 1996.

Don Doll. *Vision Quest: Men, Women & Sacred Sites of the Sioux Nation.* New York: Crown, 1994.

Joseph R. Dominguez and Vicki Robin. *Your Money or Your Life: Transforming Your Relationship with Money and Achieving Financial Independence.* New York: Viking, 1992.

Betty J. Eadie, with Curtis Taylor. *Embraced By the Light.* Placerville, CA: Gold Leaf Press, 1992.

Duane Elgin. *Voluntary Simplicity: Toward a Way of Life That Is Outwardly Simple, Inwardly Rich.* New York: Quill, 1993.

Clarissa Pinkola Éstes. *Women Who Run with the Wolves: Myths and Stories of the Wild Woman Archetype.* New York: Ballantine Books, 1992.

Stephen Foehr. *Eco-Journeys: The World Guide to Ecologically Aware Travel and Adventure.* Chicago: Noble Press, 1992.

Donald Gelfand. *Aging and Ethnicity: Knowledge and Services.* New York: Springer, 1993.

Ed Gillespie and Bob Shellhas, eds. *Contract with America: The Bold Plan by Rep. Newt Gingrich, Rep. Dick Armey and the House Republicans to Change the Nation.* New York: Times Books, 1994.

Taro Gomi. *Everyone Poops.* Brooklyn, NY: Kane/Miller Book Publishers, 1993.

Kim Johnson Gross, Jeff Stone, and Julie V. Iovine. *Chic Simple Home.* New York: Knopf, 1993.

Richard J. Herrnstein and Charles Murray. *The Bell Curve.* New York: Free Press, 1994.

Tom Hill and Richard W. Hill, Sr., eds. *Creation's Journey: Native American Identity & Belief.* Washington, DC: Smithsonian Institution Press, 1994.

James Hillman. *The Soul's Code: In Search of Character and Calling.* New York: Random House, 1996.

E. D. Hirsch, Jr. *The Schools We Need and Why We Don't Have Them.* New York: Doubleday, 1996.

Cheryl and Wade Hudson, comps. *Kids' Book of Wisdom: Quotes from the African American Tradition.* East Orange, NJ: Just Us Books, Inc., in press.

Derek Humphry. *Final Exit: The Practicalities of Self-Deliverance and Assisted Suicide for the Dying.* Secaucus, NJ: Hemlock Society, 1991.

Julie Miller Jones. *Food Safety.* St. Paul, MN: Eagan Press, 1992.

Laurie Beth Jones. *Jesus CEO: Using Ancient Wisdom for Visionary Leadership.* New York: Hyperion, 1995.

Bradford P. Keeney. *Everyday Soul: Awakening the Spirit in Daily Life.* New York: Riverhead Books, 1996.

David Kirk. *Miss Spider's Tea Party.* New York: Scholastic, 1994.

Elisabeth Kubler-Ross. *On Life After Death.* Berkeley, CA: Celestial Arts, 1996.

Christopher Lasch. *The Revolt of the Elites and the Betrayal of Democracy.* New York: W. W. Norton, 1995.

Seymour Martin Lipset. *American Exceptionalism: A Double-Edged Sword.* New York: W. W. Norton, 1996.

Gay Matthaei and Jewel H. Grutman. *The Ledgerbook of Thomas Blue Eagle.* Charlottesville, VA: Tomasson-Grant Publishers, 1994.

Thomas Moore. *Care of the Soul: A Guide for Cultivating Depth and Sacredness in Everyday Life.* New York: HarperCollins, 1992.

Bill D. Moyers. *Genesis: A Living Conversation.* New York: Doubleday, 1996.

Jun Nanao. *Contemplating Your Bellybutton.* Brooklyn, NY: Kane/Miller Book Publishers, 1995.

Sherwin B. Nuland. *How We Die: Reflections on Life's Final Chapter.* New York: Knopf, 1994.

Michael Philips. *The Seven Laws of Money.* Boston: Shambhala, 1993.

John Price. *The Abundance Book.* Carlsbad, CA: Hay House, Inc., 1996.

Philip Pullman. *The Golden Compass.* New York: Knopf, 1996.

James Redfield. *The Celestine Prophecy: An Adventure.* New York: Warner Books, 1993.

Rachel Naomi Remen. *Kitchen Table Wisdom: Stories that Heal.* New York: Riverhead Books, 1996.

Wess Roberts. *Leadership Secrets of Atilla the Hun.* New York: Warner Books, 1989.

Wess Roberts and Bill Ross. *Make it So: Leadership Lessons from Star Trek, The Next Generation.* New York: Pocket Books, 1995.

Sarah Rossbach and Lin Yun. *Living Color: Master Lin Yun's Guide to Feng Shui and the Art of Color.* New York: Kodansha, 1994.

Bonnie Miller Rubin. *Time Out: How to Take a Year (or More or Less) Off Without Jeopardizing Your Job, Your Family, or Your Bank Account.* New York: W. W. Norton, 1987.

Louis Sagar, Lisa Light, and Marti Sagar. *Zona Home: Essential Designs for Living.* New York: HarperStyle, 1996.

Elaine St. James. *Simplify Your Life: 100 Ways to Slow Down and Enjoy the Things that Really Matter.* New York: Hyperion, 1994.

David Scheinkin. *Path of the Kabbalah.* New York: Paragon House, 1986.

James C. Simmons. *The Big Book of Adventure Travel.* Santa Fe, NM: John Muir Publications, 1995.

Deborah Tannen. *Talking from 9 to 5: How Women's and Men's Conversational Styles Affect Who Gets Heard, Who Gets Credit, and What Gets Done at Work.* New York: Morrow, 1994.

Deborah Tannen. *That's Not What I Meant!: How Conversational Style Makes or Breaks Your Relations with Others.* New York: Morrow, 1986.

Judith C. Tingley. *Genderflex: Men and Women Speaking Each Other's Language at Work.* New York: AMACOM, 1994.

Bruce Tulgan. *Managing Generation X: How to Bring Out the Best in Young Talent.* Santa Monica, CA: Merritt Publishing, 1995.

Steve Wall. *Shadowcatchers: A Journey in Search of the Teachings of Native American Healers.* New York: HarperCollins, 1994.

Miriam Weinstein. *Making a Difference College Guide: Outstanding Colleges to Help You Make a Better World.* San Anselmo, CA: Sage Press, 1994.

Carolyn Wesson. *Women Who Shop Too Much: Overcoming the Urge to Splurge.* New York: St. Martin's Press, 1991.

Jim Willard and Terry Willard. *Ancestors.* Boston: Houghton Mifflin, 1997.

Pat Williams and Jim Denney. *Go for the Magic: The Five Secrets Behind a Magical, Miraculous Way of Life.* Nashville: Thomas Nelson, Inc., 1995.

James Q. Wilson. *The Moral Sense.* New York: Free Press, 1993.

Alan Wolfe. *Whose Keeper?: Social Science & Moral Obligation.* Berkeley, CA: University of California Press, 1991.

Robert Wright. *The Moral Animal: The New Science of Evolutionary Psychology.* New York: Pantheon, 1994.

Genichiro Yagyu. *The Holes in Your Nose.* Brooklyn, NY: Kane/Miller Book Publishers, 1994.

Genichiro Yagyu. *The Soles of Your Feet.* Brooklyn, NY: Kane/Miller Book Publishers, 1997.

Paul M. Zall, ed. *The Wit & Wisdom of the Founding Fathers: Benjamin Franklin, George Washington, John Adams, Thomas Jefferson.* Hopewell, NJ: Ecco Press, 1996.

Sandra L. Zimdars-Swartz. *Encountering Mary: From La Salette to Medjugorje.* Princeton, NJ: Princeton University Press, 1991.

PERIODICALS

Adbusters
1243 West 7th Avenue
Vancouver, BC V6H 1B7
Canada
800-663-1243
604-737-6021 fax
adbusters@adbusters.org
www.adbusters.org

Advertising Age
Crain Communications, Inc.
740 Rush Street
Chicago, IL 60611-2590
800-678-9595
www.adage.com

Atlanta Journal Constitution
72 Marietta Street
Atlanta, GA 30302
404-526-5151

Aromatherapy Quarterly (U.K.)
P.O. Box 421
Inverness, CA 94937-0421
415-663-9519
aromaqtlymag@easynet.co.uk

Autograph Collector magazine
Odyssey Publications, Inc.
510-A South Corona Mall
Corona, CA 91719-1420
800-99-ODYSSEY
909-734-9636 fax
www.autographcollector.com

Bereavement
8133 Telegraph Drive
Colorado Springs, CO 80920
719-282-1948
719-282-1850 fax
grief@usa.net
www.bereavementmag.com

BirdWatcher's Digest
P.O. Box 110
Marietta, OH 45750
800-879-2473

Boston Globe
P.O. Box 2378
135 Morrissey Blvd.
Boston, MA 02107-2378
617-929-2000

Brandweek
ASM Communications, Inc.
1515 Broadway
New York, NY 10036
212-536-5336

BusinessWeek
1221 Avenue of the Americas,
39th Floor
New York, NY 10020
212-512-2000
www.businessweek.com

Chicago Tribune
Tribune Tower
435 N. Michigan Avenue
Chicago, IL 60611
800-TRIBUNE
www.chicago.tribune.com

COLORS
70 Rue des Archives
75003 Paris, France
70214.2344@compuserve.com

Country
P.O. Box 991
Greendale, WI 53129
800-344-6913

Crone Chronicles
P.O. Box 81
Kelly, WY 83011
307-733-5409
307-733-8639 fax
AKCrone@aol.com

Daedulus
136 Irving Street
Cambridge, MA 02138
617-491-2600
daedalus@amacad.org

The Denver Post
1560 Broadway
Denver, CO 80202
800-336-7678
www.denverpost.com

Details
632 Broadway
New York, NY 10017
800-627-6367
www.swoon.com

Esquire
250 West 55th Street
New York, NY 10019
212-649-4020
212-265-0438 fax

Factsheet Five
P.O. Box 170099
San Francisco, CA 94117-0099
415-668-1781

Family Circle
110 5th Avenue
New York, NY 10011
800-627-4444

Fast Company
77 North Washington Street
Boston, MA 02114
617-973-0300
www.fastcompany.com

Fat Girl: the zine for fat
dykes and the women who
want them
2215-R Market Street #197
San Francisco, CA 94114
www.fatgirl.com/fatgirl

Fortean Times (U.K.)
Distributed in the U.S. by
Eastern News Distribution, Inc.
2020 Superior Street
Sandusky, OH 44870
800-221-3148
www.forteantimes.com

Fortune
Time, Inc.
Time & Life Building
Rockefeller Center
New York, NY 10020-1393
800-621-8000

George
1633 Broadway, 41st Floor
New York, NY 10019
212-767-6100
212-767-5622 fax

Gifts & Decorative Accessories
Geyer-McAllister Publications, Inc.
51 Madison Avenue
New York, NY 10010-1675
212-683-7929
212-689-4411 fax

Harper's Magazine
666 Broadway
New York, NY 10012
800-444-4653

Health
2 Embarcadero Center, Suite 600
San Francisco, CA 94111
415-248-2700
800-274-2522

Hollywood Reporter
5055 Wilshire Boulevard
Los Angeles, CA 90036-4396
213-525-2000
213-525-2377 fax
www.hollywoodreporter.com

I.D.
(International Design magazine)
440 Park Avenue South, 14th floor
New York, NY 10016
212-447-1400
212-447-5231 fax
IDMag@aol.com

JAMA (Journal of the American
Medical Association)
515 North State Street
Chicago, IL 60610
800-262-2350
ama-subs@ama.assn.org

Journal of Clinical Psychiatry
Physician Post Graduate Press
P.O. Box 752870
Memphis, TN 38175-2870
901-751-3800
901-751-3445

Journal of Democracy
1101 15th Street NW, Suite 802
Washington, DC 20005
202-293-0300
202-293-0258 fax
www.ned.org

Journal of Nursing Jocularity
P.O. Box 40368
Mesa, AZ 85274
www.jocularity.com

JUICE!
c/o Au Juice
Box 9068
1434 Spruce Street
Berkeley, CA 94709
510-548-0697
getjuice@aol.com

Latina
1500 Broadway, Suite 600
New York, NY 10036
212-439-7271 English
212-439-7272 Español
212-439-7273 fax
Latinamag@aol.com
www.latina.com

Living Large
Kathleen Madigan
P.O. Box 1006
Elgin, IL 60121

Martha Stewart Living
20 West 43rd Street
New York, NY 10036
212-522-7800
mstewart@marthastewart.com
www.marthastewart.com

Midwest Living
1912 Grand Avenue
Des Moines, IA 50309-3379
800-678-8093
mwl@dsm.mdp.com
http://midwestliving.com

Minnesota Women's Press
771 Raymond Avenue
St. Paul, MN 55114
612-646-3968

Modern Bride
249 W 17th Street
New York, NY 10011
212-462-3472

Modern Maturity
AARP
601 E Street NW
Washington, DC 20049
mmletters@aarp.org

Mother Jones
731 Market Street, Suite 600
San Francisco, CA 94103
800-334-8162

Ms.
MacDonald Communications Corp.
135 West 50th Street
New York, NY 10020

Nature (U.K.)
U.S. Office:
   345 Park Avenue South
   New York, NY 10010-1707
U.K. Office:
   Porters South
   4 Crinan Street
   London N1 9XW U.K.
   44-0-171-8334000
   44-0-171-8434596/7 fax
nature@nature.com
www.nature.com

New Age Journal
P.O. Box 488
Mount Morris, IL 61054-0488
815-734-5808
editor@newage.com

New Choices
Retirement Living
Publishing Co., Inc.
28 West 23rd Street
New York, NY 10010
212-366-8800

New Moon
P.O. Box 3620
Duluth, MN 55803-9905
218-728-5507
800-381-4743
newmoon@newmoon.duluth.us
www.newmoon.org

The New York Times
229 West 43rd Street
New York, NY 10036-3959
800-NYTIMES

People
Time, Inc.
Time & Life Building
Rockefeller Center
New York, NY 10020
212-522-0794 fax
editor@people.com
www.people.com

The Quest
P.O. Box 270
Wheaton, IL 60189-0270
800-669-9425

Sassy
Petersen Publishing Co.
6420 Wilshire Boulevard
Los Angeles, CA 90048-5515
213-782-2950

Seventeen
850 3rd Avenue
New York, NY 10022
212-407-9700

Simple Living
2319 North 45th Street, Box 149
Seattle, WA 98103
206-464-4800

Spin
Camouflage Associates
6 West 18th Street
New York, NY 10011-4608
800-829-9093

Spy
49 East 21st Street, 11th floor
New York, NY 10010
800-727-9808

Star Tribune
425 Portland Avenue South
Minneapolis, MN 55488
612-673-4000
www.startribune.com

Sunset
80 Willow Road
Menlo Park, CA 94025
800-777-0117

Technology & Learning
Miller Freeman, Inc.
600 Harrison Street
San Francisco, CA 94107
415-356-3389
415-908-6604 fax
editors@techlearning.com

Tikkun
P.O. Box 1778
Cathedral Station
New York, NY 10025
212-864-4110

Time Out New York
627 Broadway, 7th floor
New York, NY 10012
212-539-4444
212-673-8382 fax
TimeOutNY@aol.com

Travel & Leisure
1012 Avenue of the Americas
New York, NY 10036
212-382-5600

USA Today
1000 Wilson Boulevard
Arlington, VA 22229
703-276-3400
703-247-3139 fax

US News & World Report
2400 N Street NW
Washington, DC 20037-1196
202-955-2000
www.usnews.com

Utne Reader
1624 Harmon Place
Minneapolis, MN 55403
612-338-5040
info@utne.com
www.utne.com

The Washington Post
1150 15th Street NW
Washington, DC 20071
202-334-4740
www.washingtonpost.com

Weekly World News
600 East Coast Avenue
Lantana, FL 33464
561-540-1001
561-540-1084 fax

Wired
520 3rd Street, 4th floor
San Francisco, CA 94107-1815
415-276-5000
415-276-5150 fax
info@wired.com
www.wired.com

Working Woman
135 West 50th Street
New York, NY 10020
212-445-6100

Worth
575 Lexington Avenue
New York, NY 10022
212-751-4550

YM (Young & Modern)
375 Lexington Avenue
New York, NY 10017-5514

acknowledgments

Iconoculture has been from its very beginning a unique collaboration. This book would not have been possible without the open-mindedness, high-speed modems, and flexibility of the following people:

Our creative consultants, Jane Mueller, Michael Doyle, Shannon Pettini, and Paul Fabian; our tireless copy editor, Jana Branch; and our jack-of-all-trades assistants, Marta Patterson and Kirk Olson. Special thanks to our publisher, Susan Petersen, and our editor, Mary South, for not sending us to detention when we told them we had seen the future but our dog ate it.

While we have many clients and subscribers to acknowledge, we first want to thank a few key people. These marketing and advertising mavens were our very own early adopters, and we are fortunate to call them friends and colleagues. For your initial support and continued confidence in the voodoo that we do, thanks to:

Jodie Ahern, editor/writer; Nigel Carr, Director of Brand Planning, Kirshenbaum Bond & Partners; Christopher Celeste, V.P. Business Development and Strategic Planning, HMS Partners; Steve Chinn, Planning, TBWA Chiat/Day LA; everyone at *Country Living* magazine; Bill Cummins, formerly Sr. V.P., Director of Account Planning, Rubin Postaer and Associates; Robin Danielson, President and Head of Strategic Planning, Mad Dogs and Englishmen; Janine Davis, Director of Account Planning, Ketchum Advertising; Gayle Fuguitt, Director of Marketing Research, General Mills, Inc.; David Griffith, Associate Director of Account Planning, Rubin Postaer and Associates; David Johnson, Meredith Corporation; Steve Kaplan, Editor, *Minnesota Journal of Law and Politics*; Lorraine Ketch, Planning Director, Leap Partnership; Steve Leneveu, Planning Director, Leap Partnership; Linda Lewi, V.P. Brand Marketing, The Rockport Company; Harvey Mackay, CEO, Mackay Envelope Company; Pat Marzi, Senior Partner Planning and Research, Ogilvy & Mather; Terry Murphy, Consultant; Paul Neal, Sr. V.P./Director of Strategic Planning, Cole & Weber; Pat Palmer, Director of Account Planning, Rubin Postaer and Associates; Karen Serrati, Ph.D., Senior Marketing Research Analyst, American Century; Carol Ann Shindelar, *Star Tribune*; Lori Smith, Director of Marketing, Givaudan-Roure; Myra Stark, Sr. V.P. Creative Research and Consumer Insights, Saatchi & Saatchi Advertising; Heidi Vail, Associate Director of Account Planning, Rubin Postaer and Associates; Susan Virtue, V.P. Creative Fragrance Director, Givaudan-Roure; and Ron Zemke, President, Performance Research Associates.

The following forward-thinking companies were the early believers looking for those juicy nuggets from our cultural lazy Susan. For all the "atta boy" phone calls, personal insights into the consumer psyche, and fascinating tidbits from your own anthropological digs, thanks to:

ABR Information Services; ACSEC; Ad Lib; Allergan, Inc.; Amber Blocks Ltd.; American Century; American Express Financial Advisors; American Honda Motor; Arista Records; Ammirati & Puris/Lintas; The Araz Group; *Architectural Digest*; Avery Dennison; Avis Rent-a-Car System, Inc.; Award Baking International; Bartle, Bogle, Hegarty; BBDO LA; Berklee College of Music; Berry Brown Advertising; Big Apple Brokerage; Bison Baseball, Inc.; BMG Classics; Borders Perrin & Norrander; *Boston Herald*; Brain Reserve, Inc.; Brighton Development; Burger King Corporation; Burson-Marsteller; Calhoun Square; Cameron Studios; Campbell Mithun Esty; *CBS This Morning*; Chiat/Day; CIGNA; Cincinnati Bell; CME Promotion Marketing; The Coca-Cola Company; Coca-Cola Foods; Cole & Weber; Coors Brewing Company; Coty, Inc.; Dayton Hudson Corporation; DDB Needham; Denticator International, Inc.; *Details*; Deutsch, Inc.; The Dial Corp.; Disguise; Doskocil Specialty Brands Co.; Dow; DV International Inc.; Euro RSCG Tatham; Evans Group; Fallon McElligott; *Family Circle* magazine; Fleishman-Hillard; Foote Cone & Belding; Fox News Channel; Frances Meyer, Inc.; Fuqua & Eyre; General Mills; The Gillette Company; Givaudan-Roure; G & J USA Publishing; Goldberg, Moser & O'Neil; The Goodman Group; Goodwill Industries; The Graphic Solution; Grey Entertainment; Grinnell College; GSD&M Advertising; GTE; GTE Mobilnet; Hallmark Cards, Inc.; Hal Riney & Partners; Hasbro; Hill Holliday; Hunt Adkins; IBM Consulting Group; I, Brute Enterprises, Inc.; Incentive Management; The Integer Group; International Family Entertainment Inc.; Intoto; J. Hunt & Faltz; Jim Henson Records; JOICO Labs; Jordan, McGrath, Case & Taylor, Inc.; Jostens, Inc.; JPM Chicago, Inc.; J. Walter Thompson; Kanawha County Schools; Kelly Services; Kirshenbaum Bond & Partners; Kruskopf Olson Advertising Inc.; Lane Community College; Larsen Design & Interactive; The Lawlor Group, Inc.; Lennox Industries; Lexington Furniture Ind.; The Limited, Inc.; Lintas New York; Livingston & Company; Lowe & Partners/SMS; Loring Patrnership; Lynnhaven Mall; Mackay Envelope; Mad Dogs & Englishmen; The Marketing Source; The Martin Agency, Inc.; Martin/Williams Advertising, Inc.; Mary Kay Cosmetics, Inc.; Mall of America; McCann-Erickson; McCracken Brooks; Meadowbrook Lane, Inc.; Media Loft, Inc.; Meredith Corporation; Merkley Newman Hartly; Messner Berger McNamee Schmetterer; *Milwaukee Sentinel*; MINNEGASCO; *Minnesota Journal of Law and Politics*; Minnesota Public Radio; Mobil Oil; Mona Meyer & McGrath; Motorola AECG; The Musicland Group; Nestle Beverage Co.; *New York Times*; NIKE, Inc.; Nickelodeon; Northwestern National Life; Ogilvy & Mather Advertising; Olympus; O'Neal & Prelle; Pagano Schenck & Kay; Parkhill Marketing; Pat O'Neil Investment, Inc.; The Pearlstein Group; Pedersen Gesk, Inc.;

People magazine; Peterson Milla Hooks; Petersen Publishing Co.; Pet Incorporated; The Pillsbury Company; PINK; Plasti-Kote Co., Inc.; *Philadelphia Daily News*; The Procter & Gamble Company; Publicis/Bloom; Quest Business Development Group; Radio Consultants; R & B Commercial Management Co.; RCA Records; Relia Star; RFI/Sigma, Inc.; The Rockport Company; Rodale Press, Inc.; Rogers Corporation; The Rouse Company; The Rowland Company; Rubin Postaer and Associates; Saatchi & Saatchi Advertising; *St. Paul Pioneer Press*; Sears Roebuck & Co.; *Seattle Times*; Senechal, Jorgenson, Hale & Co.; Sense of Design; The Seven-Up Company; The Signature Group; Southwestern Bell Telephone; SK & R Advertising; Source Food Technology; Spiegel, Inc.; *Star Tribune*; SULZER METCO; Sunrise Corporation; Taco Bell; Target Stores; Target Base Marketing, The M/A/R/C Group; Team One Advertising; Tenneco Packaging; Tracey-Locke, Inc.; *Twin Cities Business Monthly*; Tycoon, Inc.; Tyson Foods; University of Minnesota–Morris; *Us* magazine; United States Air Force; *Utne Reader*; UV Color; Valleyfair; Versus Strategy Group, Inc.; *Wall Street Journal*; WCCO-TV; Weider Publications, Inc.; Wells Rich Greene/BDDP; Wendy's International, Inc.; WestGroup Inc.; WHO–TV 13; Wieden & Kennedy; William Eisner Associates; Winkler McManus; Wisconsin Public Radio; Wolverine Worldwide; *Woman's Day* magazine; Words at Work; and Young & Rubicam Inc.

Here's to those special personal pals, those true-blue folks who inspired us as tikes, as mates, as bloats over beers. Without your pep talks, belly laughs, and cauldrons of hot coffee and English Breakfast tea, this book could never, ever be. Thanks to:

The Abes: Bruce, Tony and Kirsten, Nedret, Dee, Sue, Lisa, Anni, Lou, and Missouri; the Dyer clan: Willie Mae, Little Pat, Gene, Bunnie, Kurt, Mary, Travis, and Taylor; Dorothy and Gordon Davis; Susan and John Spring; Susan Greer Donohue; Piggsy and Dave Lucas; James, Lorrie, and Tyler Larson; James Stageberg; Susan Allen Toth; Cecily Hines; Ann Bentz; Chris LaFontaine; Wes Janz; the 2105 support team: Brad and Geneva; and Gerry Meehan.

And for all of you who photocopy, fax, or download the newsletter—we don't know who you are, but thanks for thinking we are worth the effort.

index

iconoculture®
signs of the times

Hey, smartypants! Looking for more juicy nuggets from the cultural landscape?

Subscribe to Iconoculture's bi monthly newsletter, *Signs of the Times,* **for only $19.98.***

You'll receive six issues chock-full of hot trends and actionable ideas to keep you leaps ahead of the cultural curve.

Order your subscription(s) on the Iconoweb for instant cultural rejuvenation
www.iconoculture.com or mail or fax us this form pronto!

iconoculture®
2105 Irving Avenue South Minneapolis, MN 55405
612.377.0087 voice 612.377.8168 fax

Name _____

Title _____

Company _____

Address _____

City _____

State _____ Zip/Postal Code _____ Country_____

Phone_____ Fax _____ E-Mail_____

❏ Charge my American Express

Amex # _____Expiration Date _____

❏ My check is enclosed for $19.98   ❏ Bill me for $29.98*

* Out of checks and cash? We'd be happy to bill you for a subscription rate of $29.98.

Canadian and Mexican residents add $2 postage. All other international residents add $5 postage.